If the U Fits: Expert Advice on Finding the Right College and Getting Accepted
By Kevin McMullin

Copyright © Wise Like Us, LLC., 2012
All Rights Reserved.

ISBN: 978-0-9858440-0-4
Published by: Wise Like Us, LLC

Printing History: October 2012: First Edition

eISBN: 978-0-9858440-1-1

For Rosie

The consummate Collegewise fan

TABLE OF CONTENTS

col·lege [´kol-ij]

noun

1. An institution of higher learning offering undergraduate studies that lead to a bachelor's degree (also "university" or "U").

2. An academic superstore offering undergraduate students four years of learning, growth and self-discovery.

3. Move-in day, professors, rush week, lectures, road trips, rallies, the big game, debates, concerts, majors, minors, turning 21, all-nighters, spring break, graduation day, proud parents, next steps and fond memories.

INTRODUCTION

Before coming to Northeastern, I wouldn't have even been able to dream of the opportunities it has created for me. I would have never known what I wanted to do, I would have never known what it's like to live in a city, and I'd definitely never have gained the life experiences that will inevitably help me in the future. This college changed my life.

Wes F.
Former Collegewise student, Class of 2006
Northeastern University

EARLY STARTS

Two weeks before I left for college, I wrote a 10-page instruction guide that I boldly told my 15-year-old brother had everything he needed to know about getting into college. Most of the promised wisdom came from hindsight, things I'd have done differently if somebody had told me (or if I'd ever bothered to visit my high school counselor to ask for advice). At the time, even *take the SAT Subject Test in biology right after you finish taking the class in 10th grade* felt like sage college counseling advice.

Three years later, my brother got into Harvard.

Granted, he was class valedictorian and a state champion rower. I'm sure his credentials influenced his admission more so than the printout from my Apple IIC did. But the guide was my first foray into what would eventually become my career. Today, my brother is a Harvard graduate, my mother keeps that guide in a box of family mementos and I run a college counseling company, Collegewise. As of this writing, my team of counselors and I have helped more than 5,000 students get into colleges they're absolutely thrilled to attend.

I was inspired to start Collegewise while working for a test prep company where I presented to high school students and parents about the SAT and ACT and the role of standardized tests in college admissions. The audiences were wound tighter than my hamstrings at a yoga class. No lasting good was going to come from reminding them how many applicants with perfect SAT scores get rejected every year from Princeton. So I brought a different message: relax—nobody's ever become a failure in life because of their SAT scores.

I also learned that the public's focus on the most prestigious colleges meant that most of my audiences knew almost nothing about less-famous schools. If I asked, *Does anyone know the average SAT score for UCLA's admits?* somebody yelled out the answer every time. But when I asked, *Which college has its own golf course? Where can students water ski for free using the college's boats? Where did The Simpsons creator, Matt Groening, go to college?* nobody ever got those.

MY APPROACH

There were plenty of college admissions counselors in the marketplace, but none approached it the way I saw it needed to be done. I knew if I could make the college admissions process enjoyable, it would resonate—and not just with the high achievers. I started Collegewise in 1999 and soon logged hundreds of miles driving to nine families' homes to work with students. I helped them choose colleges, fill out applications and brainstorm essays. The messages I carried with me were:

- Relax. It will be OK. You're going to enjoy this. Let's have some fun, people.

- I don't care what your GPA or your test scores are. If you want to go college and you're willing to do the work, let's get to it.

- We're not just going to focus on the 20 prestigious schools everyone else wants to attend. We're going to look around and find the right colleges for YOU, even if you haven't heard of them yet.

- You're not going spend hundreds of hours and unreasonable amounts of your parents' money in pursuit of higher SAT or ACT scores. You'll do some focused prep if you need to, take the test once or twice and then move on.

- I won't guide you to do particular activities just to pad your applications. Whether you play softball, do community service, cheerlead or work at an ice cream shop, I'll encourage you to keep doing it as long as you enjoy it.

- When you fill out college applications and write your essays, I won't try to package you, market you or do anything else that treats you like a widget capable of being reverse-engineered to impress colleges. I'll tell you to just be yourself.

- I won't do the work for you. You'll do your own college research, fill out the applications and write the essays. But like the smarter older brother who's gone through this before, I'll help you, give you advice and a little cheerleading, and relieve your parents from the project management details.

My phone started ringing. Within a year, I was working with more than 100 students, including Emily, then a competitive high school swimmer.

EMILY'S SEARCH

Every student should have a college search as enjoyable and stress free as Emily's.

Part of it was her attitude. Emily was always relaxed and in a good mood. My sense was she probably swam with a champion's effort during team workouts, but she'd still have the same happy grin whether she finished first or fifth at the big meet. That's how Emily approached everything in high school. She gave a respectable effort and then accepted the outcome, always laid back and confident that all things college and otherwise would work out just fine.

Emily took most—but not all—of her high school's AP and honors classes. She earned A's and B's. She worked hard, but not so hard to sacrifice sleep or swim time. When we decided she'd benefit from an SAT score boost, she happily obliged. She took a course and raised her score enough to make the expenditure of time and money worth it. Then in typical Emily style, she moved on with her life and never looked back at her SAT scores.

In addition to swimming, Emily loved art. Her eyes lit up whenever she told me about a new painting she was working on—or even the idea for a painting. When her art teacher displayed one of Emily's projects in the school library, it was all she could talk about. "It made me feel so successful!" she said.

Emily never asked if art or swimming would help her get into more competitive colleges. She was just doing what she loved.

Emily often came to our meetings with the pages of her college guidebook dog-eared, wanting to talk about another college that "sounded pretty cool." Sometimes it was a school's art program that caught her attention. Other times it was because she read that every Tuesday was pizza night in the dorms. Finding the right college was an adventure, not a contest to win.

Emily's final list was full of schools she was excited about—Colgate, College of William and Mary, James Madison and a few University of California schools in case she got cold feet and decided to stay in her home state. Her parents were excited, too. They told her she could go to college wherever she wanted to go—they just wanted her to be happy.

Emily's applications

Kids who are confident in their own skin always seem to put together great college applications and essays. They are most likely to let themselves be themselves. That's what Emily did. She gave colleges windows into her life, like how she'd been swimming since she was nine years old, and the way her passion for art grew in high school.

One essay prompt asked Emily to share something about herself that wouldn't be evident from the rest of her application. I remember our conversation about it:

> Emily: "Well, I can eat a *lot*. I'm kind of known for that at school."

> "Seriously?"

> Emily: "Yeah, a couple times, people challenged me to eating contests."

> "OK, now you've got to tell me about it."

> Emily: "Well, last month, one of the football players at school bet me that I couldn't eat two large pizzas and he could. So we had a contest and I won."

> "You beat him? Was he big?"

> Emily: "Oh, yeah, he's huge. People were, like, cheering me on. And his friends made fun of him for losing to a girl."

> "You should totally write about that."

Six months later, when she visited Colgate with her acceptance letter in hand, the Dean of Admissions came out of his office to greet her. "I just had to meet the girl who won all those eating contests," he said.

Emily got into almost all of her colleges and decided on Colgate. She chose Colgate not because of the art program or because the local pizza joint served $1 slices until 2 a.m. on Saturdays, but because it just felt right. Colgate and Emily were a perfect match. She graduated in 2006. *Me and Bobby McGee*, a book she illustrated, was published in 2010. And she can still put away the pizza if you challenge her.

NOT AN ARMS RACE

Some people see college planning as an escalating arms race where students must out-achieve, out-test and out-strategize the competition. They think the only acceptable outcome for their hard work is an offer of admission from a prestigious school. To them, this process isn't supposed to be fun, and stories like Emily's are anomalies.

I disagree. There's a better way to approach college admissions, and this book details the better way for you.

Collegewise has helped more than 5,000 kids—A students, C students and everyone in between—gain admission to more than 800 different colleges. Our students find schools where they can be happy and successful. They finish their applications months before their friends. They get accepted to schools they are excited to attend and receive generous—often unsolicited—financial aid and scholarships. When our students decide on their destination for the next four years, they buy sweatshirts bearing the names of their schools. Their parents slap decals on the family cars to announce their collegiate pride. They do more than just survive the college admissions process. They thrive—with less stress—and have fun along the way.

You can, too. I wrote this book to show you how.

What to expect

This is not a book about how to get into Harvard.

I start with same basic retraining–breaking down traditional college admissions notions that ruin the process for families. Then I show you how to find the right colleges for you. I reveal what colleges really look for from students, and teach you how to give it to them.

You'll learn the secrets to a successful and enjoyable high school career, tips to get better grades and test scores, and ways any student can impress teachers, counselors and colleges.

Every part of applying to college—the application, the essays and the interview—is covered. I also discuss how to pay for it with the help of financial aid and scholarships. There's even a section for your parents to suggest how they can support your search, but let you drive it.

If it's part of a successful, enjoyable ride to college, I cover it in this book.

My approach is a radical shift for some families, but it's not controversial or risky. Throughout this book, you'll hear from admissions professionals who echo my advice, and from former Collegewise students and parents who share how it worked for them.

This is college admissions the smarter, saner way.

Relax. It will be OK. You're going to enjoy this. Let's have some fun, people.

BASIC RETRAINING: HOW TO APPROACH THE COLLEGE ADMISSIONS PROCESS

I hate it, but I understand the frenzy. I have to understand it, because I watch the news, read the papers (and the books) that tell me that there is an education crisis. Except, I can't think of one student I know or have ever heard of who wanted to go to college, applied, and didn't get in anywhere. I've definitely heard students say that they didn't get into their 1st choice college, which can be frustrating, but not the end of the world. Furthermore, I don't know of a 'bad' college…There are some that might have nicer dorms, warmer climates, more access to professors, but it's all a matter of the student's taste. So what I'm saying is, there's good news. YOU ARE GOING TO COLLEGE. There. The pressure is off. Now the question is: where?

Swarthmore College
Office of Admissions blog[1]

FOCUS ON THE GOOD NEWS

"Harvard, Princeton post record low acceptance rates"

CNNMoney ran this headline on March 30, 2012, right on cue.[2] Every spring, the major media outlets run features that suggest college admissions rates are dropping—again!

The doom and gloom headlines make my phone ring. The high school students and their parents who call are so disillusioned about their college prospects. They hear that competition is fierce, that students have to be perfect to get in and that the kid who built a satellite got rejected from everywhere!

Here's the thing—the admissions squeeze is only true for a tiny percentage of colleges.

There are more than 2,000 four-year colleges and universities in this country, and the vast majority of them accept most of their applicants. In fall 2010, colleges, on average, accepted two-thirds of their applicants.[3] According to Collegeboard.com, there are 383 colleges who accept every high school student who applies. Whatever your GPA and test scores are, you can go to college if you really want to go. The only question is which one.

Contrary to what the media report, it's actually never been easier to get into college than it is today. A Stanford economics professor's 2009 study found that 90 percent of colleges are easier to get into today than they were in the 1950s and 1960s.[4] How can that be? Since 1955, the number of high school graduates has grown by 131 percent, but the number of college spots has raised 297 percent.[5] That's right—the number of available spots has outpaced the number of students vying for them.

COLLEGE MATCHMAKER

Visit the National Center for Educational Statistics "College Matchmaker" tool and see how many colleges there are to choose from: http://nces.ed.gov/collegenavigator.

Bottom line—there are more schools with more space for students than ever before.

Sure, Harvard, Columbia, Stanford, Yale and Princeton all accepted fewer than 10 percent of their applicants. You could have perfect grades, perfect test scores and a certificate verifying that it was, in fact, you who invented plutonium. You still might not get into one of those schools. That's what happens when the highest-achieving applicants from all over the world apply to the same colleges. There are just too many applicants vying for a limited number of spaces.

How many colleges are highly selective?

I consider any college that accepts fewer than 20 percent of its applicants to be highly selective. I also consider these colleges the exception, not the norm. According to the National Center for Educational Statistics (http://nces.ed.gov/collegenavigator), only 40 colleges are actually that selective. Think Ivy League and Stanford. If you change the search variable on the website to include all schools that admit at least 30 percent of their applicants, the list more than doubles to 92 schools. Change the variable to 40 percent and it more than doubles again to 186 schools. And a 50 percent acceptance rate yields more than 350 colleges.

That leaves more 1,600 schools that accept more than half their applicants.

I understand if you don't take solace in the statistics; that you're virtually guaranteed admission to hundreds of schools you haven't heard of (yet). We have a lot of ground to cover about how to find the right colleges for you and whether the most selective schools are among them.

My team and I have helped more than 5,000 students understand a fundamental truth about college admissions today: there's a school out there for you, probably one that will make you very happy. You just have to care enough about your future to want that for yourself and commit to doing the work to get there.

This book will show you how.

COMMITTEE NOTES

Myth: It's impossible for regular students to get in anymore

Impossible? Let's not get carried away. The trend toward hypercompetitive admissions often gets oversold in the news, because it disproportionately affects private East Coast universities. Admissions aren't nearly that restrictive at the vast majority of colleges. [6]

University of Wisconsin-Madison
Getting in: The not-so-secret admissions process

It's not that difficult

Remember that getting into a good college is not that difficult. It may not be a college that your grandmother has heard of, but you have a better choice of colleges and universities here than in any other country in the world. You might pause for a moment and appreciate that. Notice all those young people moving here from China and Korea and the Philippines and Egypt and Nigeria and other places? They know that you can get a splendid education in the United States with nothing more than a basic understanding of English and a willingness to work hard. The vast majority of colleges accept most of their applicants, and some good ones still have empty spaces in September. [7]

Jay Mathews
Washington Post

WORRY LESS ABOUT COLLEGE

When families arrive at Collegewise for the first time, many of them are stressed and overwhelmed. The students worry about finding a school that will accept them with their 2.8 GPA or that their perfect credentials won't be good enough for a prestigious college. They're scared of making a mistake, and they're not having much fun with college planning. That's why the first piece of advice I almost always give to them is simple—relax.

You live in the country that has the most coveted and accessible system of higher education in the world. More than 40 percent (1.3 million) of the 3.2 million students who graduated from high school in 2010 enrolled in four-year colleges or universities.[8] Two-thirds of high school graduates who apply to college get in. You're almost certainly going to college no matter what your GPA or SAT score. Wherever you go, it'll be an intellectual supermarket where you can learn, explore, discover, meet people and have fun for four years. You, not the name of your college, will get to determine just how successful you are after graduation.

A student's college future is serious business. But that doesn't mean the process of finding and applying to college can't be an exciting time that families can enjoy together. Have enough confidence in yourself to know you're going to work hard and be successful wherever you go. You'll enjoy high school a lot more, and you'll be more successful getting into college.

Worrying constantly about whether your SAT scores are good enough for Yale, or how many APs it takes to get into Duke, or what Stanford wants you to say in your essays just make you focus on the wrong things.

More than 5,000 students have come through the Collegewise offices and just about all of them ended up with college options they were excited about. College admissions tip No. 1: relax.

Work hard. Worry less. It's all going to be OK.

PUT YOURSELF IN CHARGE

You're the one who's going to college—not your parents or your high school counselor. You shouldn't expect anybody else to do the work for you. The more you take charge of your college future, the more successful you're going to be.

It's your job to care enough about your future to research colleges. It's your job to fill out your applications and write your essays. It's your job to make sure you meet all your deadlines and follow up with the colleges to make sure they've received your materials. If these things aren't taken care of, it's not going to affect anyone more than it affects you. That's why you need to be in charge.

I'm not saying you have to do all of this alone. You should absolutely ask for advice from people you trust. Your parents and your counselor, in particular, should be on your support team. They can answer questions, cheer you on, help you make good decisions and even review your work. But don't let them do the work for you. Don't wait for them to research college application requirements, fill out your applications, or call the admissions offices to ask questions for you. Those are your jobs, not theirs. Your college future is too important for you to be a passive bystander.

The more you do for yourself during the college admissions process, the more successful that process is going to be. You'll find colleges that fit you rather than having them chosen for you. You'll have better answers when those colleges' applications and interviewers ask you why you've decided to apply to their schools. And most importantly, you'll get accepted to more colleges that you're excited about.

Once you get to college, nobody's going to run your life for you. So this is the time to show colleges, your parents, and yourself that you're mature enough to take charge of your own future.

WORK, WORK, WORK HARD

While I do spend a lot of time at Collegewise telling our students to relax, I have never once told a student that it's OK not to work hard.

Effort is the great equalizer. Your success in life will have much more to do with the amount of effort you put in day-to-day than your GPA, SAT score or whether or not you went to a famous college. I tell our Collegewise kids that once they put out an effort they can be proud of, they earn the right to relax and have faith that everything will be OK.

Behind most success stories, you'll usually find a tale of hard work. The Beatles were just a struggling high school band in 1960 when they were first invited to play in Hamburg, Germany. By the time they hit it big four years later, they'd performed live approximately 1,200 times, sometimes for as long as eight hours a night. Most bands today don't perform 1,200 times in their entire careers. The Beatles weren't *The Beatles* until they worked hard enough to earn it.[9]

When he was growing up, writer and actor Seth Rogen (from Superbad, Pineapple Express and 50/50) worked hard at being funny. When he was 12, he signed up for a stand-up comedy class. When he was 13, he and a friend wrote the original screenplay for Superbad which, years later, became a major motion picture. By the time he got to high school, people were paying him to do stand-up comedy at bar mitzvahs, parties and bars. When he was 16, he won the Vancouver Amateur Comedy Contest.[10] He wasn't just the funny guy at school. He took classes to learn how to be funny, worked jobs to practice his comedy and even entered contests to see how he stacked up against other comedians. That's a lot of effort.

If you take challenging classes and put in the effort, it doesn't matter if your GPA isn't perfect. You'll be smarter and even better prepared for college because of your effort.

If you've spent every Saturday of the last two years volunteering in a program that helps elementary school kids at inner city schools with their homework, does it really matter in the grand scheme of things whether Cornell says, "Yes"?

You've worked hard, you've helped people and you deserve to be proud of that. College admissions officers will notice, too.

Lack of effort holds you back

Just like hard work will always take you someplace, a lack of effort eventually catches up with you. If you refuse to work hard and get by with C's through high school and college, the kids who go to Harvard are going to have huge advantages over you after graduation. But it won't be because they went to Harvard and you went to a less famous school. It will be because they worked much harder than you did.

Even the most successful people were never great at everything they tried. But just about all of them worked hard to get where they are. When he was 27, Mark Cuban, the current owner of the Dallas Mavericks basketball team, got fired from his job as a computer salesman. So he started a software reseller and system integration company called MicroSolutions out of his apartment and stayed up late every night learning as much as he could about new software. Seven years later, he sold MicroSolutions for $6 million.[11] Not a bad turnaround.

We all have natural strengths and weaknesses. We can't all get perfect grades, be award-winning musicians or make it in Hollywood. But YOU get to decide how hard you're willing to work. Putting in the effort will always take you to good places.

THINK ABOUT THE BIG PICTURE

Many kids prepare for college by focusing only on short-term gains. They take an extra AP class because that will boost their GPA. They volunteer at the homeless shelter because they want more community service hours. They visit a teacher after class to ask how to get extra credit so they can get an A. They're preparing for college like mercenaries—everything they do is based on short-term advantages they think can help them get what they want. That's like getting married so you can combine two incomes to buy a nicer car. Mercenaries miss the bigger picture.

Just about everything you do to prepare for college has bigger life implications, too.

- When you work hard in your classes in high school, you become smarter and better educated.

- When you find and commit yourself to activities you enjoy, you discover your talents, learn to work with other people and enjoy life outside of the classroom.

- When you learn how to do things for yourself without relying on your parents, you become more independent and better prepared to live on your own.

- When you find a subject that interests you and dive in to learn more, you see for yourself just how rewarding learning can be when you let your interests take you there.

- When you struggle in a class and approach your teacher for help, you learn how to advocate for yourself and how to seek out assistance when you need it.

- When you try your best and still come up short, you learn how to handle that failure or disappointment and then move on.

When you take all those lessons with you to college, you get more out of the experience. As you go through high school and plan for college, don't just focus on what admissions advantage you're getting. Think about the life advantages, too. There's no guarantee anything you do will get you into one particular school. But everything you do gives you a bigger life advantage. Those bigger advantages guarantee that you'll get in someplace and that you'll also be more successful once you get there.

It's not just about getting in

...scheduling every minute of your life in order to get into college is nutty; and most importantly, it's a dumb way to live your life. If you're doing all that stuff because you love it, have a passion for it, and/or can't bear to live without it, fine by me. Trying to join every single activity that MIGHT give you some miniscule assistance in some mythical admissions process, however, is deeply misguided. [12]

Andrew Flagel
Dean of Admissions
George Mason University

BE A KID

Your high school career should be about lots of things, and preparing for college is certainly one of them. But a lot of high school students are so stressed about college that they're not enjoying their lives. You need to have a little fun, too.

In 2012, The Princeton Review surveyed more than 12,000 college applicants. Seventy-one percent of them said their stress levels were "high" or "very high" (up 2% from 2011, and up 15% from 2003, the survey's initial year).[13] Studies by the University of Kentucky found seniors in high school average less than seven hours of sleep a night, and only five percent of high school seniors average eight hours.[14] That kind of overstressed, overworked and overscheduled lifestyle is hazardous to your mental health, as well as to your college admissions chances.

You can't produce great work constantly. Your brain and your body need time off when you're not being measured and evaluated. So read the occasional gossip mag. Listen to music. Play video games. Throw a Frisbee. Throw water balloons at your siblings. Teach yourself to play guitar. Sketch. Write poetry. Watch bad television every now and then. Spend time daydreaming, exploring and exposing yourself to things that seem fun or interesting. Goof off with your friends. Be a kid for crying out loud.

Think you're too busy for the luxury of downtime? Consider this: Berkshire Hathaway CEO Warren Buffett, one of the richest people in the world, plays a mean ukulele and gives lessons to a girls' club in Omaha, Neb.[15] Secretary of State and former First Lady Hilary Clinton does crossword puzzles.[16] And almost all of 134 Nobel laureates in chemistry have had an enduring hobby, from chess to insect collecting.[17] If they can find downtime and enjoy things just for fun, you can, too.

A former Collegewise student wrote his entire college essay about how much he liked to sing country music in the shower. He said he actually looked forward to doing it every day after baseball practice. His mother would knock on the door and yell, "Honey, are you having a rock concert in there?!" It was his time to do something that had absolutely nothing to do with getting into college, and he enjoyed every second of it. He also got accepted to his first-choice college, University of San Diego.

Yes, colleges want students who know how to work hard. That's why they accept students who've taken challenging curriculums, done well, and made some substantial commitments to outside activities. They also want students who are happy and well-adjusted kids who know how to enjoy their lives.

CREATE YOUR OWN MAGIC FORMULA

Some students spend their high school years searching for the magic formula for admission to their dream college. The logic is that if they combine the right mix of classes, test scores and activities, say the right things in their essays, talk to the right people and apply under the right major, they'll be a sure thing. Their high school years become a complex game of strategy in the hopes of gaming the system and getting into their dream schools.

In fact, a magic formula for college admissions doesn't exist. If it did, someone would have discovered and profited from it already.

There's nothing wrong with being goal oriented. But trying to reverse engineer yourself to please particular colleges won't work. Making every decision in high school—from what classes to take, to which activities to do, to what to write in your college essays—based on what you think will impress your dream colleges is a terrible way to stand out. And it's certainly no way to make you happy.

College admission is a personal, often subjective process. It might seem unfair that your favorite colleges won't just tell you exactly what to do to get admitted. But this is the way the world works, too. There's no magic formula for getting a job at Google, either. Learning the right skills, working hard and getting good experience will improve anyone's chances of eventually getting to work at the Googleplex. But there's still no itemized checklist to follow.

Work hard. Do what you love. Select appropriate colleges and present yourself honestly. That's the only college admissions strategy that works.

COMMITTEE NOTES

There is no formula

Trying to define admissions with a formula is like trying to define life with a formula. It's like trying to explain poetry using calculus. It would take the human component out of it, which is perhaps the most important part.[18]

Ben Jones
Former Director of Communication
Office of Admissions
MIT

It is not a game to be played

The application process is not a "reward" for the hard work you've put in during high school. (The rewards are the grades you've earned and, ultimately, the education you've acquired.) It is not a game to be played, and for all the strategizing people think works, the gaming approach is one that is fairly obvious to us and doesn't usually yield a positive result. [19]

Swarthmore College
Office of Admissions blog

THINK MORE WHAT THAN WHERE

Going to college is important. It's a life-changing experience that's worth just about any reasonable sacrifice you and your parents can make so you can go. The difference between life with a college degree and life without one is huge. (In 2009, the median of the earnings for young adults with a bachelor's degree was $45,000; for those with a high school diploma or its equivalent was $30,000.[20]) That said, the name of the school on the degree won't be nearly as important as what you do while you're there.

You can passively go through your college years, study enough to get by and have a little fun. Or you can take advantage of the fact that you have four years of virtually unlimited opportunities to learn whatever you want to learn, discover your real talents, find mentors, build work experience and have *a lot* of fun.

Case in point: a former Collegewise student—a male—went to the University of Arizona where he tried out and made the practice squad of their NCAA Division I *women's* basketball team. The coach saw advantages to having her starters practice against players who were bigger and stronger. So the team held open tryouts for guys who'd played basketball in high school. Our student got full athletic privileges, including priority registration and free tutoring. When he graduated and started applying for jobs, he told us that every single interview he went on asked him about playing women's basketball. He was gainfully employed in marketing for a major league baseball team less than three weeks after graduating from college.

Other former Collegewise students have worked with a professor to find an AIDS vaccine, built a working submarine with other mechanical engineering majors, worked as a resident advisor and spent an evening counseling a student who was considering suicide, and tripled the fundraising revenue as a volunteer at a non-profit. All were significant life experiences. Not all of these happened at prestigious colleges.

Every college will give you opportunities to learn, explore your passions, develop your talents and create a remarkable experience for yourself. It will be up to you to take advantage of the opportunities and extract the value your college has to offer, whether it's atop all the college ranking lists or some tiny school your friends have never heard of.

The key is finding a college that's right for you—one with an environment where you can really be happy and successful.

FINDING FITS: HOW TO FIND THE RIGHT COLLEGES FOR YOU

Instead of sticking to colleges that I already knew about, my Collegewise counselor encouraged me to research a large number of different kinds of colleges. Some I had never even heard of before. When I was doing the research, I figured out what I was really looking for in a college, and what I didn't like about some colleges. My counselor would not accept BS answers, even though at first I tried to give some. She pushed me to really consider what I liked and disliked about each college. I received acceptances from 11 universities and 9 offered me academic scholarships. I committed to SMU and accepted their Provost Scholarship award. If not for my college research, I would never have known about SMU.

Aaron F.
Former Collegewise student, Class of 2012
Southern Methodist University

HOW TO CURE NAMEBRANDITIS

BEWARE OF POPULAR OPINIONS

Trying to convince some people that Harvard isn't necessarily better than a less famous school is like trying to convince the guy sleeping in line outside the Apple Store that the iPhone isn't a better product than a Blackberry. No matter how much evidence you show them to the contrary, some people just won't be convinced. That's fine—they have the right to keep seeing the world the way they see it. If that sounds like you (about the colleges, not the phones), let's just agree to disagree.

The students we work with who get into Ivy League schools, paradoxically, tend to be less enamored with the schools' prestige and more enamored with the opportunities for learning. As soon as we hear a kid say, "I want to go to an Ivy League School," it's almost a certainty that he just won't have the intellectual curiosity to get there. He's in love with the image, not with the learning.

Students convinced that prestigious colleges are the best colleges are also the ones who spend high school trying to please a short list of dream schools that will most likely reject them. Then they are absolutely crushed if those schools say no. That's giving an awful lot of power to just a few colleges.

Good kids who work hard deserve better than that.

Just to get them out of the way, here are my responses to a few biases I hear every now and then from people suffering from namebranditis (my term for the affliction that causes sufferers to fall overly in love with only prestigious, name-brand schools).

"C'mon. How can you say that prestigious colleges aren't great schools?"

I'm not saying they aren't great schools. I'm saying their prestige doesn't make them better schools.

You can get a fabulous education at Princeton, Stanford, Harvard, Duke, University of Chicago, UC Berkeley or any other highly selective college. All of them will surround you with opportunities to learn, grow, and meet intellectual, driven, interesting students. I've worked with students who went on to these schools and were blissfully happy. There's no scam there.

But so much of the pressure about getting into college today comes from the belief that prestigious colleges who reject almost everyone are somehow better schools; that people who get into prestigious colleges are destined for success and those who get rejected are starting life deep in the end zone. There's very little evidence to support such a belief.

The University of Iowa's Ernest Pascarella coauthored *How College Affects Students*, an 827-page analysis of hundreds of studies on how various colleges affect students, including intellectual growth, moral development, career advancement and economic impacts. "We haven't found any convincing evidence that selectivity or prestige matters," Pascarella said.[1]

Another study by Pascarella and George Kuh of Indiana University showed that selective schools don't systematically employ better educational practices than less selective schools do. In fact, in three areas—the number of essay examinations given, instructor feedback to students and having a supportive campus environment—selective schools actually scored worse.[2]

There are at least 100 other colleges whose offerings are indistinguishable from those at the prestigious colleges. You can get the same education and opportunities from less-selective schools. It's just going to be up to you to put the work in to benefit from your time there. What you do in college is more important than where you go.

"I've worked really hard in high school. Why should I settle for a less-selective college?"

If you've worked really hard in high school, the last thing you should do is settle. I'm not saying you should lower your standards. I'm saying there are more schools out there that meet your standards than you may think.

You should go to a college you're excited about. You should go to a college where you'll be surrounded by other students who care enough about their future to have worked as hard as you have. You should go someplace where you can meet people, have fun, find what you're good at and get a little smarter every day. You deserve those things, and good news: more than only 40 schools in the country can give them to you.

Yes, there are vast differences between the colleges that accept almost nobody and those that accept almost everybody. I understand most high-achieving students wouldn't be happy attending a college full of underachievers. But you've got to go pretty deep down the list of more than 2,000 US colleges before those differences become noticeable, deeper than 30 or 80 or even 100. Just because a school isn't as prestigious as an Ivy League school doesn't mean it's full of substandard students.

Applying to a short list of prestigious schools and then just hoping one will take you gives control of your college destiny to a few highly selective colleges. You've worked too hard for that.

"Most people who graduate from prestigious colleges seem very impressive."

I agree. But is that because they went to prestigious schools? My bet is they worked hard to become impressive before they ever went to college.

In March 2009, *The Boston Globe* reported that Harvard received a record 29,112 applications for the Class of 2013. Among the applicants, 3,700 were ranked first in their high school senior class. Harvard only has 1,655 spaces in the freshman class. There's no way around that math. Most of those applicants were rejected.

Will anybody be surprised if those 1,655 Harvard freshmen eventually go on to do great things in their lives? I don't think so. I'm not saying Harvard didn't give them a great education. But Harvard isn't putting lipstick on a pig. Those students' future successes were born from qualities they developed long before they ever took up residence near Harvard Yard. I'm talking about their work ethic, interest in learning, character, persistence, and maybe even their personality and charm.

What about the 27,000 amazingly brilliant and accomplished applicants Harvard rejected for the Class of 2013? Are they doomed to substandard lives now that they won't have Harvard degrees? Of course not. They're too brilliant and accomplished to be left behind.

Smart, hard-working, passionate kids will almost certainly make something of themselves wherever they go.

"You can't beat the connections you get from going to a prestigious college."

It's not like the prestigious colleges give you an all-access membership card to a club that hires for all the great jobs. Valuable connections are a product of doing the difficult work to earn them, not by attending a school with a famous name.

Lots of less-famous schools will give you the opportunities to learn from great professors, meet mentors, get involved, discover your passions, and work hard enough to impress people who will help you take your next step after graduation. It's going to be up to you to earn those connections, whether or not you're at a famous school.

PARENT TO PARENT

Sometimes kids know best

When our daughter began examining her college options, we thought she should apply to our alma mater and schools with highly recognizable names—it was the best assurance of employment upon graduation. She shocked us when she told us her favorite school was one of which we had never heard. It possessed a liberal arts emphasis and was clear across the country. We dismissed it, thinking there was no way she'd go there. Well, she is completing her sophomore year at that college and loves it. She completed an internship in Spain last summer and is looking forward to a summer of classical studies in Greece this year, one typically attended by grad students. She has grown in ways we would have never imagined. She is making an impact, following her own path, not ours, but a promising one just the same. Sometimes our kids do know best. It's their life and there's a point at which you have to trust and support their decisions.

Carol S.
Mother of Becca, former Collegewise student, Class of 2010
St. John's College (MD)

COMMITTEE NOTES

Are prestigious colleges life changers?

In general, the most elite products like college are overrated as life changers. It turns out that merely getting into Harvard is as good an indicator of future success as actually going. It turns out that being the sort of person that can invest the effort, conquer fear and/or raise the money to capture some of the elite trappings of visible success is what drives success, not the other way around. The learning matters a great deal, and especially the focused effort behind it. The brand name of the institution, not so much. [3]

Seth Godin
Best-selling author and blogger

DO A SUCCESS SEARCH

Here's a good way to learn more about just how many colleges, famous and not-so-famous, can lead to success. Ask successful adults in your life where they went to college.

Pick five adults you know and respect that are doing something you find interesting—your family doctor, your boss at your internship, your dad's business partner, etc. Ask them where they went to college and what they majored in. If you don't want to ask them, Google them. Either way, connect the dots from where they started and where they are now.

I promise you'll find there isn't a lot of correlation between how successful they are and the relative prestige of their colleges. Some of them may have gone to prestigious schools, but a lot of them won't have. Like most successful people, they probably got where they are today by working hard and making the most of opportunities that presented themselves along the way.

These conversations can also lead to some interesting revelations about college, what they got out of their experiences, and the roles their schools played in getting them where they are. Case in point: a dad and his daughter were leaving my office once and he saw a Grinnell College pennant on my wall. He said, "That place changed my life. I wouldn't be where I am today if I hadn't gone there."

Grinnell is a small liberal arts college in the middle of rural Iowa. The school has a good sense of humor about their location and their lack of Ivy League prestige—they sell T-shirts in the school bookstore that read, "Where the hell is Grinnell?" on the front, and "Who the hell cares?" on the back.

The Collegewise dad is a neurosurgeon.

Look outside the family circle

If you're not convinced by your immediate circles that a degree from a prestigious college is not a prerequisite for success, take the time to look up some famously successful people. Take 30 minutes at the computer and do a success search.

Would you say that someone who gets into Harvard Law School is on a pretty successful track? According to the school's website, the students enrolled at Harvard Law for 2010-2011 came from 261 undergraduate institutions, including dozens of not-so-name-brand colleges (e.g., Adelphi, Cal State Northridge, and Mary Washington).[4]

When the 2011 Nobel Prize winners were announced, I wondered where they went to college. Here's what I found: there were 10 Nobel Prize winners in 2011. Four went to prestigious colleges. Three went to less-famous schools. One went to a school I'd never heard of, and two didn't go to college at all.

You can test this theory yourself. Look up where the governor of your state or the mayor of your town went to college. Pick a company whose products you like and find out where their leadership went to college. Type the name of your hero into Google and see what you find.

I recently googled "President of the American Medical Association," a position I suspect everybody would agree connotes success. His name: James L. Madara.

He went to Juniata College in Huntingdon, Pennsylvania, home of the annual Mountain Day, a surprise day in the fall when classes are canceled and students head to the local state parks for a day of slip 'n slide, crafts, music and other outdoor activities.

Some of the happy and successful people in the world went to prestigious colleges, but there are many, many more that did not.

WHERE DID TOP CEOS GO TO COLLEGE?

Colleges and universities where CEOs of the top Fortune 500 companies in 2012 earned their bachelor's degrees[5]

Forbes rank	Company	CEO	College attended
1	Exxon Mobil	Rex Tillerson	University of Texas at Austin
2	Wal-Mart Stores	Michael Duke	Georgia Tech
3	Chevron	John Watson	University of California, Davis
4	ConocoPhillips	Ryan Lance	Montana Tech
5	General Motors	Daniel Akerson	US Naval Academy
6	General Electric	Jeffrey Immelt	Dartmouth
7	Berkshire Hathaway	Warren Buffett	University of Nebraska-Lincoln
8	Fannie Mae	Michael Williams	Drexel University
9	Ford Motor	Alan Mulally	University of Kansas
10	Hewlett-Packard	Meg Whitman	Princeton

HAVE SWAGGER—IT'LL SERVE YOU

The prognosis for a bad case of namebranditis is not good. You're less likely to enjoy the high school years. You'll be stressed throughout the college admissions process. Worst of all, you probably won't get into those prestigious schools you want to go to so badly.

People who get into highly selective colleges don't worship at the altar of prestige. They have too much confidence for that. They know they're going to be successful wherever they go. That confidence and immunity to namebranditis lets them find the right schools for them.

Getting into college is a lot like dating. Confidence is contagious. A little swagger is good.

The kid that worries that his life will be over if Princeton says, "No"—guess what? No swagger there.

The kid who makes all his decisions in high school based on what he thinks Stanford wants? No swagger.

The kid who works like crazy because he wants to be successful at whatever he tries; the kid who gets A's but really just wants to be challenged and intellectually stimulated as much as possible; the kid who can't wait to go to college and knows wherever he ends up, both he and the college will be lucky to have found each other? Now, that kid has some swagger.

Swagger personified

I worked with a student, Marcello, who had all the characteristics needed to take his best shot at some highly selective colleges. He had perfect grades, near-perfect test scores, a voracious appetite for learning and an excitement about all the opportunities waiting for him in college. He was likeable, self-effacing and a standout water polo player. Marcello had swagger.

He told me during one of our meetings, "I figure if I can leave college with a degree in electrical engineering and four years playing division I water polo, I'll be unstoppable."

He was right.

What he didn't say: "If I get into Stanford..."

A prestigious school wasn't going to decide for Marcello whether he would be successful. He was going all the way, with or without them. That's swagger.

Marcello went to Stanford. Today, he thrives at a capital management firm. I don't understand a single word of his job description, but I'm sure he does.

Don't believe that a prestigious college has the power to decide whether or not you're going to be successful. You get to make that decision for yourself. Act like it. A little swagger serves you well.

START WITH *WHY* COLLEGE?

Highly selective colleges are always going to be absurdly picky. Every year, they receive tens of thousands of applications from the most qualified students from around the world. Only about 10 to 20 out of every 100 applicants get in. That's not going to change.

So you have a choice to make. You can insist the only acceptable payback for your work is admission to a prestigious college, decide that anything else will be a disappointment and spend your high school years desperately trying to please a very short list of colleges.

Or you can reject that thinking. You can reject the idea that prestigious schools are the best—that if you don't get into Brown, you failed. You can have enough confidence in yourself to believe if you work hard and treat people right, you'll be successful wherever you go to college. You can embrace the idea that hundreds of colleges will almost certainly take you exactly as you are. And you can have enough swagger to know that if Yale, Stanford or Princeton says no, you'll just fulfill your envisioned college experience someplace else.

The cure for namebranditis is to think about why you want to go to college and acknowledge that there are a lot of schools that could give you what you're looking for. Show college admissions committees that more than going to a school with a famous name, you want a chance to learn and surround yourself with smart, interesting people.

If you had to attend a top tier school to have a good life, we wouldn't have more than 2,000 colleges in this country where people pay good money to attend. Protect yourself from namebranditis. It's not where you go to college. It's who you are and what you do while you're there that counts.

WHAT DO YOU WANT IN A COLLEGE?

LOOK FOR YOUR FIT

A college can be ranked in the top 10 on the *US News & World Report* college rankings, have Nobel Prize-winning professors and a beautiful campus with gothic architecture. But that doesn't mean it's a good school for you. What college utopia is for one student could be four years of unhappiness for another. That's why savvy college shoppers are out to find the schools that fit them, not necessarily the ones that their friends, the rankings lists or the press claim are the best.

The college-bound are spoiled with choices. You have more than 2,000 colleges to pick from and there's no way you could ever investigate all of them. That's one reason so many of the students I've met initially default to applying to prestigious schools—they don't know what else to look for and assume that those schools must be great. Again (say it with me!): prestige is hardly a measure of a college's quality. It's an even worse measure of whether or not you would be happy and successful at a particular school.

The right school

The right school for you is the one that sends you back home for your first holiday break gushing about how much you love college. It's the place where you're excited about what you're learning in class and completely fulfilled with the life you lead outside of class. It's the one where you learn more about yourself and what you're good at, where you change from a high school kid to a confident young adult, and where you make the college memories you'll (perhaps selectively) tell your own kids about one day. Most importantly, it's the school that four years later sends you from graduation excited and prepared for life after college, but also just a little sad to say goodbye to what's been such an amazing home.

There are some other compelling advantages to looking for and finding the right colleges for you. First: it can help you get in.

More than half of colleges surveyed by the National Association for College Admissions Counseling said that when making admissions decisions, they give moderate to considerate importance to a student's demonstrated interest in the school.[6] The yield rate—the percentage of admitted students who decide to enroll—is an important statistic for most colleges because they need to fill their freshman classes, preferably with students that are good fits for the school. That's why so many schools have started asking applicants to answer essay prompts about why they're interested.

> ### KID TO KID
>
> #### Find your fit
>
> I know some kids that got hooked on a reach school because of the name. That doesn't mean anything. There are so many good colleges that many people haven't heard of! I applied to six target and safety schools. I got into all of them and all but one of my reach schools. I can promise that all seniors will find some safety or target school that they love. They just have to put the effort into finding the schools for them.
>
> Kyla N.
> Former Collegewise student,
> Class of 2012
> Chapman University

Students who've done a thoughtful college search and found the right schools have much better answers for this question than the old standby, "It's a good school."

Second: it may pay. Since part of finding the right school is zeroing in on colleges where your chances of admission are strong, you'll have a better chance of getting favorable financial aid and scholarships. I write more about this in the "Affording College" section. Short version: schools are often more generous with aid money for applicants they are particularly interested in enrolling, often regardless of whether or not you demonstrate financial need.

Finally, students who thoughtfully search for the right colleges tend to have less stressful application processes. They have a list of colleges they're excited about, plenty of which are well within their admissions reach. They feel more in control of their college destiny because they're not at the mercy of admissions decisions from a long list of highly selective colleges.

Finding the right colleges takes some time. My Collegewise students do it by thinking a lot about themselves and what they want their college experiences to be like, even if they can't articulate it perfectly. They are engaged in the process and do the work to learn about potential colleges. That's how they end up at the right places.

You won't be certain a college is right for you until you actually get there and become a student. But if you do a thoughtful college search and look for the right fits, you're much more likely to end up at the right place for you.

START YOUR SEARCH BY JUNIOR YEAR

Few 17-year-olds have a perfect answer to the question, "What are you looking for in a college?"

How could you? You haven't *been* to college yet.

Picking a school is a little bit like marrying someone without dating. Just like you're probably not going to find your soul mate based on one questionnaire, finding the right colleges to apply to takes time. That's why I always suggest students start their college search in earnest during their junior year.

Finding the right colleges to apply to is a process. You have to take the time to think about what you want from a college. You have to look around and do your research. You have to go to college fairs, visit some colleges and ask your counselor and your parents for advice. You'll have to trust your gut about which schools are really right (or wrong) for you. And you must have faith that all this looking and thinking will pay off in the end. That's the way big, life-changing decisions work. That's also why it's best to not wait until senior year to seriously think about where to apply.

There's no quick-and-easy way to find the right schools for you, and delaying your search will inevitably lead to stress and application chaos. Start looking during your junior year. That will let you enjoy the search without being rushed. And the age-old saying about finding the person you want to marry applies: when it happens, you'll know.

Here's what to expect

Most colleges host informational sessions led by admissions officers. Held on campus or locally when colleges visit high schools and college fairs, these sessions can be a great way to learn more about schools that interest you, or to find out about a school you're not yet familiar with.

Info sessions give a broad overview of the college—the size and geographic representation of the college, popular majors, the average class size, special academic programs and activities many of their students take advantage of.

It's the presenter's job to get the audience interested in the school. So you'll also hear about any distinctions the college is proud of, like where they're ranked on the US News & World Report list, or if the college was named one of America's greenest campuses, or how many Nobel Prize-winning professors are on campus.

While it's a good idea to bring any questions you have about the college, you're not likely to get answers to questions about your chances of admission, like, "Are my SAT scores high enough?" The presenter isn't in a position to evaluate your candidacy in that setting and will be hesitant to say anything that could later make you feel misled when you get your admissions decision.

Instead, ask questions about the admissions process and the typical student the college admits. That will allow the presenter to give you the information they're comfortable sharing, like whether or not interviews are offered, the ranges of GPAs and test scores for admits, and the importance the school places on essays and letters of recommendations.

Think of a college information session like a more personal version of a brochure. You may not be able to decide whether or not the college is right for you based on the session alone. You learn more, you get questions answered by a live human being and you get clues about whether or not you want to do even more research about the school.

EVALUATE YOURSELF, TOO

Choosing a college is a lot like buying a gym membership. You can enroll in the most expensive, well-equipped gym in town, but if you never go to the classes, never meet with the trainers and only work out sporadically, you can't blame the gym if you're still out of shape six months later. A college can promise you the world, but none of it is going to mean anything if you don't take advantage of what's offered once you're there. You can't just evaluate colleges. You have to evaluate yourself, too.

A college can offer you lots of personal attention in small classes, but if you aren't the kind of student who will raise your hand and participate or who will ask questions and talk to professors during their office hours, you may not benefit from what the college is providing you.

A big-city college setting like New York, Chicago or Washington, D.C., may not benefit you if you're not excited to take advantage of what those cities have to offer, like opportunities to do internships or experience local culture.

If a college promises a diverse student population from all 50 states and 28 different countries, are you excited to be around people who are different from you? Do you want to hear how they've grown up and learn from their perspectives? If not, you're going to miss out on one of that college's featured benefits.

When a college touts a benefit of their school, ask yourself if that's something you really want and will actually take advantage of. Be honest with yourself and with your parents. You don't have to love everything about your potential school, but you'll be more likely to find the right place if you've considered the fit between both parties.

COMMITTEE NOTES

Make your own Harvard

... the larger problem with ranking colleges is that it is based on the premise that attending college is like an amusement park ride: a passive experience where the student picks the most thrilling ride he can handle, straps in, and holds on to his digital camera. College is nothing like that. When students go to college—any college—they take classes. Some of those classes are taught by brilliant professors, some are taught by lousy professors, and some are taught by graduate students. What they get out of their education is a function of the effort they put in. It's possible to go to the number-two ranked college and get a terrible education, just as it's possible to go to number 180 and get a wonderful education.

Zac Bissonnette
Author, Debt-Free U

START WITH THESE 10 QUESTIONS

I've always thought it's unfair to ask high school students what they're looking for in a college. It feels like asking people to explain what they're looking for in a car when they haven't actually driven one yet. So I ask students to answer, in writing, these 10 key questions about themselves. (Writing forces you to think harder about your answers.)

You may not know yet what you're looking for in a college, but you do know yourself better than anyone else. The questions are a good starting point to get you thinking about what you might like from your college experience. Your responses can also help you focus your initial college search.

As you go through your college search, you can come back to what you've written and consider how, if at all, your perspectives have changed based on what you've learned. Keep coming back and revisiting your answers, and you'll be a lot better prepared when colleges ask you to explain why you've decided to apply.

Some students don't have answers for all of these right away, which is fine. Just write "Not sure" or even "Don't care." Those answers may change the more you learn about colleges.

1. Why do you want to go to college?

It's good to consider why you're doing all this, and your answer to this question can impact your college search. If you answer, "Because I want to be a journalist," it makes sense to look at schools that offer a journalism major.

If it's, "Because I've lived in the same gated community my entire life and want to experience something different," you'll want to pay attention to where the schools are located and the diversity of their student populations.

2. Do you think you're ready to go to college?

There's no shame in feeling nervous, academically unprepared or just unsure of yourself when it comes to college. But I've seen students who, instead of just being honest about their doubts, dragged their feet through the entire application process, leaving their parents to (resentfully) do all the work for them.

> **KID TO KID**
>
> **Small classes**
>
> I cannot tell you how much of an effect small classes have on your overall academic experience. Every single professor I have not only knows my name, but truly cares about my education and encourages me to come visit them during office hours.
>
> Kelly G.
> Texas Christian University

If you have similar concerns, first, be honest about it with yourself and your parents. Second, apply to at least a few colleges anyway. You apply in the fall of your senior year but you don't actually decide where—or *if*—you're going to go to college until the end of your senior year. If you're still not ready to go then, you could consider other options; but a lot can change in those six to eight months. Refusing to even apply just takes options off the table that are hard to get back later.

3. How have you done your best learning?

I like this question better than, "Do you want small classes or big classes?"

The right colleges should give you lots of opportunities to love what you're learning and how you're learning it. So think about the times in high school where you were at your intellectual best. Not just the times when you got the highest grades, but when you were excited about what you were learning.

Was it a particular subject? Was it because the teacher was great? Was it because it involved projects, competition with other students or a lot of class discussions? Or maybe it was something that didn't even happen in school but you just took the time to learn it on your own?

Your answers to this question can tell you a lot about what you might like to study, whether or not it's important that you like the teacher, and how much academic freedom you'd like to have to choose your classes.

1. What would you like to learn more about?

"What do you want to major in?" is a big question a lot of my students aren't yet ready to answer.

"What would you like to learn more about?" is less committal. It lets you consider how much you like math without necessarily deciding that you'll major in math yet. College is school, after all. It's important to consider the learning part of your future four years.

2. How hard do want to work academically?

Some schools are a lot more demanding than others. I've met students who say they want to go to Cornell but don't want to take four APs their senior year of high school because of the workload. Those students shouldn't apply to the school with a reputation as the hardest Ivy to get *out* of.

I don't think you're a bad kid if you admit you don't want to overdo the academic intensity in college, but it's worth considering before you pick your schools. When researching schools, pay attention to what the students say about their experiences. Students at MIT, Carnegie Mellon, University of Chicago and Middlebury will bring up how much they study. It's like a badge of honor. Swarthmore College even prints T-shirts that read, "Anywhere else it would have been an A...really." That's a clue.

3. Do you have any idea what you want to do with your life?

I haven't met many successful adults who discovered their career paths when they were 17, so I don't think it's a problem if you can't yet answer this question. But if you already have a future career in mind, it should probably be a key criterion to consider when picking colleges.

Do a little career research and find out where people successful in the field went to college and what they studied. You might be surprised by what you find. For example, Google and Apple employ more graduates from San Jose State than they do from Berkeley, UCLA or MIT.[7]

4. What would you like to do on a typical Tuesday night in college? What about on a typical Saturday night?

I think this is a fun question because it's not necessarily the same as "What activities do you want to do in college?" The answers to this one draw out everything from the types of students you want to be around to where the campus is located to what you want to major in.

When we ask our Collegewise students, we get answers like, "Playing video games with my new friends in the dorms," "Talking politics in the coffee shop," "Heading into the city to do something fun," "Building a working robot with the other engineers," and "Going to the big football game."

This question also gets at just how comfortable you are with the idea of students drinking and doing other things they may not tell their parents about. With some notable exceptions, like the military academies and strict religious affiliated colleges, a certain percentage of kids at every school are going to find a way to have their good ol' college fun. Just how prevalent do you want that kind of fun to be?

You're only in class for a couple hours a day at most in college. The rest of the time, you're living your life on (or off) campus with your fellow students. Think about what you'd like to be doing in your free time and look for where that will be possible (See "50 Things You Can Do in College" if you need help brainstorming).

5. Do you want to go to college in a place that's different or similar to where you live now?

This one hits on everything from your city and state, to the size of your town, to the type of people in your community. College can be a four-year opportunity to live in a different place very different from where you live now. But that's not the right opportunity for everyone. It's good to consider just how much change you want to take on when you go to college.

One of my former Collegewise students said he wanted to be someplace very different because, "I've lived in the same gated community my entire life and gone to school with the same group of kids since I was five."

When he later applied to college, he mentioned that need for change in a lot of his "Why do you want to attend this college?" essays. One of those essays began, "I have never met anyone from Arkansas, and I think it's about time that I do."

6. Do you want to be with students who are like you or different from you?

Differences can come in lots of forms, like ethnicity, sexual orientation, where people are from, their religious beliefs (or lack of them), their politics, whether or not they drink or use drugs, etc.

Some colleges are a lot more diverse than others, and it's a good idea to consider whether or not you want to be with people who may be very different from you. A popular college application essay question asks you to describe how you'll contribute to the diversity of the campus community. Schools that ask that question tend to be proud of their diverse student population and look for students who want to become a part of it.

7. What's your family's college budget?

I cover this topic in more detail in the "How to Get Financial Aid and Scholarships" section. For now, here are two key considerations: First, talk to your parents and get a sense for how much they can afford to help send you to college. It's normal for some parents to be reluctant to discuss finances with their kids, but you can't do a responsible college search without knowing your family's financial limits. If your parents are uncomfortable discussing it, ask them to share the budget in "round numbers." That feels a little less financially invasive.

Second, don't automatically eliminate any college that's over your family's budget. You won't know the amount of any potential financial aid package until you are actually admitted. You can estimate it (see: "Meet the Net Price Calculator"), but the package could later be influenced by other factors, like your strength as an applicant. It would never be a good idea to apply to a long list of schools your family couldn't possibly afford. But don't cross every school off your list that exceeds your family's budget, either.

Talking politics

Weekend afternoons are spent doing homework or sitting in my friends' rooms listening to blues and jazz stations as we sip black coffee over political discussions.

Alex H.
Former Collegewise student, Class of 2010
American University

Hitting the town

Life at the University of Denver is always lively; there's a ton of activities to do on the weekends right on campus, including things like movie nights and just finding different things people are doing in their dorms...there's always something going on. Still, if you're looking for more to do, you can head downtown with the light rail which is right across the street from the north side of campus. I'm practically never bored here.

Matt P.
Former Collegewise student, Class of 2011
University of Denver

Going natural

I spend my weekends hiking through the forest with friends, climbing an 80-foot tree, exploring the caves on campus, going down the Hobbit Hole, swinging on tree swings, camping in the forts built by students, swimming in the Garden of Eden and seeing AMAZING concerts at The Catalyst (Rebelution, Jenny Lewis, Matisyahu, Mason Jennings!). If you're someone who is down for adventures, loves nature, would attend drum circles on the full moon, cares about what's happening in the world, and is ready for a good time that doesn't involve theme parties...then Santa Cruz is the place for you.

Anne Marie S.
Former Collegewise student, Class of 2008
UC Santa Cruz

Cheering at the big game

Football is big at Boston College and everyone is really into supporting the football team. Weekends during the fall are all about football. Go BC!!!!!!!

Sammy M.
Former Collegewise student, Class of 2010
Boston College

HOW TO LEARN MORE ABOUT COLLEGES

BEWARE OF COMMON SEARCH DERAILERS

There are some common myths about colleges that can derail your college search if you subscribe to them. Here are the five I hear over and over again, and why I recommend you overcome them early on.

1. "There's no personal attention at large universities—you're just another number."

Plenty of the students I talk with rave about the personal attention they get at their large schools—they just have to *ask* for it. If you go to a university with 25,000 undergraduates, it's nobody's job to force personal attention on you. If you don't show up to class, if you don't make appointments with an academic advisor, if you don't reach out to the departments that offer academic, health or emotional support, you won't get any personal attention. But it won't be because nobody at the school was willing to help you.

One of my former Collegewise students went to a large university and made what he thought was a startling discovery. He visited his professors weekly during their office hours just to ask questions and talk about the material. "A lot of my professors say that I'm the only student who visits them during office hours," he says. "I don't know why everybody doesn't do it. Sometimes, they even *tell* me what's going to be on the test!"

And what about the criticism that you can't graduate from a public school in four years? That students get shut out of the classes they need and have to go on the five- or six-year plan?

It's certainly true for some students. But here's a test. What if your parents dropped you off at a large university and told you, "If you graduate on time four years from now, we'll give you $1 million." What would you do?

> **KID TO KID**
>
> **Big schools give attention, too**
>
> I have had great professors so far. Teachers are always willing to work with you or have you come by their office hours if you need the extra help.
>
> Natasha K.
> Former Collegewise student,
> Class of 2011
> University of Oregon

My guess is you would make sure that four years later, you were skipping across the stage to collect your diploma and million-dollar payday.

Does it take some extra effort at large schools? Sure. You'll need to visit your academic advisor regularly. You might register for five classes every semester expecting that one or two of them won't be available, but thereby ensuring that you're still carrying a full load of courses. You can't fail classes (because then you'll need to repeat them) or change your major four times. But you can finish in four years if you want to.

I'm not pushing big schools here—they are absolutely not right for everybody. But don't rule them out because you've been led to believe that attending a large university sentences you to an impersonal education.

2.   "I should pick colleges based on my major."

If you're going to college to become a mechanical engineer, your future major will drive your college selection. It would be nonsensical for you to apply any school that didn't have a mechanical engineering major.

But I recommend students be realistic—and honest—about just how sure they are of their intended major before they let it take primacy in their college search.

Many of my former Collegewise students changed their majors while they were in college. According to Dr. Fritz Grupe, founder of MyMajors.com, 50 percent of college students who declare a major before they start college end up changing majors.[8]

If you think you want to major in business and you apply to nine colleges based mostly on the reported strength of their business majors, what happens if you later decide you don't like being a business major?

Here's a great way to factor your choice of major into your college search. Visit the websites of a few schools that interest you and read about the major you're considering. Find the list of the required courses you'll have to take, along with the descriptions of what is taught in each course. Read what the department's mission is, and what they promise their graduates will learn during their time there.

If that suggestion sounds like a tedious homework assignment, you're probably not all that excited about the major you claim to be considering. There is absolutely nothing wrong with that. At least then you'll know you shouldn't let that major alone determine whether or not you should apply to a school. You might consider a different intended major, applying as an undecided major, or picking schools that have one or two years of general education requirements so you can sample a lot of different subjects before you have to decide.

On the other hand, if reading about a major gets you even more excited about the subject and the school—if you wish you could just start those classes as soon as possible—you're probably on to something. In that case, give your intended major a little more weight during your college search.

3.   "It will hurt my chances of admission if I apply as an undecided/undeclared major."

I often hear concern from students that applying as an "undecided/undeclared" major will make them less appealing than an applicant who declares what she wants to study. Parents often share the concern, which is likely why they often ask me if Collegewise has a career or aptitude test a student can take to find out their strengths. (We don't offer any such tests.) As long as you apply to the right colleges, you won't have to worry.

I think it's perfectly normal for high school students not to know what they want to major in. If that sounds like you, look for "undecided" or "undeclared" as an option when you visit schools' websites, and maybe even look for a statistic about how many students enroll without declaring a major.

Schools won't hide whether or not they're welcoming of students who are undecided on their major. Consider this excerpt from Marquette University's website: "Undecided about a major? You're not alone. In fact, 'undecided' is our most popular major. We've found over time, however, that few students are truly undecided. Most have many ideas and interests they wish to pursue in college.

That's why we prefer to say 'multi-interested.' With more than 100 majors at Marquette, we'll help you to choose a major or minor combination that matches your interests and skills. We think you'll find that a liberal arts education will not only prepare you for meaningful work, but for a purposeful life as well."[9]

Most schools that offer undecided/undeclared options will probably require you to begin with general education requirements (classes that everyone has to take regardless of their major) so you can try different things. And as long as you select a major by the end of your sophomore year, you'll be fine.

I'm all for allowing students time to decide their majors, but that doesn't mean you shouldn't at least consider what you might like to study. Many schools, including those that welcome major-undeclared applicants, require admissions essays asking you to describe your academic interests. And if a college interviewer asks you what you're interested in studying, it doesn't look very mature to just shrug your shoulders and say, "I have no clue." In those cases, tell them what you're at least considering studying, why that's interesting to you, and why you'd like to keep your options open.

4. "The higher a school is ranked, the better it is."

US News & World Report began publishing its annual college rankings in 1983. Today, the list is the juggernaut of college rankings. In one month after the 2011 rankings were announced, the *US News & World Report* website got 10 million visitors who found out that Harvard and Princeton tied for the No. 1 spot.[10]

It's big business. Yet if you look at the methodology of the rankings, it's hardly scientific. Some of the criteria include the average SAT scores of admits, the admissions yield (what percentage of admits decide to enroll), and a peer assessment score, which asks deans and college presidents to rank their competition on a scale from one to five.

How does the president or dean of one school know how to rank an entirely different college, one that's his or her competitor? That's like asking the CEO of McDonalds to rank Burger King's food.

Best-selling author, Malcolm Gladwell, summed up the flaws of the *US News & World Report* rankings in a 2011 *New Yorker* article:

> There's no direct way to measure the quality of an institution—how well a college manages to inform, inspire, and challenge its students. So the US News algorithm relies instead on proxies for quality—and the proxies for educational quality turn out to be flimsy at best.[11]

My bone to pick

My problem with college rankings, beyond the fact that they're so subjective, is when a student or parent accepts them as gospel and won't consider schools that aren't ranked high enough. That doesn't just eliminate dozens, even hundreds of schools that might be good fits, but it also guarantees the student will apply only to those colleges that reject most of their applicants.

Don't let *US News & World Report* tell you where—or even worse, where not—to apply to college. The rankings are controversial, they change every year, and they have nothing to do with whether or not a school is right for you.

USE THE RIGHT COLLEGE SEARCH TOOLS

As you start to investigate colleges, it's helpful to have a good toolbox. Here are five sources I recommend students use to research colleges. I'm presenting these in order of suggested use, the latter ones on the list being more appropriate once you've found potential college fits.

1. Collegeboard.com

It seems appropriate that the same company that produces the SAT and AP tests also offers a way for students to use process of elimination for colleges. The site has a fairly comprehensive college search function that lets you select the attributes you want in a college (e.g., size, location, majors, selectivity, etc.) and see a complete list of those schools that match your chosen criteria.

So if you're wondering, for example, which small colleges on the East Coast have fraternities, intramural lacrosse, on-campus housing and a major in music industry management, you can search Collegeboard.com and find the 13 schools that have what you're looking for.

2. The Fiske Guide to Colleges

Fiske is the former education editor of the *New York Times*, and his guide profiles more than 300 of the country's most popular colleges. Anytime you want to investigate a particular college you don't know much about, The Fiske Guide is a great place to start. Each school gets an objective, easily digestible two- to three-page write-up about the college's mission, strongest programs, admissions information, campus life and housing options. Think of the Fiske Guide as a way to get a quick overview of a college so you can decide whether or not you want to learn more.

3. Unigo.com

Unigo is a (mostly) free website designed for today's multimedia college searcher. In addition to a short write-up about life at each school, it also features videos of current students discussing their experiences at their respective schools, links to blogs and online newspapers, campus pictures and video tours.

The sell for me on Unigo is that our Collegewise students love using it. It makes researching colleges less like a homework assignment and more like watching YouTube. The site also offers for-pay college counseling online, and the ability to pay college students to chat with you one-on-one about their schools.

I don't use those services with students so I can't speak to their quality, but the free portions of the website are excellent.

4. The colleges' own websites

I put this toward the bottom of the list because I find most colleges' websites to be terrible places to *start* learning about a school. It's hard to get past the marketing lingo like, "We seek to empower students to utilize critical thinking and technology to make meaningful contributions in a globally changing world where..." seriously, at what point did I lose you?

But once you have a sense for what you want and you've identified some schools that seem to offer those qualities, the colleges' websites are the best source of information to investigate those offerings.

5. Scattergrams

A scattergram is a graph that shows you the GPA, SAT or ACT score and admissions result for students at your high school, grouped by college. So you can pick a school and see what the numbers were for the students who've applied in recent years, and whether they were accepted, rejected or wait-listed. It's a quick, visual way to get a sense of how your numbers stack up against those of other applicants from your high school, and you can get at least a basic sense of your chances of admission.

Some high schools put together their own scattergrams, and others use a company called Naviance. Ask your high school counselor if your school has any of this data available to you. Remember that even if your school doesn't have this data, your high school counselor often knows what the results have been for students in recent years, and she can often tell you how you compare to other applicants.

Wikipedia lists

Wikipedia's write-ups about colleges usually list "notable alumni" for each school. It's a good reminder that graduates of the least famous of colleges can go on to be CEOs, coaches, politicians, professors, scientists, published authors, actors, inventors, professional athletes, astronauts, entrepreneurs, news anchors and presidents of other colleges.

CLICK KEY SECTIONS ON COLLEGE WEBSITES

If a college sounds intriguing after reading about it in the Fiske Guide and researching it on Unigo, it's time to visit the college's website. Once you get there, here are 10 key clicks to find the information many students want to know.

1. About

The "About" section is the best place to get basic facts, like how many students attend, how many majors are offered and how ethnically diverse the campus is. It also often explains the college's mission, which can be revealing.

For example, some colleges exist to prepare students for their chosen careers, some promise a broad education with plenty of reading and writing, some have religious affiliations that want students to grow in their faith and some have specialized offerings like designing your major with an academic advisor.

2. Life at.../Student life/Campus life

Here's where you'll find information about clubs, dorms and what there is to do on campus. Watch for traditions, too—they can tell you a lot about the student population and what they care about.

For example, you won't have to spend long on Ohio State's website to see how many traditions revolve around rooting for the football and basketball teams. In the meantime, students at Reed College annually celebrate "Nitrogen Day" because it's apparently an "underappreciated element." Those traditions are good signs that Ohio State and Reed are two very different colleges.

3. Academics

Here you'll find what majors are available and where you can look up the classes of the major you're considering. If you're already serious about a potential major, pay attention to the eligibility requirements for that major—if it's a popular choice, some schools make you attend for a year or two and complete certain courses satisfactorily before you can declare it.

4. Student stories

Some schools have testimonials or even videos of current students sharing their experiences at the school. Of course they're going to pick students who really like it there. (Nobody ever says, "I hate this place—I want to transfer" in one of those videos.) But if those students make comments about their schools that make you think *That's what I'm looking for in my college*, it's a good sign you're on the right college search track.

5. Undergraduate admissions

Here's where you find everything you need to know about applying to the school, from the recommended high school classes, to what tests do you need to take, to the deadlines and application options.

On many college websites, this information can be surprisingly hard to find. Your first click is usually "Prospective Students," "Admissions" or "Apply," (even though you're not actually applying yet). Eventually you'll get the option to select "Undergraduate Admissions."

Unless you're a college student looking to transfer, you're looking for information for "First-time Freshmen." Make sure you pay attention to any "Frequently Asked Questions" sections here, too. They often share a lot of information about the application process and what the school looks for in a competitive applicant.

6. Office of financial aid

This section tells you about the cost of attending the school and how to apply for financial aid. To find it, your first click is usually "Prospective Students," then "Undergraduate Admissions," then "Financial Aid," "Cost and Aid" or "Affording (insert name of college here)."

A word of caution: Many schools claim to meet "100 percent of demonstrated financial need," which certainly sounds good. But that doesn't mean they just give money to everyone who needs it. You have to qualify for need-based aid, and not all financial aid is free money. It can also come in the form of loans or work study.

If you want to see how much aid people really get and how much is free vs. loans, look up your college using the National Center for Educational Statistics "College Navigator" tool, found here: http://nces.ed.gov/collegenavigator/

7. Blogs

Many colleges have begun hosting blogs on their websites that are updated by current students and/or admissions officers. These can be particularly helpful as you move into the application process, as they'll even post reminders and advice for applicants.

8. Potential contacts

If you have an interest in a specific department, club or organization, the website for the group often includes the email address of the person in charge.

Maybe you want to know more about how many open slots there are in the marching band every year, or how you go about getting involved with the school paper, or if you have to try out to play on the club rugby team? Why not drop an email and ask? You'll learn more about what you really want to know, and you'll have some additional fodder if the college later asks you why you're applying.

I have just three warnings about this practice: (1) Don't bug/stalk people—one email ought to do it; (2) Ask a specific question, rather something general like, "Can you tell me about the school newspaper?" (3) Don't do this just as a strategy to show interest in a school—do it because you really want to know something.

9. Request more information

Don't miss links that invite you to request more information or to be added to the mailing list. That way, you'll be alerted if the college is planning a visit to your high school, the alumni are holding a local event for interested applicants, or admissions officers will be staffing a table at a local college fair.

Many colleges also track all of your contact like emails, visits and attendance at local events to get a sense of your level of interest. Submitting an inquiry form counts as a contact, and the alerts you'll get will give you even more chances to show your interest as you get closer to applying.

10. Anything else important to you

As you start to make a mental wish list of what you're looking for in a college, you'll probably have particular things you want to look for on the websites, like the countries you could visit in a study abroad program, whether or not there's support for students with learning disabilities or how popular fraternities and sororities are on campus. Don't be afraid to veer off on your own cyberspace path and look for things that interest you.

EVALUATE YOUR ADMISSIONS CHANCES

As you learn about colleges that seem like potential fits, it's good to get a sense of your future chances of admission. Some less-selective public schools will come right out and share their admissions formulas—take the required classes, get the required GPA and test scores, and you're in. But here's how to evaluate your chances when the selection process isn't as definitive.

1. **Type the college's name and "class profile" into your favorite search engine.**

What you're looking for is the information about the most recent class of freshmen who enrolled. The data will usually be labeled by the year that class will graduate from college (example: "Entering Freshmen Profile: Class of 2016"). Then bookmark or print up that page.

2. **Type the college's name and "common data set" into your search engine.**

The Common Data Set is a standardized questionnaire to which many colleges have posted responses. Bookmark or print that page.

3. **Using one or both those sources, find this information about the college's current freshmen:**

- The SAT/ACT range for the middle 50 percent;
- The average high school GPA;
- How many freshmen were in the top 10, 25, 50, etc. percent of their high school class; and
- The overall percentage of applicants accepted.

4. **Interpret the data.**

The acceptance rate of a college gives you an idea of where your GPA and test scores need to be to have a good chance of admission.

> ### Double-check guidebook data
>
> Don't rely on a college guidebook to judge whether or not your GPA and test scores are in the academic range. Those books take a long time to produce and can have admissions data as much as two years out of date. The college's website and the common data set are usually more current.

If the acceptance rate of a school is at least 50 percent, and your GPA and test scores are about the same as the middle range for the freshman class, I would consider that a "target school" for you. I'm not guaranteeing you'll get in, but the odds seem to be in your favor.

If the acceptance rate of a school is between 35 to 45 percent, your grades and test scores would need to be near the high end of the range to consider that a target school.

Any college that accepts fewer than 20 percent of the applicants is a highly selective school and usually a reach for just about everybody.

This isn't an exact science, as many of these schools will also be looking at activities, letters of recommendation, essays and your interview, all of which can influence a decision. It's also important to remember the posted numbers include everyone who was admitted in the freshman class, including highly recruited athletes and kids whose parents pay for buildings on campus. Those students don't necessarily have inferior qualifications, but it's fair to say those in special interest groups have something the colleges want, which sometimes makes grades and test scores less important.

5. Compare your findings with your school's data.

Once you have this preliminary sense of your chances at a particular school, that's a good time to investigate the scattergrams (if your school has them) to see how the applicants from your high school have fared. If your school doesn't have scattergrams, visit your high school counselor, show her the data you've collected and ask if she has any feedback about your chances of admission.

HAVE FUN VISITING

For many high school students and parents I meet, the idea of visiting colleges feels more like a homework assignment than it does an adventure. They feel pressure to visit ALL the colleges they're interested in, to turn every visit into an intense fact-finding mission, and to do all of it while the colleges are in session as opposed to over the summer. Those expectations can make college visits stressful and not nearly as fun as they should be. So here are some visit tips to help you enjoy what should be a positive part of the college search process.

1. No need to visit all your chosen schools before applying.

"Visit all your schools before you apply," is great advice in theory. But it's just not practical, especially if you're applying to colleges far away (and in many different directions from your home). Remember that you can also visit colleges after you apply, and even after you get accepted.

You apply to most colleges in the fall of your senior year. You hear back around March, and you usually have until May 1 of your senior year to make a decision. That means there are five to seven months after you apply when you can still visit colleges.

Before you apply, gravitate toward schools near places you're visiting anyway, like for a sports tournament, a band competition or even a Thanksgiving weekend at Uncle Frank's house. That will get you the most bang for your visit buck.

Also, prioritize visiting schools you aren't yet convinced of. This gives you the chance to fall in love or decide they're not right for you. The rest, you can save until after you apply.

2. Don't limit your visits to "reach" schools.

Many of the students I meet plan visits to only their top choices, which all too often are schools most likely to reject them. Instead of widening their college choices by visiting schools where their chances of admission are solid, they're narrowing the pool by renewing vows to dream schools.

If you love Duke, if you've cheered on their basketball team since you were 12 years old and simply cannot envision a universe where you wouldn't apply to Duke, you don't need to fall any deeper in love with Duke by visiting the campus. Spend this time visiting other colleges, preferably some more likely to love you back. Baylor, Gonzaga, Syracuse and Michigan State have great basketball teams, rabid fans, and a lot less competition for spots in the freshman class. If your Duke admission comes through in the spring, *then* go see the home of the Blue Devils.

3. A summer visit is better than no visit.

Some students are told to only visit a college when it is in session; that visiting over the summer doesn't give you the same feel as when the campus teems with students. There's some truth to it—a lot of colleges are deserted over the summer and it's absolutely not the same as if you were there in the fall. But it's not easy to put your high school classes and activities on hold to go see colleges, so the visit-while-it's-in-session logic doesn't always hold up.

If you can visit a college during the school year, do it, especially if you want to sit in on a class, get a sense of whether a big school's population is too much for you or do anything else that only is revealed when students are there. But if you just want to see the campus or find out just how small the college's small town really is, a summer visit is probably fine, and certainly better than not visiting at all. Before you make the trek, just check the college's website to make sure they'll be offering tours while you're there.

4. Don't see more colleges in one trip than you can handle.

It's possible to commit college-visit overkill by trying to see too many colleges in one trip. I remember one student only somewhat sarcastically recalling her family's marathon college tour: "We saw four colleges the first day, another four the second day, and I was like, 'I don't want to go to college anymore—I just want to go home,'" she said.

I understand why this happens to families. If you're going to take the time to travel someplace to see colleges, it makes sense that you should see as many as possible as long as you're there. But the average person wouldn't enjoy seeing nine amusement parks in three days, either. So be realistic about just how much college touring you can really handle.

I'm a college junkie who will see schools anywhere I happen to be visiting. But even I can't see more than two or three in a day before I'm ready to do something else.

5. If you're not having fun, you're doing it wrong.

Some of the advice about visiting colleges you read borders on the absurd. "Take the tour, listen to the admissions presentation, sit in on a class, eat in the cafeteria, interview a faculty member, stay overnight in a dorm, visit the athletic facilities, tour the library, visit the surrounding community..." The list goes on.

I can't imagine my Collegewise students wanting to do all of those things, or finding the time to do them for every college on their list. It's not realistic. I've never met a student who said, "That college visit wouldn't have been nearly as valuable were it not for this two-page checklist I brought with me."

Yes, it's a good idea to contact the campus tour offices and make some formal arrangements for your campus visits. Once you're admitted, there will likely be some schools that deserve more time to give a thorough evaluation, maybe even one that includes a visit to a class and an overnight stay. But until that time, most college visits don't need to be so rigorously planned. Gut instincts are surprisingly accurate when visiting schools.

Have a little fun

Take the tour, look around, maybe have lunch on campus and try to imagine what it would be like to attend. Most importantly: enjoy yourself. Looking at colleges is like getting to shop for your own birthday present. If you're not having fun, you're doing it wrong.

CONNECT THE DOTS LATER

Some of the best parts of college can't be summed up on the schools' websites.

Yes, you're going to college to get a degree. But each spring, when our Collegewise counselors survey our former students who are in college and ask them how they're enjoying their college lives, the vast majority don't talk about the picturesque campus or the 12:1 student faculty ratio or the fact that there are more than 300 clubs and organizations on campus—typical website material. They talk about new friends, finding mentors, living in dorms, discovering their talents, being independent, taking road trips, going to football games, having fun and being proud of what they're doing.

There's no predicting the future with certainty. If you think about the five best experiences you've had in high school, how many of them could you have predicted back in eighth grade? Whether your highlights are academic, social, athletic or something else, chances are they may make perfect sense looking back, but would have been difficult to predict in advance. Many of the best parts of college will be a lot like that.

In his commencement address at Stanford in 2005, Steve Jobs, the founder and former CEO of Apple, said, "Again, you can't connect the dots looking forward; you can only connect them looking backwards. So you have to trust that the dots will somehow connect in your future. You have to trust in something—your gut, destiny, life, karma, whatever. This approach has never let me down, and it has made all the difference in my life."

Plenty to look forward to

When you start your college search, remember some of the parts may not get mentioned on the websites or during the tours. Accepting that you can't connect all the dots now—that they'll connect later—will also help you realize just how many places you could have a great college experience.

If you need some inspiration, here are 50 things you might get to do in college, each of which have been experienced firsthand by at least one former Collegewise student or current Collegewise counselor.

1. See how many straight nights you can eat spaghetti.
2. Be a resident advisor in the dorms.
3. Do research in physics with a professor.
4. Meet your future husband or wife.
5. Meet the person who will one day be your maid of honor or best man.
6. Paint your face in the school's colors for the big game.
7. Have a professor who tells you that she sees great potential in your work.
8. Enjoy late night conversations with your new friends in the dorm.
9. Create memories with your friends that will make you smile when you're 50.
10. Write for the campus newspaper.
11. Sit with a professor during her office hours and realize you're chatting with the person who wrote the textbook you're using in class.
12. Play mud football games on Sundays.
13. Study abroad in Italy. Or Greece. Or Australia.
14. Eat late night pizza in the dorms.
15. Take road trips.

16. Play intramural basketball games—at midnight.
17. Choose classes you want to take.
18. Pull an all-nighter studying with your friends.
19. Go to parties—good ones.
20. Participate in campus traditions.
21. Sing (obscene) songs to your college's rival at the homecoming game.
22. Work a part-time job at the campus coffee shop, the library, or at the restaurant in town.
23. Discover your academic passions.
24. Play in the school's marching band.
25. Participate in the engineering Olympics.
26. Feel like you're getting a little smarter every day.
27. Realize that you are actually excited to attend your classes.
28. Leave everything you didn't like about high school behind.
29. Go on a camping trip with your new friends.
30. Find an internship in a career you're considering.
31. Meet mentors who will help you reach your potential.
32. Celebrate the end of finals week with your fellow students.
33. Take a class that has absolutely nothing to do with your major just because it looks interesting.
34. Join a fraternity or sorority.
35. Participate in an outdoor education program.
36. Go to the school's football games. Or the basketball games. Or the hockey games.
37. Spend Thanksgiving with a friend's family because they live closer to campus.
38. Camp out to get basketball tickets.
39. Eat food for dinner that would make your mom cringe.
40. Write a senior thesis on a subject you get to pick.
41. Spend your summer getting career experience in your major.
42. Study in the park—in between Frisbee tossing.
43. Excel academically and enjoy what you're learning.
44. Make the kind of friends you know will be in your life for a very long time.
45. Do community service with your college friends.
46. Find your natural talents and interests.
47. Discover what you want to do with your life.
48. Do things that, one day, your kids won't be able to imagine Mom or Dad doing.
49. Graduate and marvel at how far you've come, how much you've grown, and how much you've learned over the last four years.
50. See how proud your parents are at your graduation.

HOW TO FINALIZE YOUR LIST

STRIVE FOR BALANCE

A lot of students create college lists that are heavy on schools where they don't have a good chance of being admitted—"reach" schools. That sets them up for maximum disappointment when decisions arrive and they face a very real chance of not getting in anywhere. You deserve better than that. Make sure your list is mostly composed of "target" and "safety" schools.

At Collegewise, we define a "target" school as one where the students who got in last year look very similar to you on paper. So we think you have a good shot, too. A "safety" school is one where all signs point to an almost certain admission.

Target and safety schools should make up at least two-thirds of your college list. With more than 2,000 colleges to choose from, even C students can find plenty of colleges where they have a good chance of being admitted. A balanced list makes you more confident and excited about your college future. It puts you in charge instead of just crossing your fingers and hoping that enough colleges say yes.

I recommend students apply to one or two reach schools, four or five target schools and one or two safety schools. A balanced list like this takes the pressure off. You'll be likely to get into two-thirds of your schools. You can focus your application energy on schools most likely to admit you. You'll have more options of schools to attend and financial aid offers to compare. And you won't just leave your college fate to chance by applying to a long list of reach schools and hoping for the best.

Don't play the lottery

Some students think the best way to improve their chances of getting into one of their reach colleges is to apply to as many of them possible. They hope that by submitting 20 applications to reach schools, their odds of winning an admission improve dramatically. But getting into reach schools isn't like a state lottery system where your odds of winning improve (however marginally) the more often you play. I see plenty of students who get into reach schools every year, but I've never seen one do it by playing the lottery. Here's why:

Our Collegewise students who get admitted to reach schools do it by selecting one to two reaches that are the best matches for them, schools where they have a sincere, thoughtful answer to the question, "Why do you want to attend this school?" Lottery players never have a good answer to that question for all the schools on their reach list.

Applying to too many reach colleges also dilutes the quality of all your applications. No student is as energetic on the 20th application as she was on the first five. And no teacher or counselor wants to do the work of completing letters of recommendation for a long list of colleges that aren't realistic options for you.

You, too, high achievers

Some schools are reaches for even the highest achievers. Those 40 colleges that reject almost all of their applicants routinely turn away straight-A students. When your counselor tells you that the Ivy League schools, Stanford, Amherst, Northwestern, Notre Dame, Georgetown, the Naval Academy, or any of the other highly selective colleges are reaches for you, don't take it personally, even if you're the highest achiever in your senior class. You should be proud of the work you've done. Your hard work won't change the fact that those schools will get far more qualified applicants than could ever be admitted.

Even seemingly perfect kids still need balanced college lists. If you have a couple schools you really like that are out of your reach, take your best shot. Everyone deserves to aim high. But never let reach schools make up more than one-third of your college list. Your college future is not the place to play the lottery.

If there's one regret you want to avoid during the application college process, it's being rejected from most (or all) of your colleges and wishing you'd applied to more schools that might have taken you. That's an easy regret to avoid no matter what your GPA and test scores are.

COMMIT LATER

When a Collegewise family experiences some anxiety about whether or not a particular school should go on the student's list, we remind them that applying to a college doesn't necessarily mean the student must go there.

Applying is like asking a college on a date. You're not yet formally committing to a full-blown relationship. That might sound obvious, but recognizing that applying to a college is different from actually deciding to attend can relieve common doubts or even family disagreements.

I've heard:

> "I think I want to be a journalism major, but I'm not positive."

> "My parents want me to stay closer to home, but I want to go farther away."

> "That school is too expensive."

You apply to college in the fall of your senior year, but you almost certainly won't decide which one you'll attend until the end of your senior year. That's a lot of time to think about how committed you really are to journalism, to discuss with your parents whether or not you're ready to leave home and to see what kind of financial aid package arrives.

You should always have good reasons for applying to any school, and you shouldn't go crazy and apply to 20 colleges. But if you have a few schools you're not sure of, remember that you don't have to be sure yet. For now, you're just applying.

GET YOUR COUNSELOR'S APPROVAL

Deciding which colleges to actually apply to is one of the most important decisions you make in college planning. And while there are many people who can give you good advice about what colleges you might like, one of the best sources of advice about your chances of admission is your high school counselor.

Your high school counselor doesn't just know you—she knows college admissions. She knows which students from your school have been admitted to which colleges in the past. She knows how you stack up against those students. That's not information you can get from friends, a college guidebook or even the colleges themselves.

So make an appointment with your high school counselor and show her your list. Ask her what she thinks your chances of admission are, and give her permission to be honest. Listen to what she has to say, even if you don't like the answers.

It's fine to ask for clarification so you can better understand. But you are not allowed to get all torqued up if every school on your list only accepts 15 out of every 100 students who apply, and your counselor says your odds of admission are slim.

The best time to visit your counselor and get approval? May of your junior year, not the fall of your senior year, for three reasons:

1. Counselors are at their busiest during the fall. It's a new school year, students are still getting their schedules adjusted and the seniors are coming in with all their requests for college application support.

2. If your list is out of whack, you'll have the summer to do more research and find appropriate replacements.

3. If your list is approved (or mostly approved), you can start on your applications and essays over the summer.

Additional advantages

There are some additional advantages to getting your counselor's approval of your list. If you're eventually deferred or wait-listed, your counselor may be able to call the school and find out information about your chances of being admitted in the next round. But you're a lot more likely to have your counselor on your support team if she approved the list in the first place.

Bottom line: make sure you have a balanced college list of target schools. It's fine to have a few schools that are out of your admissions reach, but the best way to end up with choices you're happy with is to apply where your chances of admission are strong. Don't get that advice from friends, hearsay or any other source. Your counselor is a great source for that information, and your college list is too important not to ask the question.

LOVE YOUR LIST

Admissions uncertainty makes a lot of applicants apply to schools they're not that excited about. They just feel better knowing they have a lot of applications out there. You're probably not going to *love* every college on your list equally, but it's good to be in full-blown *like* with every school on your list. Don't apply to any school just to see what happens.

If you'd rather go to juvenile hall than actually attend one of your safeties, why bother applying? Focus your safety schools on those you'd actually be excited to attend. If you can't find safety schools you like, you've got namebranditis, not a lack of good options.

If you apply to all the Ivy League schools just because they're prestigious, you don't really like those schools. You like the *idea* of those schools.

If you load up your college list with lots of options that you haven't researched because you're afraid you won't get into enough schools, relax and trim the fat off your list. Applying to schools you're not really interested in just makes more work for you and takes time away from your applications to schools that mean more to you. If you've done your college soul searching and had your counselor approve your list, you'll be fine.

COMMITTEE NOTES

Fall in list love

Here is my advice: Love your list. In the landscape of higher education, there is no excuse for feeling "bleh" about a school you apply to. Honestly, if you can't see yourself going there, why spend the effort writing essays, filling out forms, and shelling out application fees? Love your list. Pick schools that deserve your talents but do not abandon reality. 'Safety school,' 'match school,' and 'reach school' should still be phrases running through your head. However, should loving your safety school be a foreign idea? Imagine getting that first acceptance letter and genuinely being thrilled...whoa...[12]

Justin Pike
Tufts University admissions officer

PREPARING: HOW ANY STUDENT CAN BECOME A MORE COMPETITIVE COLLEGE APPLICANT

The students who thrive at Stanford are those who are genuinely excited about learning, not necessarily those who take every single AP, Honors, or accelerated class just because it has that name. [1]

Stanford University
Our Selection Process: Academic Preparation

HOW TO PLAN A COLLEGE-PREP SCHEDULE

CHALLENGE YOURSELF SANELY

According to a 2010 survey of colleges, grades in college preparatory courses and strength of curriculum were the top factors in admissions decisions.[2] It's not surprising. The football games and late nights in the dorm help make college memorable, but it is school, after all. The best way to show a college that you can handle the school part is to take challenging classes in high school and get the best grades you can.

Take the most rigorous courses you can handle. For some students, that might mean taking a fourth year of math, foreign language or science that you weren't required to take. For high achievers, it might mean taking honors, Advanced Placement or International Baccalaureate courses.

Don't pad your GPA with easy courses in the hopes of impressing colleges. That's like trying to get an athletic scholarship by choosing to play against only the weakest competition you can find. No college coach wants the wrestler who managed to beat a long list of the worst wrestlers in the state. And no college wants a student who backs away from an academic challenge in pursuit of an easy A. B's in hard classes are better than A's in easy ones.

How rigorous a class schedule? Most colleges have a description of their recommended academic preparation on their websites. It's often listed in the FAQs found in the admissions section. Just about all of them advise to choose a demanding curriculum. Here's an example from James Madison University's website: "Students with solid achievement in four or more academic courses each year of high school will have a distinct advantage in the admission process. Competitive candidates for admission will have taken upper level coursework (i.e., Honors, AP, IB, Dual Enrollment) in the core academic areas when available in their high school."[3]

I believe hard work, a little stress and even occasional late-night studying are healthy experiences for high school students. College academics are likely to be more—not less—challenging than what you've done in high school, and enrolling in a rigorous curriculum helps you get ready for what you'll face later.

But you should still challenge yourself in a sane way.

If you have to stay up until 2 a.m. every night just to keep up, that's not sane—you're overscheduled.

If you're putting out a lot of effort and you're getting C's (or worse), your classes are too difficult.

If you're constantly worried about school, if you can't name a favorite class or teacher and if you're working so hard that you can't wait for the year to be over, it's not worth it. You're challenging yourself, but you're sacrificing sleep, fun and sanity to do it. It's not worth it. You're giving up more than the challenge will pay back.

Hard work shouldn't hurt

Hard work should feel good. It should give you a sense of pride and accomplishment, not leave you tired and demoralized. No college wants to admit a student who's academically burned out.

Vanderbilt University offers this advice on their website:

> If your high school offers any advanced, honors, Advanced Placement, or International Baccalaureate courses, it's recommended you pursue those as appropriate. You should challenge yourself without getting in over your head.[4]

Every year, I see B and even C students who've taken no AP or honors classes and still get accepted to plenty of colleges. The University of Mississippi (Ole Miss) states on its website that nonresident applicants with a 2.50 GPA or higher in a college preparatory curriculum (no APs or honors required) and composite ACT score of 20 or higher (or 950 or higher on the SAT Critical Reading/Mathematics only) will be granted regular admission to the university.[5]

If you're a Mississippi resident, the numbers are even friendlier—2.50 high school GPA and a score of 16 on the composite ACT (or 760 on the SAT critical reading/mathematics).

The better your academic performance, the more college options you will have. Challenging yourself sanely means that you enroll in the most difficult classes *you* can handle. Don't lock yourself into a curriculum that ruins high school for you. If you already have, talk to your parents and your counselor about making some changes so you can start challenging yourself sanely.

ASK FOR A DROP OPTION

At most colleges, students can jump in and try a course for a couple weeks to see if they like it. If they don't want to take the course for any reason, they can drop it. As long as they do so within a specified trial period, there are no negative impacts on their academic records. Savvy high school students find out if their schools will let them do the same.

Some high schools have a stated policy about how long you can stay in a particular course before you drop it. Other schools leave it up to counselors to decide on a case-by-case basis. No matter where you go to high school: (1) know what the policy is, and (2) ask about the option before you begin a course—not out of necessity after you get a D+ on your first exam.

When you ask your counselor, make it clear you're asking because you want to take an academic risk and challenge yourself, not because you want an escape hatch if you blow it and don't study for your tests. For example, if you're picking classes for next year and you're unsure about AP Chemistry because you tend to struggle in your science courses, tell your counselor about your concern. Let her know you really want to try the course, but you're wondering if you'd be allowed to drop it if AP Chem got the best of you. The drop option should encourage you to embrace a challenge.

If your counselor gives you parameters in which you could drop the course, jump in and do everything you can to not exercise that option.

Even if your counselor tells you there isn't a drop option, you'll establish yourself as a student who's academically self-aware enough to anticipate challenges and mature enough to discuss them.

COMMITTEE NOTES

Embrace a challenge

It's usually easier to drop down from a more-rigorous track to a less-rigorous one; so if you're on the fence, challenge yourself with a more-rigorous load, and drop down if it ends up being too difficult to handle. We love students who embrace a challenge. [6]

Swarthmore College
Office of Admissions blog

FOLLOW YOUR FAVORITE SUBJECTS

When planning a course of study with a counselor at Collegewise, students often ask questions like:

"Which one: AP US History or AP Chemistry?"

"Should I take a fourth year of language?"

"Can I take AP Psychology instead of AP Calculus?"

When you have questions like that, here's a good place to start: ask yourself where your interest overlaps with the biggest challenge.

If you don't want to take both AP US History and AP Chemistry simultaneously, pick the one that looks more interesting to you, dive in and learn as much as you can.

If you're not sure whether to take a fourth year of language, ask yourself how much language really interests you. If you're a lot happier learning math than you are Spanish, or if your geometry teacher was one of the best teachers you've ever had and she also teaches calculus, consider trading Spanish and taking calculus.

If you want to take AP Psychology instead of AP Calculus, be honest about why you want to do that. If it's because AP Psychology just isn't as hard as AP Calculus and you still want the extra grade point from an AP class, you're not exerting the effort or following an interest.

Admissions officers want to see flashes of your academic interests. College interviewers routinely ask about your favorite subjects and teachers. The students who've thought about their favorite subjects and worked especially hard in them always have the best answers to those questions.

COMMITTEE NOTES

When challenges meet interests

My take: first, you should try picking courses because they interest and challenge you, and not just to get into a school, since there are plenty of schools and just maybe you should focus on the best learning for yourself. The Collegeboard seems to want EVERY student to take AS MANY AP COURSES AS POSSIBLE. I think that leads to a bit of insanity, and maybe a complete lack of a life. I do think, however, that it's great to challenge yourself when given the opportunity and the interest. I've mentioned before that one thing to consider is how much you think a course might drop your grades. If it's going from an A- to a B+, I wouldn't sweat it. If you're pretty sure taking the AP is going to drop from a solid B to a low C or even risk a D, I think that may be a bad decision. [7]

Andrew Flagel
Dean of Admissions and Associate Vice President for Enrollment Development
George Mason University

HOW TO GET BETTER GRADES (AND STUDY LESS)

MAKE CLASS TIME STUDY TIME

You know that kid who says he barely studied for a test and still gets an A? One way he does it: he makes the most of class time.

Imagine you knew at the conclusion of every class there would be an immediate test on the material. What would you do differently? You'd really pay attention. You'd try to soak up every piece of information and commit it to memory. If something wasn't clear, you'd ask a question. And you'd look for cues from your teacher about what material will be tested—cues including:

- Anything the teacher writes on the board.

- Anything the teacher repeats, makes a big deal of or emphasizes in any way (sounds like, "This was a crucial turning point for the United States in World War II").

- Anything your teacher discusses at great length (if you're studying the Great Depression all week but spend two days on the reasons for the stock market crash, that's a tip).

- If your teacher goes to the trouble to make a handout.

- If your teacher spends a lot of time talking about something that isn't mentioned anywhere in the textbook.

The in-class study time adds up fast. Let's say your math teacher gives a test every three weeks. If you're in that class for one hour a day, five days a week and you treat it like study time, you'll already have studied 15 hours by the time your test arrives.

How much additional studying will you need to do? Not much. You'll be that kid who studies just a little bit for the test and still does well.

START BEFORE YOU NEED TO

If you start studying for a biology test before you need to, you'll find the concepts you're still not sure about and be able to visit your teacher after class to clear them up before the test.

If you start writing your essay for English class before you need to, you can ask your teacher to read a rough draft, and you can incorporate her feedback.

If you start your history project before you need to, you'll have more time to research it and put it together. You'll be able be able to practice your delivery and get to sleep earlier the night before.

Starting late lets the deadline decide when and how you spend your time. Starting early puts you in charge. You get to decide when to start and how much time to spend. You can work in short, focused bursts instead of one frantic marathon. You won't have to miss out on fun activities with your friends because you have a project due in two days.

Don't cop out and say that you work best under pressure. The president's speechwriter doesn't wait to start writing the State of the Union until even the week before it's presented. Great work takes time to produce. The first step is to have the discipline to start something before you need to.

ELIMINATE STUDY-TIME INTERRUPTIONS

If you're answering emails, texting or checking Facebook every five minutes while trying to study, you're going to spend a lot more time than you need to get your work done.

Students age 8 to 18 today use entertainment media almost eight hours a day.[8] That's almost as many hours a day as the typical adult spends working a full-time job, and it can have consequences.

Driving while using a cell phone reduces the amount of brain activity associated with driving by 37 percent.[9] Text messaging creates a crash risk 23 times worse than driving while not distracted.[10] Nobody's going to get hurt because you text while doing your history homework. But if using your cell phone makes it harder to drive safely, I have to imagine it would also affect your ability to solve chemistry equations.

A suggestion: next time you sit down to do your homework and study, eliminate all your potential electronic distractions. Turn off your phone and shut down your computer. If you need your computer to do the work, close your email and instant messaging, and log out of Facebook.

If your house is bustling with activity and you can't concentrate, find a quiet place where you won't be disturbed, like a library. Then take note of how much faster you get your work done and if the quality is better.

Disconnecting doesn't hurt

I've had students tell me they need to be reachable, that it's not OK for them to turn off their phones. My response: heart surgeons and emergency response teams may need to be available 24/7 for emergency calls. A high school kid does not. Do you answer texts or email while you're quarterbacking the football team, performing in the school play or giving a speech to run for class president? Of course you don't. And I suspect no lasting social damage ever was done during those unreachable hours.

This skill of eliminating interruptions and letting yourself really focus on your work will be even more valuable in college. If you can be the kind of student who can turn a two-hour break in between classes into effective study time, you'll buy yourself two hours of free time that evening for other projects, activities or good old-fashioned college fun.

When you have important work to do, eliminate all interruptions until you're done. You'll do better work and you'll finish faster. All the emails, texts and Facebook posts will still be there when you're done. And you can reply to all of them without the work hanging over you.

KID TO KID

No multitasking

I always like to think of myself as good at multitasking, but I'm not. I don't think anyone is. When doing homework or any work for that matter, checking Facebook or Twitter for two minutes turns into 30. And texting my friend back quickly ends up in a long conversation. Turning it all off and focusing on my work allows me to go to bed before 11 p.m. every night.

Caroline C.
Collegewise student, Class of 2013

MAKE ACADEMIC WORKOUTS INTENSE

Two types of members you'll see at the gym are:

1. The one who hits the workout hard for 45 minutes, works out like his hair is on fire, doesn't talk to anyone, and usually leaves tired, sweaty and disgusting.

2. The one who's in no rush to get out of there, who half-heartedly lifts a few weights, talks to people, checks himself out in the mirror, runs a few minutes on a treadmill, watches the TV, repeats the cycle a few times, showers and talks with guys in the locker room about the "brutal two-hour workout" he just finished.

The first member is in much better shape and spends half as much time at the gym as the second guy. He gets more done in less time, with better results because he's focused.

What if you approached your homework and studying like the first gym member?

Study skills author Cal Newport got straight A's at Dartmouth while studying less than all of his friends. He says academic success is not about how many hours you spend studying, but rather how focused you are when you do your work.

Here's Newport's formula:

Work accomplished $\neq$ time spent studying

Work accomplished = time spent studying x intensity of focus

Good studiers want to maximize every moment of study time. They'd rather spend two focused hours studying than five unfocused hours. So they eliminate their interruptions, throw themselves into the work and study for a short period of time like they're academic career depended on it.

I learned the value of this when I was teaching SAT classes in college. If I gave students 25 math problems to practice in class, some students would dive in like it was the real SAT, while others would get distracted or just zone out. But if I said, "You're going to take a 30-minute timed math section from a real SAT," every single student focused hard for those 30 minutes, even those who were easily distracted. Adding a time limit made them focus, and they always scored better because of it.

No marathons

Just like how that hard-charging gym member could never go five hours straight, good studiers don't study in long, marathon sessions. They know that once they start to get tired, they lose their focus and will ultimately have to spend even more time to learn the material. So they break up their work into small, focused bursts.

Newport recommends you take a 10-minute break for every hour worked, and never work more than three hours (with 10-minute breaks) before taking significant time off.

Treat your mental workouts like your gym workouts. Focusing and going hard will always give you better results in less time.

Read Cal Newport's blog post about the concept of "hard focus" here: http://calnewport.com/blog/2007/07/26/the-straight-a-gospels-pseudo-work-does-not-equal-work/

ASK FOR HELP

Students who earn the best grades are often also the ones unafraid to admit when they just don't get it.

There's no shame in asking for help. So if you didn't understand a single equation in your algebra II class today, ask the teacher for help.

If you studied really hard and still did poorly on your chemistry test, meet with your teacher to find out where you went wrong.

If you're having trouble in a number of your classes and think you might need to make some changes, talk with your counselor and get her advice. Students who are willing to ask for a little extra help when they need it are the ones who impress teachers, counselors and colleges.

Here are five tips for making help time more productive.

1. Start by being a good kid.

If you've blown off your homework, haven't paid attention in class or just haven't tried all that hard, don't expect your teacher to save you two weeks before the final just because you ask for help.

Most teachers will go far out of their way to help a good kid who's struggling. So start by being a good kid. If you haven't done your part and still want to ask for help, be honest about it. Tell your teacher you know it's your own fault you're in a mess, and explain you'd like some help turning yourself around.

2. Don't wait to ask.

If you didn't understand your trigonometry homework last night, why wait a week or two (or even worse, until after your next test) to ask for help? This isn't a problem that's going to go away on its own. The longer you wait, the deeper the academic hole you're digging. Ask for help early and you may find that one 10- to 15-minute chat with your teacher is all you need.

3. Be specific.

Help your teacher help you by pointing out not just what you're struggling with, but also what you feel confident about. It sounds like this: "Here's my test from last week. I got every problem with only one variable right, so I think I'm OK there. But I just fell apart on every problem with two variables. Can you show me what I'm doing wrong?"

That's like process of elimination for your teacher. It makes it easier for him to identify exactly what to focus on to help you improve.

4. Make it stick.

When you leave the meeting with your teacher, the material you just got help with will be fresh in your mind. But you still have to make that understanding permanent. So after the meeting, go back over your last homework assignment or test and redo what you got wrong. If you really want to make sure you've mastered it, pretend you have to teach it back to your class the next day. Then stand up in your room and actually teach it (don't laugh—it works). That will make your newfound understanding permanent.

5. Thank your teacher the right way.

After a help session, make sure you tell your teacher how you made that understanding permanent.

"Thanks so much for helping me yesterday. I went back through my test last night and redid all of the multi-variable problems, and I got all of them right. I really appreciate your help."

Successful students do this for two reasons: (1) it's a nice thing to do, and (2) it earns a reputation as a good kid who works hard. That's never a bad reputation to have with your teachers, especially the next time you need help.

USE OLD TESTS AS STUDY GUIDES

Tests are teachers' ways of measuring what they think is most important. Think about that for a second. Isn't that the most crucial information you could know if you want to do well in a class? And even though you can't (legally) get your hands on a test before your teacher gives it, here are a few ways your old tests make great study guides.

Know where you've been.

Each test you get back is like a blueprint for you what you need to review. So go back through it and figure out what went wrong and why. Review any comments your teacher made, including the positive ones (that's where you were so good your teacher felt compelled to mention it). Reviewing your last test is especially helpful in math, science and language courses where new material tends to build on material you've already covered.

Learn your teachers' testing tendencies.

How much of the reading was actually tested on the last exam? What did your teacher seem to care most about? How much of what was tested actually came from the homework assignments? Pay attention to those tendencies and adjust your studying accordingly.

Anticipate finals.

When it's time to study for final exams, you simply could not purchase better, more revealing study guides than your old tests. They pretty much come out and tell you everything your teacher thought was most important about all the material you've covered that semester. If it was important enough to put on a test before, it's probably important enough to ask you about again.

Never throw away an old test.

TEACH IT BACK

The best way to learn something is to get to a point where you could teach it to someone else. So if you want to be prepared for an exam, pretend you have to stand up in class and teach it tomorrow.

When you study as if you'll have to actually teach it the next day, you can't just passively review the material. You really have to think about it. How would you explain it? What would you focus on? What parts do you think your classmates would have questions about, and how would you answer them?

Scott Young, author of *Learn More, Study Less*, got straight A's in high school and in college even though, as he claims, he studied far less than any of his friends. One of the ways he did it was to constantly explain the material out loud or on paper, not just when he studied for a test, but also when he was doing his assignments.[11]

If you can't explain something clearly and confidently, you don't know it yet. That's why this technique is so powerful. You might passively review material in your textbook and really think you understand it. But when you try to teach it back, anything you don't fully understand gets exposed. Once you can stand up in your room and actually teach how to balance quadratic equations in front of an imaginary class, you really know your equation balancing.

Once you see how well this works to prepare for exams, take it a step further. Every night as you do your homework, pretend that you have to go in and teach the material the next day. You'll understand the material better the first time. Anything you don't understand will be immediately exposed and you can ask your teacher about them the next day. Best of all, you won't need to study nearly as much for exams because you'll already be able to teach the material.

If you can teach it, you know it.

HOW TO PROVE YOU'RE COLLEGE-READY

OFFER MORE THAN A TRANSCRIPT

For colleges, selecting a freshman class is a lot like betting on horses. As anyone who's spent time at a racetrack will tell you, a horse can have a winning record, the right physical attributes and a 26-pound jockey who can get a horse to play blackjack, but still come in dead last at the Kentucky Derby.

Taking hard classes and getting good grades are good indicators that you have the potential to succeed academically in college. But there are other things you can do to show that you will actually live up to those standards once you enroll and the academic race starts.

For example, a good high school GPA isn't worth much to a college if you don't like school and can't wait for it to be over. But a B or even C student who takes responsibility for his academic shortcomings without making excuses, who thrives in a particular subject and uses those opportunities to show his teachers and counselors his potential, is showing evidence that he could succeed in the right major at the right college.

Colleges will certainly pay close attention to your transcript. Those asking for teacher and counselor letters of recommendation, responses to essay questions and interviews with alumni are looking for evidence of academic potential that your transcript might not reveal.

In this section, I suggest how to show that potential.

TAKE CHARGE OF YOUR HIGH SCHOOL EDUCATION

College will give you the chance to completely take charge of your own education.

You can major in whatever interests you. You'll have hundreds of potential classes to choose from and an academic advisor who can help you plan the perfect schedule. If you need help in a course, you'll be able to visit your professors during their office hours when you can sit down personally with someone who's a subject of his or her life's work. If you really enjoy a particular professor or course, you can follow that interest the next semester.

All of those opportunities to focus your attention lay ahead. You don't have to wait until college to start. High school is a good time to start taking charge of your academic life. You don't have to just passively accept whatever courses are handed to you. Play a more active role in designing your education.

Visit your counselor at least once a semester to get advice about which classes to take. If you're having trouble in a course, visit your teacher to get some advice instead of letting your parents do that for you. If you really like your AP European History teacher, ask the teacher what other classes she teaches, then talk to your counselor and request to be put into those courses.

More engaged

When you take charge of your education, you're more engaged. You're more likely to enjoy your classes and teachers, do better in school and be excited about the idea of learning in college. You'll have better success getting into college, too.

One of the topics colleges ask teachers and counselors to discuss in letters of recommendation is the applicant's preparedness for college academics. You don't just demonstrate that readiness by getting good grades. You also demonstrate it by showing that you're ready to make your own academic decisions.

Your education is yours, not anyone else's. You wouldn't let your parents pick out what you wear to school every day or let your counselor tell you which friends to hang out with. Don't let them make all the decisions about your education, either.

I'm not saying you should ignore their input and just do whatever you want to do. But it's never a good idea to let somebody else decide what you learn and how you learn it. That's your job.

10 UNUSUAL COURSES FOR COLLEGE CREDIT

Colleges are like academic supermarkets—you can learn whatever fancies you. Here are a few examples of real classes you can take in college.

1. **"Special Topics in Literature: The Twilight Saga"**
   University of Alabama

2. **"Philosophy and Star Trek"**
   Georgetown University

3. **"Music, Video Games, and the Nature of Human Cognition"**
   NYU

4. **"The Joy of Garbage"**
   Santa Clara University

5. **"Topics in Comparative Media: American Pro Wrestling"**
   MIT

6. **"Tree Climbing"**
   Cornell University

7. **"The Stand-Up Comic in Society"**
   Johns Hopkins

8. **"Getting Dressed"**
   Princeton

9. **"The Simpsons and Philosophy"**
   UC Berkeley

10. **"Elvish: The Language of Lord of the Rings"**
    University of Wisconsin

GET TO KNOW YOUR COUNSELOR

A 2010 study by the Gates Foundation suggests a majority of high school students believe their guidance counselors don't give them sufficient advice about colleges or careers. Half of those surveyed rated their counselors "poor or fair" at helping students with the college application process. Nearly half said their counselors made them feel "like I was just another face in the crowd."[12]

I think the study says more about students than it does about counselors.

I often hear students and parents say they don't feel well supported by their high school counselors. Yet whenever I ask one of those families if they've ever actually requested an appointment with their assigned counselor, most of them haven't.

Do these families wait at home expecting their doctor or dentist to show up and give them a check up? I hope not. Why should you expect your counselor to track you down and force you to talk about your college future?

A day in the life

First, let's face some facts. In 2010, only 26 percent of public schools reported employing at least one counselor (full or part time) whose exclusive responsibility was to provide college counseling.[13]

Public school counselors surveyed were able to spend only 23 percent of their time on postsecondary counseling in 2010, and even their private school counterparts only spent about half their time on college counseling.[14]

The Gates Foundation study also pointed out that the student-counselor ratio nationally is 460 to 1 (in California, there are nearly 1,000 students for every high school counselor). If you feel ignored by your counselor, it might have more to do with how many students are at your school and how many responsibilities your counselor has than it does with a lack of interest in helping you.

So what should you do?

Get to know your counselor

Take initiative. Schedule meetings with your counselor, and don't wait until your senior year to do it. Starting early will help you establish a relationship with your counselor so she can get to know you and give you even better advice.

If you have just two 10-minute meetings each semester and do that from the day you enter high school, you'll have more than two hours of one-on-one time with your counselor by the time you apply to college as a senior.

There's no need to schedule a formal meeting more than once or twice a semester. But you can also make contact with your counselor outside of those meetings. If you're really enjoying a class or teacher she recommended, stop by and thank her. Email her about the colleges you've visited and tell her which ones you liked. Say hi to her in the hallways and at the homecoming dance where she's a chaperone.

Even if you attend a high school with a huge student population, counselors will always remember and appreciate a nice kid who goes out of his or her way to talk to them.

Another advantage of building this relationship: just imagine how much more she could say about you when you ask her to write a letter of recommendation to college.

Are there some bad high school counselors? I'm sure there are (just like there are some bad doctors, lawyers and accountants). But the vast majority of counselors I've met are good people who want to help kids succeed. Give your counselor the opportunity to do that for you and you'll probably be pleasantly surprised.

FIVE QUESTIONS TO ASK YOUR HIGH SCHOOL COUNSELOR

When you first visit your high school counselor, here are five questions to get your college planning started.

1. Am I taking the right courses to be competitive for college?

2. What are some appropriate colleges for me to look at?

3. Are any college reps visiting our campus this semester?

4. Does the counseling office do any college planning presentations or have any guidance materials that I should take advantage of?

5. Are there any special instructions you like students to follow when requesting transcripts, school reports or anything else from your office?

RISE ABOVE THE GRADE GRUBBERS

Counselors, teachers and college admissions officers use a term to describe some students: "Grade grubbers." You don't want to be one.

Grade grubbers are so obsessively focused on their GPAs that they're not interested in learning—they just want the A. They'll only participate in class discussions if participation is counted toward a grade. They'll only do an outside project or extra reading if they get points for it.

When a grade grubber gets a B in the class, he doesn't ask the teacher how he could actually improve his work and do better; he asks what extra credit is available so he can get an A. And if that doesn't work, a grade grubber's parents aren't above waging a "My son needs an A in this class" argument with the teacher and counselor.

It's not that grade grubbers don't work hard. But if all you care about is the grade, and you'll resort to anything to get that grade, it's like volunteering for a community service project just to collect the hours for your resume, not caring at all about the people you're actually helping.

Grade grubbing is a selfish way to go through school. It's hard for teachers and counselors to really like grade grubbers.

Love to learn

The opposite of a grade grubber is a kid who loves to learn. Those kids work hard and get good grades, too, but they do so more because of their own curiosity than an agenda to get into prestigious colleges.

It might be a student who loves literature and takes some college-level creative writing courses during the summer; who participates in her English classes and talks to her teacher after school about books; or who's a happy, self-described lit geek who can't wait to join a book club in college so she can stay up late talking Shakespeare with others just like her.

Colleges love students who enjoy learning new things and take initiative to learn them. It doesn't matter whether it's math, literature, science, cooking, automotive repair, computer programming, woodworking, dance—if you find it interesting, feed your curiosity. Show colleges you're not just a high achiever but also a curious learner.

Even if you're not a straight-A student, show colleges what you're capable of when you're learning what you want to learn. A C student who loves his video production class and takes a summer course at a local film school has just given colleges something else to notice besides his GPA.

William's story

My former Collegewise student, William, took this advice. He was a straight-A student who had two passions—science and cooking. When he found a summer course at UC Irvine called "Food Science," it was like someone had created a course just for him. He enrolled (over his mother's urging that he take calculus instead) and later wrote his college essay about how much he loved learning about the chemical reactions that make bread rise and the physics explanation of why adding salt to water makes your spaghetti cook faster.

William was admitted to his first choice—Stanford University.

There's nothing wrong with being focused on your GPA. But real learners see academic rewards as a byproduct of their work ethic and curiosity.

Nobel Prize v. learning

Richard Feynman was a physics professor at Caltech who worked on the atomic bomb and was a member of the team that investigated the Space Shuttle Challenger disaster. After he won the Noble Prize in 1965, he gave an interview: "I don't know anything about the Nobel Prize," he said. "I don't understand what it's all about...I've already got the prize. The prize is the pleasure of finding the thing out."[15]

Imagine what he would have said to a kid who was taking AP Calculus just so he might have a better chance of getting into an Ivy League school.

No student loves every class in high school. But teachers love a kid who works hard for a grade *and* is sincerely interested in the material. Those students make the class experience better for everyone. The grade grubbers just take what they need to get the A. But the learners give something back with their enthusiasm.

It's easy for teachers and counselors to write great letters of recommendation for learners. And it's easy for colleges to admit them.

Maximize strengths over fixing weaknesses

Too many students I meet spend almost all their time trying to improve in their weaker subjects, which they'll probably never love or be great at.

If they get straight A's except for one B in chemistry, they don't celebrate the A's—they get a chemistry tutor.

If their SAT scores don't rise to what they'd hoped for after working with a tutor, they jump back into tutoring and try it again.

I once worked with a student who was a competitive sailor and earned nothing but A's except for the B's in his math courses. No matter what I said to him, he spent more time with his math tutor than he did on his boat. He never did get an A in math and spent a lot more time frustrated with numbers than he did being fulfilled by racing.

What would happen if you spent less time trying to fix your academic weaknesses and put more time into your best subjects? How much better could you be in your stronger classes? How much time would you free up to read a book you've wanted to read, to do an even better project in a class you really enjoy, to take a college level course in your favorite subject, to write your own computer program or to learn how to sew?

We're taught from a young age that we can be great at anything if we put our minds to it. Research has even shown that 77 percent of parents in the United States think that a student's lowest grades deserve the most time and attention.[16] The reality is we can't all be great at everything.

In my sophomore year of high school P.E., we ran a timed mile. The fasted kid in the class (who was on the track team) finished in 4:35 and then ran another two laps to "cool down." I finished in 7:15 and felt like my aorta had exploded. No knowledgeable track coach would have said I could go the Olympics as a miler one day if I put my mind to it. We all have our natural strengths and our limits.

Strengths improve most

During the 1950s, the Nebraska School Study Council supported a statewide research project that compared three different techniques to improve students' reading speeds. Of the 6,000 tenth graders who participated, the ones who improved the most (from 300 to 2,900 words per minute) were those who were the fastest readers at the *beginning* of the study. The slower readers improved a little, but not nearly as much as those who were fast when they started.[17]

I'm not suggesting slow readers should give up reading all together. But if a slow reader might have natural talents for math, music, art or science, doesn't he deserve to keep developing those strengths and potentially be great at them?

When you focus more on strengths than you do on weaknesses, you're likely to enjoy what you're doing and be happier in general. The Gallup Organization surveyed more than 10 million people worldwide on the subject of employee engagement. The research showed that spending time building strengths was far more productive than logging countless hours trying to fix weaknesses. In fact, people who have the opportunity to focus on their strengths every day are six times more likely to be engaged in their jobs and more than three times more likely to report having an excellent quality of life in general.[18]

Manage weaknesses

Gallup's research doesn't argue that people should ignore their weaknesses all together. Good thing, too, because you can't just refuse to take math in high school if you aren't good at math. But their studies did show the most successful people find ways to manage around their weaknesses so they can spend more time focusing on their strengths.

Colleges don't expect you to be perfect. In fact, many schools have essay questions that ask you to comment on a time you failed or made a mistake. College of William and Mary's senior assistant dean of admission blogged, "…all of us deans were high school students too, and none of us were perfect high school students. We tripped and stumbled and struggled with courses along the way to our colleges of choice and we recognize that today's students do too." [19]

So don't spend all your time trying to cure every imperfection. Working to maximize a natural strength will always feel more rewarding than grinding through a weakness. And it's a much better way to stand out.

HOW ZUCKERBERG "LIKED" HIS STRENGTH

When he (Facebook founder Mark Zuckerberg) was about eleven, his parents hired a computer tutor, a software developer named David Newman, who came to the house once a week to work with Mark. "He was a prodigy," Newman told me. "Sometimes it was tough to stay ahead of him."... Soon thereafter, Mark started taking a graduate computer course every Thursday night at nearby Mercy College. When his father dropped him off at the first class, the instructor looked at Edward and said, pointing to Mark, "You can't bring him to the classroom with you." Edward told the instructor that his son was the student. [20]

The Face of Facebook
The New Yorker

FEED YOUR PASSIONS

Have you ever had a class that you looked forward to going to every day? Maybe the subject was one that just came naturally to you. Maybe the teacher was great and always found a way to make the material interesting. Maybe the students in the class made the discussions that much more challenging and interesting every day. Whatever the reason you enjoy it so much, great classes are big opportunities to give your best performances. Great performances show colleges your potential.

If you have a history teacher whose class you can't wait to attend every day, make it known. Put your hand up in class. Participate in the discussion. Spend extra time on the class project. Tell the teacher how much you enjoy the class, and be specific about what you find interesting.

If you really enjoy your video production class at school, find a way to deliver an award-winning performance and get really good at video production. Read how-to guides about it. Take a class outside of school at a local college or community college. Put what you've learned to use by producing great videos of water polo games, school musicals, or the graduation ceremony.

If you love Spanish, don't stop at AP Spanish. Take a college level class over the summer. Volunteer as a translator or language tutor for recent immigrants. Get a part-time job where your Spanish can be put to use.

A former Collegewise student, Justin, held a C average when he began a journalism class in his junior year. He worked hard to improve his writing, and while he didn't hold any leadership positions on the school paper, he did contribute at least one article to every issue that year. When he applied to college, his journalism teacher wrote him a letter of recommendation. Today, Justin is a graduate of San Rafael, California's Dominican College.

When you feed your passion, your teachers have more to say about you in letters of recommendation. You'll have an answer when applications or interviewers ask you about the subjects that interest you or what you'd like to know more about. And you'll have more opportunities to win academic awards, even if you don't excel in every subject.

LOSE THE EXCUSES

Whenever I hear a student say things like...

"I got a C because of a personality conflict with the teacher."

"I didn't do well in Spanish, but the language department at my school is terrible."

"I was just three points away from an A, but my teacher refused to raise the grade."

...I can't help but think the same thing any college in the universe would think: *Somebody in that class found a way to an A.*

Is it possible your class or teacher is less than perfect? Of course. Guess what—it could happen in college, too. After college, you might have a bad boss. Or a bad landlord. Or a bad mother-in-law. You won't necessarily be able to just quit your job, move or refuse to speak to your mother-in-law again. You'll need to find ways to make those situations work. High school is a great training ground for those scenarios.

If you really do have a personality conflict with a teacher, what are the other students doing differently than you are (or are not) doing?

If the language department at your school really isn't strong, what steps could you take to improve your own learning experience?

If you really were just three points away from an A—and there's no changing your teacher's position—I understand it's a bitter pill to swallow. Also, consider that lots of things, from swim meets to sales competitions at big companies, are based on cold, hard numbers, and you can't win the prize just for getting close. Instead of complaining, find out what you can do differently next time and resolve to do it.

What if the excuse is legitimate?

Sometimes your academic performance suffers for a legitimate reason. I worked with a student whose mother was diagnosed with leukemia during his junior year, and he had to care for her after school. Another student was a baseball player who got hit in the head with a foul ball and had to miss three weeks of school with a serious head injury. Their grades suffered because of real challenges, and they explained those circumstances to colleges when they applied.

It's not complaining when you do face a challenging circumstance that's out of your control. But most excuses for a poor performance in class are just that—excuses. Colleges (and future employers) don't want students who blame other people. They want the students who find solutions and make it work.

No excuses

Don't make excuses. If you've had a poor or inconsistent grade performance due to unusual or stressful circumstances, feel free to share that information with us; it can be useful. But don't strain credibility by making up false excuses. Be honest—we'll respect that.[21]

University of Michigan

HOW TO THRIVE IN EXTRACURRICULAR ACTIVITIES

CHOOSE WHAT YOU ENJOY

Many students have the impression that colleges reward particular activities. The logic suggests a student who hasn't worked at a soup kitchen or served as president of the Latin Club is somehow at an admissions disadvantage. It's not true. College admissions committees don't care which particular activities you choose to do. They're more interested in how much you care about what you're doing.

Colleges appreciate community service and leadership activities, but not more (or less) than success in or passion for athletics, art, music or any other activity that you really care about and make an impact doing. An entire college campus full of nothing but leaders and philanthropists wouldn't be as interesting as a community with lots of different talents and interests.

Jerome Lucido, Provost for Enrollment Policy and Management at the University of Southern California, told *The Washington Post*, "There simply is no mold for 'what admission directors are looking for.' The important thing is to design your activities to develop and test your interests, not to please a distant admission official. Yes, we believe this!"[22]

If you want to impress colleges, show them that you have the initiative and passion to find things you love doing and then commit yourself to them. Colleges know those students will keep being engaged and involved once they get to college.

NEED SUMMER ACTIVITY SUGGESTIONS?

Colleges will also look at how you spent your summers. If you'd like suggestions, check out my blog post "50 Ways to Spend Your Summer." It's got a list of potential activities, all of which are free or low cost.

http://www.wiselikeus.com/collegewise/2012/04/50-ways-to-spend-your-summer.html

---

KID TO KID

Choose what you enjoy

I never joined a club at school because none of them appealed to me, and I didn't have the dedication or athleticism for any of the sports. However, I did find a way to be a part of the school community. During my sophomore year, I struggled with anxiety and depression. As a part of my recovery, I volunteered to speak to health classes about my illness. I've spoken to many classes after two years, and it has been among the most rewarding experiences of my life. It helped me get over my anxiety, help people who are struggling with what I went through, and have a subject for a college essay, all in one. I'm glad I found a way to be active and helpful in my school community.

Ben C.
Former Collegewise student,
Class of 2012
Western Washington University

COMMITTEE NOTES

When I was in high school, we were convinced that there was some sort of extracurricular checklist used in admissions offices. You had to have service, athletics, something creative, leadership and something academic on your resume. I'm happy to report that with 715 student organizations on the books at UVA, we have no specific preferences when it comes to activities. We have mainstream groups that probably mirror the ones you have at your high school and we have fringe-y ones that you probably never dreamed of before.[23]

Assistant Dean of Admissions
University of Virginia

SHOW PASSION

Some students worry about doing *enough* activities to show colleges. They want to sign up for as many clubs on campus as possible so they can pad their resumes and look involved. But long lists of activities don't impress colleges. Real commitment does.

It's not hard to join a lot of clubs. Anyone can show up to a few meetings just so they can add to the activity sections of their college applications. What's impressive is the student who finds a few activities she really cares about and commits to them. Colleges know it's that committed student, not the compulsive joiner, who's more likely to make the same kinds of contributions once she gets to college.

Tony Bankston, Dean of Admissions at Illinois Wesleyan University told *The Washington Post*, "Students who have a passion for something are significantly more likely to make a more significant contribution to the campus community. They are not only more likely to get involved, but they are also more apt to bring new initiatives to campus or bring about improvements to existing clubs or programs. Passion is more likely to breed action."[24]

Time investment

When you list your activities on your application, most colleges will also ask you to estimate how many days a week, and how many weeks a year, you spend doing each one. That's why the sheer number of activities that you do is less important than the commitment you make to each one.

The tennis player who spends almost all her free time on the court is still impressive to colleges even though she may only be listing one activity on her application. Commitment quality beats activity quantity. Game. Set. Match.

Many colleges, including more than 450 that use the standardized Common Application also require applicants to write an essay about an activity that's been important to them. The students who have the best answers to that question are always the ones who give a lot of time and energy to do something they care about, whether it's playing water polo, working at an ice cream shop, acting in school plays or taking karate classes.

Hobbies count, too

Hobbies can be activities, too. If you invest a lot of time and energy into a hobby you enjoy, colleges will be impressed (as long as the hobby isn't prohibited by law).

I worked with a student who spent a lot of time fishing. He and his dad would take regular trips together that they'd plan months in advance based on the season and what kind of fish would be likely be biting. During his junior year, he took up spear fishing and spent a lot of time learning how to do it. He wrote his college essay about his hobby and titled it, "Gone Fishin'." Today, he's a graduate of California's Loyola Marymount University.

So don't worry whether or not you have *enough* activities. Are you doing things you enjoy? Are you spending quality time and energy to do them? Then relax. What you do within your activities is more important than how many activities you do.

Real commitment

You certainly do see what I call "serial participators" who are in every club and organization to either get their picture in the yearbook the most times or perhaps stuff their resume for the college application. That superficial participation can't be sustained in college and is not impressive. [25]

David Lesesne
Dean of Admissions and Financial Aid
Randolph-Macon College

No laundry lists

We are always suspicious of students with laundry lists of extracurricular activities because it suggests that the student is not developing an in-depth engagement with any one activity. Also, it suggests a level of frenetic busyness that may be more about building a college resume than about genuine interests on the part of the student. [26]

Eileen Brangan Mell
Worcester Polytechnic Institute

STAND OUT FROM THE CROWD

Have you ever noticed that certain clubs and organizations are particularly crowded? I've met a lot of students who join the Key Club or National Charity League because, well, everyone else seemed to be doing them.

There's nothing wrong with joining any popular activity if that's what you really want to do. But if you're just doing it because everyone else is, why not stop following the crowd and do something different?

I've met a lot of kids who have volunteered at hospitals. But I've only ever met one who also worked as an emergency medical technician. She wrote her essay about her first night on the job in the back of a speeding ambulance when she did chest compressions on a 19-year-old motorcycle accident victim who had just gone into full cardiac arrest. She got accepted to her first choice—University of San Diego—where she studied psychology.

Lots of kids go to expensive summer programs at colleges. But I've only ever met one who spent his summers taking history classes at his local community colleges for $20 per unit. He got to know one of the professors who shared the reading assignments for her upper division course on George Washington. That student didn't care whether any college would look favorably on it—that's not what it was about for him. He was just obsessed with history and wanted to know more. He went to Yale, where he majored in history, and then to Georgetown Law School.

Lots of kids play an instrument in the high school jazz band. But I've only ever met one who also played trumpet in a real mariachi band. He wasn't doing it to put it on his college applications—he just liked playing good music (and wearing the authentic mariachi outfit). He went to Occidental College and studied economics.

Those students weren't necessarily smarter, more talented or harder working than all their classmates. And they weren't trying to game the process and do things they thought would help them get into college. They just took otherwise common interests to uncommon places.

Bottom line: doing your own thing on your own terms can be a lot more enjoyable than following the crowd—and a better way to stand out.

MAKE AN IMPACT

One of the more popular essay topics colleges now require is some version of, "How will you contribute to our campus community?"

The best responses to that question come from students who aren't just involved in activities, but actually make an impact on the people, teams and organizations they're involved with.

Making an impact means the team, club, job or group is different with you there, and they'd notice if you stopped showing up.

If you're the MVP quarterback, the editor-in-chief of the newspaper or the founder of a successful food drive, you're making an impact. But impact isn't reserved for the superstars. The second stringers, the B students, and the club members without leadership positions can make an impact, too.

The staff writer on the school newspaper could take a journalism class at a college and then offer to share the material with the rest of the writers on the paper once he completes the course.

The second-chair oboe player in the orchestra could convince the conductor of the local community symphony to come to one of their music classes to talk about life as a professional musician.

A B student in physics could organize an all-star team of classmates to compete in the county-wide high school physics Olympics.

Colleges have a term for these kids: "High-impact applicants." They know these students make positive contributions to their classes, organizations and fellow students. People would notice if they stopped showing up.

How a bench warmer made an impact

One of my former Collegewise students said he was the worst player on his water polo team. He played about three minutes of actual game time in high school. But he ran the fundraiser to buy parkas for the team. He volunteered to hold the video camera when the coach wanted to start recording games. Most importantly, he loved being on the water polo team.

My student brought a great attitude to practice every day even though he knew he'd never play, and he won the coach's award two years in a row. He wasn't a good player, but the team would have missed him if he stopped showing up. He wrote his college essay about his experience as the worst player on the water polo team and was accepted to almost all of his colleges.

If you stopped showing up to your part-time job, soccer practice, rehearsals for the school play or your art class after school, would the group be missing something important?

If not, start looking for opportunities to make an impact. Become indispensible and leave a legacy.

Make an impact

Colleges are more interested in the student's passion, the authenticity of the student's involvement, and the impact they've had in their communities, teams, or organizations. Sometimes that means they've only done 1 or 2 things, but they've been involved in a way that has fundamentally impacted those organizations. That to me is more important than being involved in 20 clubs and not having impacted any. [27]

Angel B. Perez
Dean of Admissions
Pitzer College

LEARN WHEN AND HOW TO QUIT

A lot of students think that once they start an activity, they should never quit because it would look bad to colleges. But colleges don't want you to just plod through something for the sake of sticking it out. Successful people not only know how to commit to things, but also how to quit.

You change a lot while you're in high school. A club or activity you joined as a freshman might lose some of its oomph by the time you're a junior. Good quitters can sense when an activity, a job, a project or a relationship isn't going anyplace good or is just making them unhappy. So they quit and move on, and they don't beat themselves up about it.

One of my former Collegewise students was a standout football player, but he quit right before the start of his junior year. Football was making him miserable. He realized he just wasn't the type of guy who would ever enjoy, as he put it, "doing something where he was regularly congratulated for trying to take someone's head off."

My student wanted to do other things that he thought would make him happier. So he quit, joined a steel drum band at his high school and started volunteering at his church. He went on to attend and graduate from Notre Dame.

When you give time and effort to an activity, it should give something back to you. If you hate every second of marching band practice and are pretty sure that lugging your tuba around every day after school has caused permanent damage to your spine—stop. Don't march in the band anymore. Find something else that you enjoy with lighter equipment.

When quitting pays big

Knowing that quitting is an option can also strengthen your commitment to things you really care about. The online retailer Zappos bribes new employees to quit. "The Offer," as it's known at Zappos, is the brainchild of CEO Tony Hsieh. Every new call center employee at Zappos goes through a four-week training program during which time they earn their full salary. At the end of the program, Zappos offers $4,000 to any new hire who wants to quit. Only about 2 to 3 percent of the people take the money and run.[28]

By giving new employees an easy way to quit, Zappos fills its ranks with people who really want to be there.

Are you doing an activity that your heart's just not in anymore? If the answer is, "Yes," why are you still doing it? Why not find something you love enough that you'd never take the bribe to quit?

Keep in mind, not all quitting is good. If you love being on the volleyball team, but quit just because you didn't get picked as the starting setter, maybe you should stay and work to earn your spot back?

You get to choose which activities you do outside of class. If you make the wrong choice, or if what used to make you happy just isn't working for you anymore, don't be afraid to be a good quitter and make a different choice.

On good quitting

Sometimes it's refreshing to see the student who, for example, gave up the violin he had been playing for years because he wanted the time to try soccer. Continuity is not a virtue unto itself. Scattered evidence of a curious mind can be more impressive than singular achievements from routinized commitments.[29]

Henry Broaddus
Dean of Admissions
College of William & Mary

GET A JOB

I make one amendment to the rule of thumb that one activity isn't more important than another. I think every teenager should have a part-time job at some point in high school. And I don't mean a job you don't have to apply for at your mom or dad's company. I mean a regular, honest-to-goodness, flipping burgers, bagging groceries, ringing a cash register, sweeping the floors kind of job.

Kids who have part-time jobs learn a lot. They learn how to deal with angry customers, how to show initiative and how to work well with people. I've read some wonderful college essays from kids who worked at fast food restaurants and talked about how good it felt when they got promoted to shift manager and didn't have to take orders at the drive-thru anymore.

Every admissions officer I've ever asked about this has agreed it's hard not to like a kid who scoops ice cream or pours coffee or takes tickets at the movie theater to make some extra money.

A teen that gets a regular part-time job almost certainly has no ulterior motive. There's rarely a hidden strategy to impress colleges when a student chooses to serve frozen yogurt part time. You can't always say the same about the kid whose family pays thousands of dollars to send him to summer school at an Ivy League university. All the students I have worked with who discussed their part-time jobs in their applications have been very successful at getting into college.

Job market

The biggest reason I give this advice is the potential future career advantages to sweeping floors or scooping popcorn at the movies while you're in high school. It's not an easy job market out there now for recent college grads. Among the students who graduated from college in 2010, just 56 percent managed to get a job by the following spring. That compares with 90 percent of graduates from the classes of 2006 and 2007.[30]

Everybody needs their first job at some point—the job you take because you don't have any work experience and know you can't afford to be picky. Why not do that in high school? Get your first job at 16 or 17, and before you even start college, you'll have something to list on your resume and references you can give potential internships or employers.

Thrive at one job and you'll have an advantage when you look to move on to your next one. Have a string of successes by the time you graduate from college and you'll be ahead of the job-seeking competition.

A great start at McDonald's

Long before Jeff Bezos started Amazon; long before he earned more than $1 million a year as a young star at a hedge fund; long before he got degrees in electrical engineering and computer science from Princeton (before he graduated as valedictorian of his high school class); Jeff Bezos worked a summer job at McDonalds. His favorite shift was Saturday morning when he'd start by cracking 300 eggs into a big bowl. And he learned to do it with one hand.[31]

I'm guessing Bezos didn't spend a lot of time asking himself, "What would look good to Princeton?"

Find a part-time job. You'll make some money. You'll have the first item to list on your professional resume. And you'll improve your chances of getting into college without spending any money to do it.

You can't do those three things at Harvard Summer School.

Part-time jobs

We also honor and value summer jobs; for many students they are necessary and for others they can be just as important a learning experience as anything else. What's important to us in not what you chose to do for the summer, but what you got out of it.[32]

Jeff Brenzel
Dean of Undergraduate Admissions
Yale University

TESTING: PLANNING AND PREPARING FOR STANDARDIZED TESTS

Test scores don't get you in

Scores are one tool we use to help us in admissions. And yes, your grades and test scores (especially your grades) are important. But as I have said in the past, what ultimately really matters to us is who you are, what qualities you bring to the table. We want people who are academically curious and passionate, people who will bring their various talents to MIT and share them with others, people who will be good roommates, good mentors, good friends. We do not admit test scores. We admit people.[1]

Matt McGann
Associate Director of Admissions
MIT

1926

Carl Brigham, a psychologist who created aptitude tests for the US Army during World War I, after the war develops the Scholastic Aptitude Test (SAT) for use in college admissions.

1933

Harvard begins using the SAT to evaluate applicants for a new scholarship program.

1939

The SAT introduces new machine-scored answer sheets. While the SAT had always been a multiple-choice test, all of the student responses previously needed to be reviewed and scored by hand.

1958

For the first time, students may see their SAT scores. Before 1958, only high schools and colleges were able to view students' scores.

1959

Everett Franklin Lindquist, an education professor at the University of Iowa, develops the American College Testing Program (ACT) as a competitor to the SAT. In addition to math, reading and English skills, the ACT assesses students on their knowledge of scientific facts and principles.

1971

The College Board begins to mail scores directly to students' homes (they were previously sent to the high schools).

1990

The SAT is renamed so that the acronym stands for "Scholastic Assessment Test."

1993

The SAT is renamed and is no longer an acronym. The letters SAT don't stand for anything.

1996

The ACT (both the test and the company) are renamed. The letters ACT are no longer an acronym—they don't stand for anything.

2001

Richard Atkinson, president of the University of California, tells a group of fellow college presidents, "The SATs have acquired a mystique that's clearly not warranted. Who knows what they measure?" He proposes the university make SAT scores an optional part of the application for all 90,000 kids who apply each year.

2005

Partly in response to the University of California criticisms, the content of the SAT is changed. Verbal analogy questions are dropped and a writing skills section with an essay is added.

Students now get three SAT scores—Critical Reading, Math and Writing—each on a scale of 200-800. A perfect score is now 2400.

2007

Harvey Mudd College begins accepting ACT scores. The ACT is now a valid admissions test at every four-year college and university in the United States.

2009

Score Choice is introduced for the SAT, allowing students to decide which scores from multiple administrations will be sent to colleges.

2010

The number of high school seniors taking the ACT (1.57 million) is greater than those taking the SAT (1.55 million).

LEARN YOUR TESTING ABCS

Before we get into which tests to take, when to take them and how to maintain your testing perspective, let's define some terms. Below are five standardized tests you'll need to make decisions about taking. More on how to decide in "Pick a test and go with it."

1. PSAT

The PSAT is a practice version of the SAT. It's given in October at your high school and is intended to be an optional, nonthreatening opportunity to see how you might score on the SAT without having to sit for the real thing. The PSAT is also used as a qualifier for National Merit scholarships, which is good news for good test takers, but it's never used for college admissions purposes. You can learn more about it at www.collegeboard.com.

2. PLAN

The PLAN is a practice test for the ACT. It's less popular than the PSAT, and high schools that offer it traditionally do so for sophomores. Like the PSAT, it's just a practice test and doesn't impact your chances of getting into college.

3. SAT

There are three SAT sections—Math, Critical Reading and Writing (which also includes an essay), and each section is scored from 200-800. The lowest possible score you can get is 600, the highest is 2400. The national average score is about 1500 (500 in each section). You can learn more about the SAT and register for it at www.collegeboard.com.

4. ACT

Meet the Pepsi to SAT's Coke—the ACT. The ACT and SAT are two companies with competing products that are used for exactly the same purposes. The ACT has four sections: English, Reading, Math and Science. There's also an optional 30-minute essay (which you should do unless you're 100 percent certain that your chosen colleges don't want it). Each of the four sections is scored from 1-36, then they average the four scores together for your "composite score" between 1 and 36. The composite score is what you'll quote when a nosey friend asks, "What'd you get on the ACT?" The national average is about 21. All the ACT information and registration is available at www.act.org.

Colleges that require standardized tests will accept either the SAT or the ACT. And they never require you to take both.

Subject Tests

SAT subject tests are one hour tests that focus on specific academic subjects. There are 20 tests in five different areas—Math, History, Literature, Science and Languages. Each subject test is scored from 200-800. You can find a listing of all the tests at www.collegeboard.com.

About 30 colleges—most of them highly competitive—require some combination of subject tests (e.g., Math Level 1 or Level 2, and a science). Roughly 25 colleges recommend—but don't require—subject tests. And some 50 schools neither require nor recommend subject tests but are happy to look at your scores if you choose to send them.

If you're taking a challenging curriculum, especially one that includes honors or AP classes, consider taking the corresponding subject tests in your strongest subjects.

DON'T PANIC OVER PSAT SCORES

Testing panic tends to start building in December or January of high school students' junior year, when they get their PSAT scores back. It's scary to get your first big-name standardized test score, and it's easy to let anything less than a great score freak you out. I've been invited to speak at "PSAT scores-back nights" at high schools where students receive their scores surrounded by counselors, parents and several hundred of their closest friends. (No pressure.)

Relax and remember that the PSAT is just a practice test. It's like a dress rehearsal before opening night of the play. That's all. It was created to let students take a nonthreatening trial version of the SAT before they take the real thing. It can't hurt you. It can't damage your future. No student in the history of college admissions has ever been rejected by a college because she scored poorly on the PSAT.

Yes, a small number of students (about 8,000 of the 1.5 million annual test takers[3]) are awarded National Merit scholarships every year, and the PSAT scores are the first of many rounds of qualifiers. If you're notified that your PSAT scores qualify you for future consideration, that's good news. (Unless you don't like free cash.)

How colleges use PSAT scores

The only thing colleges use PSAT scores for is marketing—they buy the names of those who sit for it, so they can mail them marketing materials. If you recently took the test and checked the box that you would like to receive information from colleges, you and your mail carrier will soon see what I mean.

According to the College Board's website, more than 1,100 colleges, universities and scholarship programs[4] pay them (at a base price of $0.33 per name[5]) for student contact information, and the PSAT is one source from which they harvest the list.

How to use your PSAT scores

If you did well on the PSAT, it's good news because you will likely do well on the SAT when you take it. But for everyone else, use your PSAT scores constructively.

Maybe low PSAT scores are your first sign that you might be a better ACT taker? Or maybe you can use your PSAT score to identify the parts of the test that have you the most troubled so you can focus on those areas when you prepare for the SAT. Or use the score sheet to practice your origami swan. Those are good ways to use your PSAT scores.

KEEP TESTS IN PERSPECTIVE

Nowhere in the world of college admissions has more of the population gone so far over the deep end as they have with standardized test anxiety and the resulting preparation. Seventh graders are taking SAT prep classes. I have met families who take tutors with them on vacation so as not to break a test preparation streak. I swear I am not making that up. Be careful. You're bound to meet these people and they will either make you feel bad about your testing approach, or scare the hell out of you.

Standardized tests are just one part of colleges' evaluations of students, and they are never the most important part. The classes you take and the grades you get will always be more important than your test scores.

According to the National Association for College Admissions Counseling "2011 State of College Admissions," in order of importance, the top factors in the admission decision of colleges surveyed were: (1) grades in college-preparatory courses, (2) strength of curriculum and (3) standardized test scores. More than two-thirds of colleges surveyed did not rank test scores as "significantly important."[6]

There are plenty of colleges out there that will gladly take a good kid with average or even below-average test scores. Fairtest, an organization that works to end the misuses and flaws of standardized testing, maintains a list of 850 colleges that now make admissions decisions about substantial numbers of applicants without using the SAT or ACT. You find a searchable listing of test-optional schools here: http://www.fairtest.org/university/optional

So, you can pretty much walk into the SAT or ACT, take it cold, and as long as you don't draw dirty pictures on the answer sheet, you'll still get into college. I'm not suggesting you should completely blow them off, but test taking is not a life-or-death experience. Don't treat the scores with more importance than the colleges do.

Highly selective colleges an exception?

The students I see who agonize the most over their test scores are those who want to go to the most selective colleges. Test scores never get you into these schools—they just keep you out.

If you want to go to Yale and you have a 1520 on the SAT, your chances are going to be slim. "Higher scores are better than lower scores, of course, but even the highest scores are by no means a guarantee of admission," wrote Middlebury College Dean of Admissions Robert Clagett in the *New York Times.*[7]

So the great test taker who is sure that with just another round of tutoring, he can raise his 2250 SAT to a 2300—he's not getting himself any closer to gaining admission to a highly selective college. He's only sacrificing time that could have been spent winning a physics competition, writing a play or taking computer programming. I've seen this play out dozens of times with nervous overachievers who are convinced an extra 20 or 30 points will make the difference.

If you want to go to a prestigious college, you need to nail your standardized tests. Otherwise, you should assign about as much concern and attention to your tests as the colleges will. Care enough to plan for them, prepare and do your best. Maybe even take the test twice. Then get on with your high school career.

We won't miss test scores

In March 2005, Lawrence University adopted a test-optional policy, thereby giving students the choice to submit or not to submit their standardized test results for our admission and scholarship review. If you are happy with your test scores, we are more than happy to consider them as part of your application. If you have a strong academic record and don't feel your standardized test results are a good indicator of your academic potential, we won't miss them... and we won't assume you're trying to hide something from us.[8]

Lawrence University

Scores don't predict college success

After extensive study, researchers found that standardized test scores are not the best predictors of college success within the application. Course selection and grades are much more indicative of students' likelihood to succeed. By adopting this test-optional policy, we are further emphasizing these strong predictors in the hope of broadening our applicant pool to represent students across a range of backgrounds.[9]

Sewanee University

DON'T TAKE TEST SCORES PERSONALLY

The worst thing about standardized tests is that they make kids who don't score well feel badly about themselves. Totally unnecessary.

Standardized tests don't measure how smart you are, how hard you work or how successful you're going to be in college. Fairtest calls the SAT, "…a mind game that has nothing to do with skills necessary for higher education: it tests a tiny range of techniques, mainly how quickly you can choose among four or five answers without thinking deeply about any of them."[10]

Even the ACT's test writers admit that high school grades predict first-year college grades better than ACT scores do.[11] One study at Chicago State University confirmed that for the vast majority of the university's graduates who scored in the middle range of the test as high school students, the ACT explained only 3.6 percent of the differences in cumulative college GPA.[12]

Standardized tests measure how well you take standardized tests. That's about it. There are good test takers and bad test takers, and they sometimes have wildly overlapping levels of academic achievement.

The natural question is, of course: *why do so many colleges require standardized tests?*

They require them because they want a common yardstick to compare 3.5-GPA kids from Toledo, Tallahassee, Tacoma and every other city in the United States, not to mention international applicants.

Those kids earned their 3.5s from different high schools (and home schools) with different requirements and different teachers. But they all take the same standardized tests. It's a far-from-perfect system to compare kids; but for now, the tests remain a necessary evil. I mean: a rite of passage.

If you're a good test taker, congratulations. You have one less thing to worry about and you should show off that skill by nailing your standardized tests.

If you're not a good test taker, I encourage you (and your parents) to not take your scores personally. Don't let subpar scores make you feel badly about yourself. And please don't obsess so much about transforming yourself into a good test taker that you ignore school, the jazz band, your community service work or anything else more important to you and to many colleges.

KID TO KID

Test scores don't measure how smart you are

I was a 4.0 student, but I have always been a bad test taker and I knew that I would struggle with the ACT and SAT. I did many practice tests and had a tutor for the ACT, but the three times I took it, I got an average score every time. This was extremely frustrating, but it wasn't the end of the world. My advice is that students need to put their best effort into getting good grades. Having a higher GPA and lower test scores is better then having a lower GPA and higher test scores.

Kyla S.
Former Collegewise student,
Class of 2012
Chapman University

The SAT measures nothing

The SAT is a scam. It has been around for 50 years. It has never measured anything. And it continues to measure nothing. And the whole game is that everybody who does well on it is so delighted by their good fortune that they don't want to attack it... So it's this terrific kind of rolling scam that every so often, somebody sort of looks and says—well, you know, does it measure intelligence? No. Does it predict college grades? No. Does it tell you how much you learned in high school? No. Does it predict life happiness or life success in any measure? No. It's measuring nothing.[13]

John Katzman
Founder of The Princeton Review

PLAN YOUR TESTING CALENDAR

A quick way to get stressed about college admissions is to get to your senior year and realize you've neglected to take a standardized test that one of your chosen colleges requires.

Here's a suggested timeline to avoid that.

Now

1. Visit the websites of any colleges you are considering and review their testing requirements. This is a good way to get an admissions context for the testing plans you're about to make.

Sophomore Year

1. Take the PSAT or the PLAN—whichever one your school offers—in October. These are both nonthreatening practice tests that will make it easier for you to decide between the SAT and the ACT when the time comes to choose.

2. If you are a strong student with goals to attend a selective college, consider taking Subject Tests in June for the related courses you're completing. For example, if you're taking biology and doing well in it, you'll never know that material better than you will as you're preparing for final exams. That's the perfect time to take the Biology Subject Test.

   Even if your research in Step No. 1 indicated that none of your colleges require Subject Tests, you might still consider taking them at the appropriate times in case you later add schools to your list that do want them.

Junior Year

1. Take the PSAT in October of your junior year. It will help you decide between the SAT or ACT, and how much you should prepare for either, this spring.

2. Prepare for and take either the SAT or ACT (but not both) at least once during your junior year.

3. Consider taking Subject Tests in May or June for the related courses you're completing.

Senior Year

1. In the fall of your senior year, retake the SAT or ACT if you need to improve your scores.

Before you actually enact this plan, review it with your high school counselor. I recommend this for two reasons. First, it's good to involve your counselor in your college planning, and to show her that you're the type of student who gets organized and seeks out advice. Second, your counselor may suggest that you alter this calendar slightly. For example, I've worked with students whose schools offered "life science" instead of "biology," which impacted their chances of scoring well on a biology subject test.

What if you're starting late?

If you're reading this in the fall of your senior year and you've yet to take any tests, all is not lost. Research the testing requirements of your schools to find out what you need to take, and find out the date by which those scores need to be submitted to your chosen colleges. The SAT, Subject Tests and ACT are given in October, November and December, and most schools will accept scores from those dates.

PICK A TEST AND GO WITH IT

Every college in the country that requires standardized tests scores will accept *either* the SAT or the ACT. That hasn't always been the case (e.g., Harvey Mudd College held out on accepting the ACT until January 2007), but today, you will not find a four-year college in the United States that requires both the SAT and the ACT, and you will not find school that accepts one test but not the other.

So you have a choice—SAT or ACT—and an opportunity to play to your testing strengths by focusing only on the test you're naturally better at. That's the good news. Unfortunately, when you compare the features and benefits of the SAT and ACT, it's nearly impossible to decode which one is better for you. See for yourself:

SAT vs. ACT comparison

	SAT	ACT
Sections	Math, Writing, Critical Reading	Math, English, Reading, Science
Scoring	Sections scored from 200-800 and then added together. The highest score is 2400.	Sections scored from 1 to 36, then averaged for a composite score out of 36.
Essay	Yes	Optional
Math	Arithmetic, Algebra, and Geometry	Arithmetic, Algebra, Geometry, and Trigonometry
Tests vocabulary?	Yes	No
Points deducted for wrong answers?	Yes	No

How to choose

If you've taken both the PLAN and the PSAT, you can compare your scores of those two exams and see if you're better at one over the other.

If you haven't taken one or both of those tests, you can certainly buy the official study guides from the College Board and ACT websites, take one full-length practice test from each and compare the scores. But if you're looking for a shortcut, here are a few things I've learned from our Collegewise students' results.

- About 75 percent of our students' initial practice test results showed they scored about the same on both the SAT and the ACT. Of the remaining students, it's about an equal split between the two tests. Don't be surprised if you're not dramatically better at one test over the other.

- Kids who like English a lot more than they like math tend to prefer the ACT. Why? The SAT is one-third math. The ACT is one-quarter math. (If you don't understand what I just said, you should probably take the ACT.)

- If your math section of the PSAT was your highest score, you'll probably be better at the SAT than you will the ACT.

The students who do well in school but have to work very hard to do it tend to prefer the ACT. The kids who get A's after studying for just 10 minutes the morning of the test are usually better SAT testers.

The test prep company The Princeton Review has also created an exam called the PRA (Princeton Review Assessment). It lasts about three and a half hours and tests both SAT and ACT material. When you get your scores back, it tells if you're noticeably better at one of the exams. Most Princeton Review offices do free administrations of the exam several times a year.

Of course, you could always take both tests and show colleges your highest score. But standardized tests and their accompanying preparation take up time. You're better off picking one test and giving it your best effort.

PREP SMARTER

It's easy for students (and the parents paying the bill) to get paralyzed by the options available to them to prepare for the SAT or ACT. You have books, online courses, weekend seminars, long classes and private tutoring, to name a few. And the price tags range from free to more than the cost of many teens' used cars. It amounts to a lot of pressure.

No matter what your testing goals, time or budget, here's some advice about making your test prep choice.

Beware of prep peer pressure.

Like most things in high school, the fact that everybody else is doing something doesn't necessarily mean that you should, too.

About 25 percent of our Collegewise students don't do any test preparation, and it's not because they're all great test takers. A B student who applies to colleges loaded with kids just like him will find that his average test scores are good enough. You're not going to Berkeley, USC, NYU, Duke or Boston College without high test scores; but if you've found colleges you like and your scores are already higher than those of their admitted students, what's the sense in doing test prep?

Before you decide to prepare for the SAT or ACT, research the colleges that you're considering and find out what the average score is for students they accept. Take your list to your counselor and ask for her opinion about how your current scores (PSAT, PLAN or a practice test) stack up.

If you and your counselor decide you've found some appropriate colleges and you would benefit from higher test scores, do some test prep. But don't do it just because everybody else is doing it.

You get out what you put in.

This is one of those times when a cliché is actually true— no matter how reputable and expensive the test preparation, you'll get out of it what you put into it. That's true for any kind of self-improvement you pay for. You could hire the best personal trainer in town who worked all your friends into Olympic shape, but if you don't do the workouts (and eliminate regular servings of your beloved French fries) you're not going to get the desired results. Like fitness, good test scores can't just be purchased. The effort has to be there.

Spend wisely.

There are many low-cost preparation options, from shorter courses to books, that have all the same information taught in an expensive class. The biggest difference is if your parents buy 25 hours of private tutoring, you'll be forced to spend 25 hours preparing for it. Books and shorter courses are far more lenient on the reluctant prepper. Some kids will study for standardized tests even when they aren't forced to, but a lot won't.

If you do decide to take a class or work with a tutor, ask for recommendations from friends who've already prepared.

Don't go overboard.

The amount of time a lot of students spend studying for the SAT and ACT exams is often totally disproportionate to the tests' importance. If you're spending more time doing test prep than you are doing homework, running with the cross country team or spending time with your family—stop; it's time to do less.

Test scores are important at lots of colleges. But they're never important enough to sacrifice time that could be spent getting better grades, playing better basketball or painting better pictures.

Test preparation needs to fit into the rest of your schoolwork and your life. Choose your time of year to prep wisely and apply some good time management when you do. If you feel pressured to ignore other important areas of your life, sacrifice the test prep first.

Efforts to turn average test takers into great test takers usually don't work and make those kids feel badly about themselves. Put in some appropriate time and work hard to improve your scores. Even if you're not happy with your results, be happy with your effort. Then move on to other things you enjoy.

If there were one method that turned every kid into a standardized test-taking world champion, everyone would already be choosing that option. So pick the one that fits your schedule, budget and comfort zone.

PREP FOR LESS THAN $50

Great test prep doesn't need to be expensive. If you have the discipline to study on your own, here's an effective, low-cost way to prepare.

1. **Buy The Princeton Review's *Cracking the SAT* or *Cracking the ACT* book**
   Full disclosure: I used to teach for The Princeton Review, so theirs are the test-taking techniques I know firsthand. Each book retails for about $13 and teaches almost all the test-taking strategies you would learn in an expensive course. Spend three to four weeks learning the techniques they teach.

2. **Buy the College Board's The Official SAT Study Guide with DVD, or ACT's The Real ACT Prep Guide.**
   I recommend these because both contain official practice tests (10 for the SAT, 5 for the ACT, respectively). Each retails for about $31.

3. **Leading up to your exam, take at least one full-length practice test per week, and have someone time you to mimic the real exam.**

4. **After you score the test, go back through every wrong answer.**

Use the explanations that come with the practice test to help you understand where you went wrong for each question. And use the Princeton Review book to review how one of their strategies might have served you well for each wrong question.

For SAT testers, Sal Khan of The Khan Academy (www.khanacademy.org) has worked through every question of the College Board's Official SAT Study Guide, all viewable free on his website. It's like having a tutor right there explaining it to you.

A student who follows this system will have learned test-taking strategies, completed five to 10 full-length practice tests under timed conditions and reviewed every single incorrect answer, all for less than $50.

KNOW WHEN TO SAY WHEN

When our Collegewise students get their SAT/ACT scores, they usually ask, "Should I take it again?" Even if they're thrilled with their scores, that's still the question they ask. Standardized tests have a way of doing that to people. No matter what score you get, you always wonder if it could go higher.

Eventually, the law of diminishing returns applies itself to studying for standardized tests. Spending your entire summer preparing to take the SAT a third or fourth time just won't feel worth it if you only go up 20 points.

So, how do you know when to throw in the testing towel and put the SAT or ACT behind you? There's only a little hard science to this decision, but here are a few guidelines.

1. Did you nail it?

If you met or beat what you hoped you could score, move on. End your standardized testing career on a high note. I know it's tempting to think you might be able to eke out even more points, but there are lots of other things you can be doing to prepare for college admissions that are more important, and more rewarding, than doing more test prep.

Also, if you scored 2150 or higher on the SAT, or 32 or higher on the ACT, walk away. Those scores are good enough at even the most selective schools. Higher scores won't improve your chances, and taking the test again just makes you look neurotic.

2. Check average test scores.

Most colleges share the average test scores of the students they admit. You can find that information on their websites or on collegeboard.com. Before you make a decision about retesting, it's good to know how you compare to students your chosen colleges admit.

Also, don't forget that many colleges allow you to report your highest SAT Math, Critical Reading and Writing scores from different sittings (a practice called "superscoring"). So your highest test score may be better than you thought it was.

Here's an example. Let's say you take the SAT twice and get the following scores:

630 Math
520 Critical Reading
600 Writing
Total score: 1750

590 Math
660 Critical Reading
640 Writing
Total score: 1890

Your best SAT score from one sitting is 1890. But if the schools you're applying to look at your highest scores for each section from different sittings, your score is actually 1930 (630 Math from the first sitting, 660 Critical Reading and 640 Writing from the second sitting).

Some schools use a similar practice for ACT scores, but not nearly as many as do for the SAT. Visit the admissions sections on the websites of the colleges that interest you and find out how they use the scores. Then you can make an informed decision about taking the test again.

3. What does your counselor say?

Once you have the information about your colleges' average test scores of admitted students, visit your high school counselor and ask for her opinion about whether to take the test again. Test scores are more important at some colleges than they are at others. Your counselor can also take other factors into account, like how strong your curriculum and grades are, to give you good advice about whether or not you really need higher test scores.

4. Are you feeling optimistic, or beaten down?

Some students want to take the test again because they know they can do better. They feel they've got the testing upper hand and want to show what they can do. If you're feeling buoyed and want one more try at slaying the testing beast, have at it. But if you've done your best and spent your time preparing and now just wish you never have to take them again, do something else that doesn't make you feel so discouraged.

For most students who plan and prepare well, two times is enough for any standardized tests. When a student decides he's just got to try a third time, I tell him to go for it, but then mandate that he throw in the testing towel once he finishes. Part of managing standardized tests means knowing when to say when.

REALIZE YOUR TEST SCORES SOON WON'T MATTER

Test scores deserve some reasonable concern during your high school years. (Note: I didn't say nail-biting stress.) Here's the futility of it all: one day in the not-too-distant future, nobody will care what your SAT and ACT scores were.

Once you leave high school, SAT and ACT scores are ancient history. Nobody will care how you did. If you struggled with these tests, you'll laugh about them, not unlike the way some people have to laugh about the terrible fashion or hairstyles they chose during their teen years. Good or bad, it's ancient high school history. You move on after graduation.

Nobody has ever become a failure in life because his or her test scores weren't high enough. Millions of students with all levels of test scores have gone to college. What happens after that will have nothing to do with how you scored on those tests. Your college friends won't know or care. You will never interview for a job where someone asks you what your SAT scores were. The person you eventually want to marry isn't going to dump you if you reveal that you got low test scores back in high school.

POST-TRAUMATIC TEST DISORDER

Let test scores be ancient history

It has taken 20 years to forget the trauma of that damned test (the SAT), and looking up my scores would be like going back to Vietnam.[14]

Conan O'Brien
Late night television host
Harvard graduate

SAT and ACT scores have an influence in your life right now. But the expiration date for their influence is coming soon.

APPLYING: THE ART OF COLLEGE APPLICATIONS

Students are usually in shock when I chuckle and tell them I never expect perfection. In fact, I prefer they not project it in their college applications. Of course, this goes against everything they've been told and makes young people uncomfortable. How could a dean of admissions at one of America's most selective institutions not want the best and the brightest? The reality is, perfection doesn't exist, and we don't expect to see it in a college application. In fact, admissions officers tend to be skeptical of students who present themselves as individuals without flaws.[1]

Angel B. Perez
Dean of Admissions
Pitzer College

PART I: IT GETS PERSONAL

LOOK INSIDE THE ADMISSIONS OFFICE

Many large state universities ask for nothing more than a simple application with your biographical and contact information, and copies of both your transcript and test scores. At those schools, the evaluation is a number-crunching exercise. If you've taken the required classes, gotten the minimum GPA and test scores, you're in. The only application strategies for those schools are to fill out the information accurately and to submit everything before the deadlines.

Most of the advice I'm sharing in this chapter is aimed at the more selective colleges— including many competitive public schools—that ask for more personal information in their applications. Most ask you to list your activities and to note how much time you spend doing each of them. Many ask you to write one or more essays. Some invite you to submit letters of recommendation from teachers and counselors and to interview.

Classes, grades and test scores are always important, but these more comprehensive applications mean more personal evaluations. The admissions officers don't just crunch your numbers—they use your application to get a sense of who you are and how you might contribute on campus. How you present yourself can make a big difference.

The application review process

Most selective colleges (schools who admit less than 75% of their applicants) use some version of the following process to evaluate applicants.

In the fall as the applications begin to arrive, colleges have full-time administrative staff members who first receive and sort the various pieces and parts (applications, test scores, transcripts and letters of recommendation—all of which are sent at different times by different people) into each applicant's file. This can be a Herculean task. At Vanderbilt University, each complete file consists of about 15 pieces of paper. In 2011, the school received almost 25,000 applications, amounting to more than 372,500 pieces of paper that needed to be downloaded, printed, sorted and filed.[2]

Once a file is complete, it's handed off to an admissions officer (a "reader"). It's common for colleges to group applications by geographic region so that each reader is evaluating students from a particular territory, allowing readers to get familiar with the high schools in their assigned areas.

First read

Most readers start by reviewing the rigor of your classes, the grades you've earned, your academic standing in your class and your test scores. They'll look through your list of activities and try to get a sense of which ones meant the most to you. They'll read through your essays to get to know you a little better, read your letters of recommendation and consult your interviewer's report. During this time, readers take notes on each part of the application, and they conclude by writing a summary of your strengths and weaknesses, and anything else that was interesting or notable about you. This process can take anywhere from 20 minutes to an hour, depending on the school and how many pieces of information are part of the application.

At most schools, this first reader can recommend to admit a particularly strong student or to deny one who has no chance of admission, without discussing the applicant with the rest of the committee.

If you're the high school valedictorian and you're applying to a school that accepts B students, you're likely to be admitted right away unless there is a compelling reason not to, like a suspension from school or a shoddy application that makes it clear you're not interested.

If you apply to MIT and you have multiple D's on your transcript, you're not likely to make it past this first reading.

At most schools, a senior admissions officer has to approve this quick admit or deny it before the decision is made, but there's generally no further discussion with the committee.

The second read

If you make it past the first read, a second reader will review your application, write comments and compare her impressions of you with those of the first reader. If both readers have the same recommendation (admit or deny), a senior admissions officer will review the file and decide whether to accept the recommendation or to send it to the committee. All other applicants will be sent to the committee for discussion.

Meet the committee

The admissions committee is usually comprised of readers, regional directors and the director of admissions. This is where college admissions can get a little dramatic.

For your file to get to this point, at least one of the readers wants to admit you. But all of the other readers have applicants they want to admit, too, and at a selective college, they can't admit everybody. "In March I go into committee with my colleagues, having narrowed down my top picks to a few hundred people," said Ben Jones of the MIT admissions committee. "My colleagues have all done the same. Then the numbers come in: this year's admit rate will be 13 percent. For every student you admit, you need to let go of seven others."[3]

As your file comes up for discussion, your reader will plead your case. He or she will summarize what parts of your application were most compelling, share all the reasons why you should be admitted or why any weaknesses should be overlooked. And these discussions aren't limited to grades and test scores. Your reader might share that you were raised by a single mother or that you worked 25 hours a week during high school. She might share the part of your essay that moved her or the line in a letter of recommendation that makes her think you can succeed in college. For example, our Collegewise counselor, Arun, was an Eagle Scout in high school and used to take his share of flack from his admissions colleagues at Caltech and University of Chicago for seemingly always lobbying just a little harder for the Eagle Scouts in the pile.

The admissions committee discussions can be lengthy. Vanderbilt University has three committees running six to eight hours a day, and they average about 10 application discussions in a committee hour.[4] Eventually, your admissions decision will be put to a vote. If enough hands go up, you're in.

Given how invested readers get in their applicants, the final vote can be an emotional one. One of our Collegewise counselors, Allison, worked in admissions at the University of Redlands. She remembers lobbying hard for a student whose parents, after learning the student was gay, sent him to military school. He had a lot of academic deficiencies, but as she put it, "I thought we could save this kid and give him a chance to start over in college."

When the committee didn't agree, she went back to her office, cried and ate an entire bag of candy hearts someone had given her for Valentine's Day.

It gets personal

Schools use different variations of the system I've described, but the one constant is that a school who asks you to share personal information will reciprocate by letting real human beings evaluate you. When they do, they'll look at lots of things beyond just grades and test scores. This chapter will help you make a compelling, lasting impression on your readers that will make them fight for you in committee if that's what it takes.

PART II: HOW AND WHEN TO APPLY

MAKE SENSE OF APPLICATION PLANS

The most common application timeline looks like this: (1) you apply to college by January 1 of your senior year, (2) they give you an answer by mid-March and (3) you have to decide which offer to accept by May 1.

Roughly 450 colleges offer early application options where you apply in early November and find out by December. Some of those plans require you to make a binding promise to attend the school if you're accepted.

Many other schools review applications on a first-come, first-served system. So you don't just decide where to apply, you also have to decide when and how to apply, which can make the process that much more confusing.

Here's how to make sense of the various application plans and pick the right ones for you.

1. Rolling admissions

Rolling admissions looks a lot like regular-decision admissions with one crucial difference—rolling schools evaluate applications as they are received, then send admissions decisions back throughout the cycle (sometimes as soon as four to six weeks later).

The earlier you apply, the sooner you get your answer (and the more spaces are left to fill). Rolling admissions isn't an option you choose; it's just something that certain colleges do.

2. Early acceptance options

There are two different early acceptance options that allow you to submit an application by November 1 or 15 of the senior year and receive a decision by December 15.

Early Decision

Early decision applicants make a binding promise to the college—if you're accepted, you must enroll. In fact, students accepted to a binding early decision program actually have to withdraw all their applications from all other colleges. You can apply to as many other schools as you'd like, but because of this binding commitment, you can only have one early decision school.

I'm often asked what would happen if a student backed out of an early decision admissions. The truth is a college can't legally make you attend. But unless you can demonstrate financial hardship (which is the one reason they will let you back out), colleges have been known to carry a grudge. It's not unusual for an admissions officer to call her colleagues at an applicant's other colleges to let them know he backed out of an early decision commitment.

Years ago, I toured Stanford and the tour guide told a story of a student who enrolled at Stanford and was later found to have backed out of an early decision commitment to another school. Stanford threw him out.

Don't mess around with early decision commitments. As part of an early decision application, you, your parents and your counselor all sign a document saying that you understand what you're agreeing to. Backing out will always have consequences.

Early Action

Early action is just like early decision, but without the binding commitment. Since there's no promise to attend if you're admitted, you can apply to as many early action schools as you'd like, though some schools (most notably Harvard, Yale, Princeton and Stanford) offer "Single Choice Early Action" which, while not binding, limits you from applying to any other early programs, binding or nonbinding.

If you need to take an Aspirin, I understand. It starts to sound like a complex logic game.

APPLICATION OPTIONS

Application type	*Deadline	Is the decision binding?	If you're accepted, when do you decide?	Sample schools
Regular admissions	On or around January 1	No	May 1	Most schools offer this option
Rolling admissions	Colleges begin taking applications as early as August 15 and continue as late as March 1	No	May 1	University of Michigan, Penn State
Early decision	November 1 or November 15	Yes	N/A. If you're accepted, you're going.	Colgate, Duke
Early action	November 1 or November 15	No	May 1	University of Chicago, Villanova

*These are approximates—you should always check the deadlines for your specific schools.

SEEK EARLY DECISION IF...

Many of the students and parents I meet have heard that applying to a binding early decision program can improve your chances of getting in. They don't want to miss out on that advantage, so they feel pressured to apply early. Truth is: the extra stress may not be worth it.

Applying to a nonbinding early action program does not improve your chances at most colleges. In the fall of 2010, colleges that offered an early action option admitted those students at a nearly identical rate as those admitted in the regular pool.[5]

Applying early decision, however, can give you a nice admissions boost at some schools. Nationally, early decision schools admitted 57 percent of early applicants compared with 50 percent in the regular pool in 2010.[6] At some schools, the difference is more dramatic. Duke just comes right out on their website and tells applicants: "There is a measurable advantage in the admissions process to applying Early Decision. In 2010-2011, we admitted 29% of students who applied Early Decision and 12% of students who applied Regular Decision."[7]

That's compelling data, but it's important to understand why those admissions rates are higher before you let a potential admissions advantage convince you to apply early decision.

Early applicants are admitted at higher rates because it removes some of the guesswork for colleges. Whoever they admit early is bound to attend—the college won't lose any of those students to other schools. The most selective schools receive two to three times the number of qualified applicants than they could enroll. Most of those applicants also apply to other highly selective colleges. Admitting a higher percentage of students in the early decision pool has more to do with the college snatching up who they want the most than it does with admitting people who aren't qualified.

Advantage: strongest applicants

In my experience, the students who enjoy an early admission advantage are those who are already highly qualified and would probably be admitted in the regular pool, too.

Just because something gets easier doesn't mean it's easier for everybody. Coors Field in Denver has a reputation as the most hitter-friendly park in Major League Baseball. That's great news for Alex Rodriguez (who's hit more than 600 home runs in his career), but it wouldn't help someone like me who's happy to get a solid base hit in the annual softball friendly.

A student who is a great match for an early decision college, who would be competitive even in the regular pool, and most importantly, who is absolutely certain that she's found her collegiate soul mate might enjoy an admissions advantage applying early decision. If you fit those three criteria, talk it over with your high school counselor and strongly consider the option.

Otherwise, don't feel pressured to apply early just for the potential admissions boost.

APPLY STRATEGICALLY

Once you've identified which application plans are offered by your chosen colleges, here's how to choose the right plan and decide which applications to do first.

1. Submit rolling applications first.

I've seen many students who began their senior year having already received an acceptance from a rolling admissions school. Talk about a nice emotional boost. Imagine knowing for sure you have at least one college to attend before you've even finished the bulk of your applications. That's why I always tell students to complete their rolling applications first, even if those schools are far from their first choices. Your chances of admission will be stronger because there are a lot more spots available at the beginning of the admissions cycle than there are at the end of it (and you never know when the class will fill up).

2. Apply early (binding or nonbinding) only if you're a competitive applicant.

When you apply early, you're evaluated based on what you've accomplished by early November. What if you get your best GPA in the first semester of your senior year? What if you retake the SAT in December and improve your score by 120 points? What if you win a debate tournament or get named MVP of the field hockey team or receive a department award in physics?

Early admissions decisions will likely be made before a college can consider any of those accomplishments. If you're not confident, why not do everything you can to have your best semester yet? Nothing improves your chances more than improving your qualifications.

3. If you apply early, keep working on your other applications.

I've met students who submitted early applications in November, and then waited with their fingers crossed, leaving all their other college applications to wait until they heard back from their early school.

Sure, that's a great system if you get an early acceptance. But if you don't, you'll have to muster the enthusiasm to put all the necessary love and attention into finishing your remaining college applications, get them done in just a few weeks over your holiday break, all while nursing the emotional hangover from having a dream school reject you.

Don't do that to yourself. Complete all of your college applications before your holiday break. If your early school says "No," you'll be able to take some solace in the fact that at least your other applications have already been submitted.

Yes, if your dream school admits you, you'll have completely wasted your time on those other applications. But which problem would you rather have?

4. Apply early decision only if you are sure the school is your first choice.

Early decision was designed for students who have a clear first choice school and are willing to commit early, not as a way to gain an admissions advantage. Most seniors aren't ready to pledge their undying love to one college (fewer than 10 percent of the students at Collegewise apply early decision). If you aren't ready to make the commitment early, don't apply early decision, and don't feel badly about it.

5. **If you're certain you'll need financial aid, don't apply early decision.**

If you're accepted early decision, you give up the chance to compare offers of financial aid from other colleges. And the colleges don't have as much incentive to entice you with unsolicited aid because you're bound to attend if they take you.

PART III: COMPLETING APPLICATIONS

START EARLY

Ask seniors who've applied to college what advice they have about surviving the application process, and I promise you most of them will tell you to start early.

Students who start (and finish) their applications early have a more manageable process. They're less stressed. They have more time to write better essays. Their chances of admission are stronger at schools who admit applicants on a rolling basis. They get on with enjoying their senior year.

Another reason to start early: you're not the only person who will need time to prepare and send your application materials.

- Your counselor will need time to send your transcripts and complete your secondary school report.
- Your teachers will need time to write and send your letters of recommendation.
- The College Board and ACT will need time to send your official score reports to your chosen colleges.
- If you want someone to help you proofread your college essays or your applications, that person will need enough time to do a good job.

You may be willing to wait until the last minute and pull a few late nights to finish your applications. But the other people who'll play a role in those applications aren't likely to feel the same way. The earlier you start, the more time you give them to help you.

So, when is early?

I think it's reasonable for students to start their college application process during the summer before their senior year. As long as you've finalized your college list and gotten your counselor's endorsement that the schools you've selected are good choices, you can begin working on college applications and essays as soon as they become available.

The Common Application (www.commonapp.org), a standardized application used by more than 400 colleges, releases its updated version by August 1. Many other colleges will make their individual applications available over the summer, too. Just about every college will have its application available no later than October 1. Since most applications aren't due until January, there's no reason you should be left scrambling to meet your deadlines.

I know that working on college applications isn't anyone's idea of summer fun, but it's not going to get any easier once you start your senior year and have to balance your classes and activities.

Start early. Your applications, results and senior year will be better because of it.

Work early, relax late

By the first day of senior year, I had already completed all of my college applications. Most of my classmates hadn't even started. This made the world of difference in my first semester.

Jared G.
Former Collegewise student, Class of 2009
University of Southern California

Wouldn't change a thing

I was almost done with the most difficult parts of applications after the first month of my senior year. If I had to do it over again, I wouldn't change a thing.

Colette B.
Former Collegewise student, Class of 2010
George Washington University

The relaxed peer

It's really great to be done with everything while you watch your friends stress out over getting everything in on time.

Jeremy B.
Former Collegewise student, Class of 2010
Boston College

Months ahead of schedule

I was nearly finished with all of my college applications before my senior year even started. So while all of my classmates were freaking out about applications, I was done months ago.

Joseph K.
Former Collegewise student, Class of 2010
University of Puget Sound

GET REQUIREMENTS FROM THE SOURCE

A complete application to a college can have a lot of different parts—the application itself, a transcript, a school report, official test scores, letters of recommendation, etc. So your first step is to find out what's required from the colleges where you want to apply. The only trusted place to get that information is in the "Undergraduate Admissions" section of each college's own website.

In particular, you want to know:

- What are the elements of a complete application?
- When is the application deadline?
- What standardized tests are required for admission, and by when must you have your scores sent to the college?
- What other supporting documentation is needed for an application to be complete (letters of recommendation, transcripts, school report, etc.)?
- Are interviews recommended? If so, how do you schedule one?

It's very important that you get this information only from each college's website—don't rely on any other source. For example, if you're applying to schools on the Common Application, they list the application requirements for each college for you. I've seen several instances where the instructions on the Common Application were different from those on a college's website. For one school in particular, the Common Application listed interviews as "optional," but the school's website explicitly said that local applicants were expected to interview. When in doubt, do what the college's website tells you to do.

A lot of colleges also offer application advice or answers to frequently asked questions on their websites. When the people who will read your application offer advice, it's a good idea to follow it.

Many colleges' admissions offices also write blogs during the application process. Look for them. They not only share insight about how the process works and who the people are making the decisions, but they also share helpful tips and even answer questions.

Bookmark the blogs (or add them to your reader) and check them every couple of days.

MANAGE YOUR PARENTS

Some seniors get frustrated with their parents during the college application process. They wish their parents would back off and stop asking, probing, nagging or generally driving them crazy. You'll know this is happening if you find yourself snapping, "Mom, stop asking me about this. I'll get it done!"

Here's something you can do to keep the stress levels in your household manageable: talk to your parents about what you're doing.

You can put your parents at ease by just spending a few minutes every couple of days actually telling them what you're up to.

Tell them when you meet with your counselor, when you submit your letters of recommendation and when you visit your English teacher to have her look at your essay.

Show them the information you print out from colleges. Tell them when the deadlines are, and when you plan to submit yours.

If you need help organizing all the information, ask your parents to help—not to do it for you—but to help.

One of my former Class of 2012 Collegewise students, Ryan J., said this about keeping parents in the loop: "It virtually eliminated conflict in our house about college because my mom didn't have to nag me about anything."

Ryan went on to attend Northeastern University.

College application guilt

Some parents will gladly stay out of the college application process and let their kids handle it.

For others, stepping back and letting you take charge, especially at the time that you're doing something as important as college applications, is a hard thing to do. They worry something could go wrong, that they'll have to live with the college application guilt of not being involved enough when it counted. That's why parents ask if you've written your essays yet, and if you've started your application to Duke, and if you've seen your teachers about getting letters of recommendation. It comes from a good place.

If you feel like your parents are standing over your shoulder during this time, and it would be a lot less stressful if they would just back off a little, do the opposite of what you're inclined to do. Talk to your parents about the process, and they'll be more likely to take themselves out of it.

FOLLOW INSTRUCTIONS

I know you don't need me to tell you that it's a good idea to follow instructions. Still, it's surprising how many students forget to follow that simple advice. Following instructions is your single best application strategy.

Colleges spend months creating their applications. They write the questions, compose the essay prompts, arrange the information on the application, and decide what, if any, supporting documentation they want in addition to the application. The finished products are carefully constructed applications that will provide each college with the information they want, in exactly the way they want it presented.

That's your roadmap—do exactly what they ask you to do. Their way is the best way to apply.

Part of following instructions means resisting the urge to decide that you have a better way. Here's an example. I've met students who insisted they had far too many important activities to list in the space provided and wanted to write "See attached resume." Bad idea. Doing so would force the admissions officer to pore through your resume, all the while knowing a stack of other applications is waiting for her—applications that followed the requested format. That's just going to annoy an admissions officer, which is not your goal as an applicant.

No matter how unique you think your situation may be, no matter how much more compelling you think your candidacy would be, don't look for a better way. Colleges would prefer you do it their way. If any of the directions are unclear, call the college and ask for clarification. But make sure you've really taken the time to read all their directions and the frequently asked questions on their website.

Applying to college is stressful and can feel overwhelming at times. As long as you follow instructions, you're not going to do anything that hurts your chances of admission.

GET THE BASICS RIGHT

Most college applications start by asking for fairly basic information about you and where you go to school. Answering usually isn't challenging; but I find that students consistently make simple mistakes. Here are the top 10 mistakes and how to avoid them:

1. First/given name

It's important that the name you list on your application matches the name on formal documents like your Social Security card, birth certificate and transcript. Even if everyone in your life calls you Pat, don't write Pat if those formal documents say Patrick. Otherwise, it's easy for one of the elements of your application to get misfiled with those of another applicant with a similar name.

2. Social Security number

I've met parents who didn't want their kids listing their Social Security number on a college application because of privacy concerns. It's important to answer this question because schools sometimes match official test score reports (like the SAT and ACT) to applicants' files based on Social Security numbers. If you apply for financial aid, you'll need to put this in because it will correspond to your Free Application for Federal Student Aid (FAFSA) information.

3. Email address

Make sure it's an email address that: (1) you check regularly and (2) is appropriate. One of our Collegewise counselors who worked in admissions said she and her colleagues had a contest every year for which admissions officer would read a file with the most inappropriate email address. That's not a contest you want to win. What's inappropriate? If your college interviewer asked you, "What's your email address?" would you be embarrassed to answer? Then it's probably inappropriate.

4. Preferred Telephone

I recommend students list their home number, rather than their cell phone number. The number you list here is the one admissions officers will call if they have a question, and interviewers will use to contact you. Imagine your cell phone ringing while you're in a car with your friends, music blaring at top volume, your friends viciously taunting you for making a poor ringtone choice. The voice you hear on the phone says, "Hi, this is James, from Georgetown University, calling to schedule our interview. Is this a good time to talk?"

No, it wouldn't be.

If your family has made the switch and no longer has a home phone, or if you just feel more comfortable listing your cell phone on the application, make sure your outgoing voicemail is something you'd be comfortable with a college representative hearing.

5. Parent occupation/employer/title

"Businessman" is not an occupation. If you're not sure of your parents' occupations, ask them. It's important that they feel what you have shared is accurate.

6. Counselor information

Some colleges ask you to list your counselor's name, title, phone number, email and/or fax number.

Take the time to get this information right. Go to your school's website or visit your counselor personally to verify all of this information. "Mrs." does not count as a first name here, by the way.

If colleges have any questions about your application, they're going to contact your counselor. But a college isn't under any obligation to track your counselor down if you put in the wrong phone number or email address. Make it easy for them.

7. SAT/subject tests

Pay attention to whether the college asks for all of your scores, or just your best scores from different sittings of the exam.

8. Advanced Placement/International Baccalaureate tests

If you've taken multiple AP or IB tests, list your highest scores first. This is a subtle thing, but when a reader looks at a list of scores, you want to start strong.

9. Current year courses

List the courses in descending order of difficulty. This lets you impress the admissions officer immediately. List AP courses at the top (starting with Calculus or English if you're taking one or both), then move to honors courses, followed by regular classes (solids, followed by electives).

If you don't have any honors or AP classes, list any of the five academic solids first—English, math, science, foreign language or social science. Then list any electives.

10. Academic honors/awards

Start with your most impressive awards first. If you're not sure which one is the most impressive, list the more recent awards toward the top.

Many awards that appear as acronyms need to be spelled out, especially if they are unique to your school or your state. Admissions officers in California may know that CSF means "California Scholarship Federation," but most colleges in other states won't. The same can be said for any schoolwide or countywide award that's an abbreviation.

It's also important to describe the context of any award that a college may not understand. They know what a "National Merit Finalist" is. But if you won an award at your school called the "Aerostar Award," colleges will have absolutely no idea what that means. Help the college understand it, like this:

Aerostar Award: Two juniors selected by faculty for outstanding achievement in science.

MAKE IT EASY TO UNDERSTAND YOUR ACTIVITIES

Most colleges will provide you with a space to describe your activities and estimate the amount of time you spend doing each. Here's how to do that effectively.

1. Never submit a resume in place of actually listing your activities.

As mentioned in "Follow instructions," if you send a resume without being asked, it's like telling the college that you didn't like the way they put the application together. Don't do it. It'll just annoy them.

2. List your activities in order of importance to you.

Start with the one activity that you could never imagine your high school career without, then work your way down from there. That will help an admissions officer quickly understand what was most important to you, and likely what you spent the most time doing.

3. List only what's significant.

The applicant with the longest list of activities is not necessarily the one who's going to get in. Admissions officers want to learn about the significant ways you spent your time outside of class. If you were in the Spanish Club in ninth grade and never went back after ninth grade, it won't really help your application to list it. Leave the space blank, or use the spot to share something else more important to you.

Remember: this isn't a contest to see how much you can list. It's your chance to describe what you really enjoyed doing in high school.

4. Spell out (most) abbreviations/acronyms.

It would be hard to find someone who doesn't know what an MVP is, but there are lots of other abbreviations that only mean something to the people involved in the group that uses it. Would your aunt who doesn't work at your high school know it? If not, write it out on your application.

5. Be accurate with your "approximate time spent."

Many colleges will ask you to estimate the number of weeks per year, and number of hours per week, that you spend participating in each activity. Be as accurate as you can. Colleges aren't paying close enough attention that they'll question if two hours a week in the Spanish Club should more accurately be one hour. But if you tell them your involvement in the Spanish Club is 30 hours per week, that doesn't add up (unless Spanish Club has become your full-time job).

Don't underestimate, either. If you say you play football six hours a week, that's probably selling yourself short considering that one game alone is at least three hours. Again, just be as accurate as you can.

Also, some students who are very involved in an activity automatically enter "52 weeks per year." But you should only do that if you are honestly swimming in the pool or working at the hamburger stand or running the Key Club every single week of the year (including winter holiday, spring break and summer months). There's no need to exaggerate here, and no reason to give an admissions officer pause.

AVOID GIMMICKS

When he was working in admissions at Caltech, our Collegewise counselor, Arun, once read a student's essay she'd printed on pink paper and saturated with enough perfume to make him feel queasy (and a little creeped out).

Every year, overzealous applicants send cookies, CDs of them singing the school's fight song and applications filled out in the school's colors. The attempts make for stories that last from generation to generation in the admissions office, but not necessarily for good reason.

College application gimmicks don't work. The admissions officers may gladly eat your cookies, but that won't sway their admissions vote. Neither will sending a poster of yourself draped in the college's paraphernalia or camping out in front of the admissions office with a sign that says, "Will work for admission."

If you know a student who tried a gimmick and was accepted, remember it's likely he or she was accepted in spite of the gimmick, not because of it. Genuine interest in the school, following directions, thoughtful applications and essays, a good conversation with your interviewer—those strategies will get you closer to being admitted than even the best oatmeal raisin cookie will.

Be clear. Be honest. Be thoughtful. You may not become a college admissions tale that carries on to the next generation, but the admissions officers will be more likely to actually admit you.

By the way, that perfumed application? She wasn't admitted.

COMMITTEE NOTES

Don't be creepy

The student who years ago sent in a life-size doll who was her "best friend," equipped with a recorded endorsement of the applicant, left the admissions staff feeling like it was in a Twilight Zone episode. Creepy. Don't send brownies, T-shirts or love notes. Just write a good application, choose recommenders well, write a thoughtful, personality-infused essay and if an interview is offered, do it.[8]

Bruce Poch
Former Dean of Admissions
Pomona College

AVOID THE FIVE DON'TS

Just about every college admissions officer I've met was a nice person who would much rather admit than deny kids. But some applicants do things that earn them a quick trip to the "No" pile. Here are my top five application don'ts.

1. Don't lie.

When you sign your college application, you're signing a formal document stating all of the information is true to the best of your knowledge. If you get caught in a lie, you won't get in, or your admission will be revoked, and there will be no apologizing your way out of it.

Colleges know how to spot inconsistencies in your application and they won't hesitate to call your counselor to verify information that doesn't seem right. I met a student who'd conveniently omitted calculus from her list of classes she was taking because she got a D. Three months before she was supposed to start college, the school found out and took back her admission.

The risk of lying far outweighs any potential reward.

2. Don't write any part of your application like a text message.

Capitalization, punctuation and complete sentences are your friends. You won't be automatically rejected if you mix up "role" and "roll," but refusing to use capital letters is just lazy.

3. Don't report any of your classes or grades incorrectly.

This is a variation of the "don't lie" rule. Some schools, like those in the University of California system, ask you to input on your application all the classes you've taken and the grades you've earned. Don't even attempt it without your official transcript in hand. If you're admitted and your reported academic history doesn't match your transcript exactly, there's a good chance the school will revoke your acceptance. You won't be able to "oops" your way out of it.

4. Don't make excuses for things that were your fault.

This is especially true if a college asks you to explain any disciplinary actions that were taken against you. Accept responsibility and show them how you've learned your lesson. One of my students was suspended for fighting when he was defending his younger brother who was autistic. Still, he admitted in his explanation that he could have just walked away with his little brother in tow, and instead, he'd chosen to fight. He called it "a really stupid thing to do."

5. Don't let your parents do your applications for you.

Parents fill out applications differently than kids do, they use different words and phrases, and it's usually obvious to an admissions officer. Parents who hijack the applications are often the same ones who call the admissions office for their student, often going as far as to reveal "I'm filling out the application..." That's like your dad calling your history teacher, "I'm writing Dan's paper for him..." Do your own work.

PART IV: HOW ANY STUDENT CAN WRITE BETTER COLLEGE ESSAYS

GIVE YOURSELF A BOOST

Great college essays are equal opportunity employers. They don't discriminate on the basis of grades and test scores. The C student has the same opportunity to write great essays as the kid who's had straight A's since birth. Everybody has a story to tell. You just have to find yours and tell it in an engaging way.

By the time you get ready to apply to college, most of your high school career will be in place. You're not going to substantially raise your cumulative GPA or find a way to replenish fossil fuels. So the essays might be the one area where you can make a substantial difference in the quality of your application. Don't miss the opportunity by writing something safe and unrevealing. Start early, find stories you care about and write them in an engaging way.

Which of your extracurricular activities has had the most meaning for you?

Wrong approach: Sharing what admissions officers already know—that football is hard, that community service feels good when you help others, that being on the student government involves leadership skills.

Right approach: Treat that question as if it actually reads, "Please tell us something interesting, unusual or personally meaningful—preferably something we don't already know—about one of the activities you've listed."

Share an experience, achievement or risk you have taken and its impact on you.

Wrong approach: Choose your most impressive activity and tell a story about how the activity helped you develop admirable traits or learn valuable life lessons.

Right approach: Start with the end of the prompt in mind: "...and its impact on you." Your story needs to address this impact, and it needs to be something truthful, something you've actually said to other people. "Winning a debate tournament taught me the importance of committing to my goals" doesn't get the job done here. "Winning a debate tournament was the first time I realized that I could actually be comfortable in front of crowds" does.

Describe a person who has had a significant influence on you.

Wrong approach: Focusing too much on what makes the person so impressive, not enough on how this person has influenced you. The admissions committee doesn't need to be convinced that Martin Luther King, Jr. or Gandhi are admirable.

Right approach: Focus on the influence. Choose someone who has actually caused you to change, take action or think differently, and write about how this person influenced those events.

How will you contribute to our campus community?

Wrong approach: Visiting the college's website, finding the names of clubs or organizations that are loosely related to your current activities, and claim that you would "love to get involved." That's all hypothetical.

Right approach: Contributing as a member of a campus community simply means finding your place within it and participating. Start by thinking about the parts of college that you're most excited about, where you see yourself really thriving, and ask yourself how you'll be contributing in those scenarios, like joining student government, writing for the school paper, talking about politics with friends at the coffee shop or cooking vegetarian food with fellow meat abstainers. Explain how you know you'll like those things, and share things you're doing that are precursors to those college activities to come.

Is there anything else you'd like us to know that may not have been covered sufficiently in your application?

Wrong approach: Answering just to fill the space, often with an essay you wrote for another college. When that essay doesn't present new and compelling information, it dulls your application.

Right approach: When this essay is optional as it almost always is, don't be afraid to leave the section blank. Two thirds of my students don't respond. More information doesn't always equal a stronger application. Only use this essay opportunity to share something you would have been frustrated to leave out if you hadn't been given the opportunity.

HELP READERS KNOW YOU

The function of your college essay is not to convince the college that you're worthy of admission. It's to help readers get to know you.

Think of your college application and the accompanying essays as doing two separate but equally important jobs. The application—the transcript, standardized test scores, extracurricular activities, honors and awards and letters of recommendation—helps a college decide whether or not you're qualified to be admitted. The essays help them decide whether or not they like you.

Colleges know they aren't just admitting collections of grades, test scores and activities. They're admitting real human beings who will live and learn with a community of fellow students. They want to know how you'll fit in.

A high school valedictorian with perfect test scores and a certificate proclaiming that he founded his own country is obviously qualified. But if he seems like an arrogant jerk, a college owes it to the other students to admit a different valedictorian who seems more pleasant to be around.

Colleges ask you to write essays as a way to get to know you in ways that qualifications alone can't do. One of my students wrote about how much he loved his beat up, rusty 1988 Nissan Sentra even though it only started 60 percent of the time and had a heater that would not shut off. That essay helped him relay that he was relaxed, self-assured and likeable. He let the application do the convincing and the essay do the engaging.

One of our counselors who worked in admissions at several selective colleges described it this way: "When reading the essays, I would be asking myself, 'If I were back in college, would I want this kid to be my roommate?'"

The best way to get people to like you is to just be yourself. It's one of those clichés that's true. So don't use the essays to try to convince the college to admit you. Just answer the questions honestly and be yourself. The application tells the college about your qualifications. The essays tell them about the person *behind* those qualifications.

COMMITTEE NOTES

Almost the worst thing is for students to write to what they think we are looking for. The best thing they can do is write from the heart.[9]

Stu Schmill
Interim Admissions Director
MIT

KEEP THE FOCUS ON YOU

Every college essay prompt is designed to yield more about the same subject—you. If your essays don't help readers learn about you, you're focusing on the wrong things.

If you write an essay about how wonderful your English teacher is, you're drifting away from the most important subject. The college will learn a lot more about your English teacher than they will about you.

If you write an essay about how great the other students were at the leadership camp you attended, or how your best friend has always been there for you, or what your dad does for a living, the college is learning about people other than you. They might be impressed by the person you discuss. But that's not the desired outcome here.

Even those prompts that seem to be asking about something or someone other than yourself are really looking to learn more about you.

For example, a lot of students answer the prompt, "Why do you want to attend this college?" with an essay detailing why the college is great, how many Nobel Prize-winning professors work on campus and how small the classes are. The person reading your essay already knows this. A better response describes why the college is appealing to you.

An essay prompt asking you about a person who's influenced you is not asking why this person is wonderful. It's asking how this person has influenced *you*. What have you learned, changed or done as a result of this person's influence?

It's fine to bring other people or places into your stories, but the essays still need to be about you. Keep the focus on you. Don't drift.

HONEST BEATS IMPRESSIVE

There's nothing wrong with impressing people. But there is such a thing as trying too hard to impress people. That's where so many otherwise good kids go wrong in their college essays.

When writing their college essays, too many students ask themselves, *What would sound impressive? What do colleges want to hear?*

A staggering number of kids arrive at the same conclusion. They'll take an activity or experience they're proud of and tell a story about how it helped them learn valuable lessons or develop admirable traits. It may feel original to the writers. For admission committees, the end result is several hundred thousand unique college applicants writing identically clichéd college essays.

That's why baseball players, student body presidents and editors of school newspapers fall into the trap of writing about how their activities taught them the importance of teamwork and committing to their goals.

National Charity League members, Key Club officers and students who volunteered on blood drives end up writing about how the experience gave them an appreciation for helping others.

Students who've traveled anywhere outside of the continental United States write about how seeing a different place broadened their horizons.

Essays like those aren't just overused—they're often not honest. "Baseball taught me the importance of hard work and commitment" may technically be a true statement for a baseball player. But if that life lesson never occurred to him until he sat down to write his college essays and tried to guess what might sound impressive, it's not really true.

Colleges would rather have heard about the celebratory dinner with his family after he threw a two-hitter, or what it was like riding the bench for two years just waiting for a chance, or how he practiced his curveball two hours a day all summer until he knew it was one of his best pitches.

Don't try to guess what the admissions office wants to hear. That's the fastest way to write an essay every other kid will write. Instead, just tell the truth.

COMMITTEE NOTES

The standard type of question—tell us about yourself—led a lot of students to construct a personality that they felt would be acceptable. Some of these essays were brilliant. The students constructed a work of art. But that isn't what we want. We want to jar them out of doing the expected thing so that they really tell us about themselves. When that happens, it's wonderful.[10]

Ted O'Neill
Former Dean of Admissions
University of Chicago

SHARE THE DETAILS

To make your essay stand out and actually help the reader get to know you better, share a story the admissions officer hasn't read yet. Two ways to do that:

1. Share an experience so remarkable, no other teenager in the history of college applications has gone through the same thing.

2. Add as much detail to your story as possible so that nobody else could tell quite the same story.

Most 17-year-olds don't have a story that absolutely no other applicant could share. But your experience playing on the basketball team, running for student body treasurer, going on a family vacation in an RV, volunteering at a hospital or working a part-time job are not the same as every other kid who had those experiences. Details help you take ownership of a story and make it yours.

For example, a cross country runner doesn't own: "Cross country is a grueling sport. During the summer, I ran seven miles a day just to get ready for the season."

But she would own: "Last summer, I ran the seven-mile loop through the hills behind my house so many times that the park ranger actually knew my name. (I know hers now, too—it's Karla.) When I was gone for five days on vacation with my family, Karla later told me she'd started worrying that something might have happened to me on the trail. She actually considered doing a search."

If you can't come up with enough details to own a story, it's probably not the right choice for a college essay. That doesn't mean the subject wasn't valuable in some way. If you played varsity basketball for two years and loved every minute of it, list it proudly on your application. But if you can't think of a basketball-related story you own, pick a different topic for your essay.

FIVE OF MY ALL-TIME FAVORITE ESSAYS

1. Jack P. opened his essay with a description of the snow cone business he started at age 10 with his little brothers, a business whose original sign—complete with the unfortunate typo, "Snow Cons"—was still stored in their garage. It was a charming start to an otherwise serious essay, and the detail ensured that no other essay in the stack of applications would start exactly the same way. He went to Princeton.

2. Chad M. wrote an essay about his favorite player on the soccer team he coached for mentally challenged kids, Steven. He admitted that coaches weren't supposed to have favorites, but Chad just couldn't help himself. Steven was his brother. The admissions committee never would have known about Chad's special relationship with his brother had he not shared it in his essay. Chad went to the Air Force Academy.

3. Mike M. wrote about working part time at a hamburger stand throughout high school. That essay began, "I make a mean hamburger. In fact, I'm a professional. I've got four years of professional hamburger-making experience." He'd been the lead in several school plays and was applying as a drama major, but his essay let the reader learn about another activity that had become just as important to him, even if it wasn't as impressive as his acting credentials. He attended USC (University of Southern California).

4. Sarah S. wrote that while she had never been on a date, she was still a proud, fully fledged nerd, one who couldn't wait to attend a college where every lunch table was full of "eligible nerd bachelors." She titled her essay, "I'm with The Banned." I can't imagine anybody reading that essay and not liking a kid so self-aware and comfortable in her own skin. Sarah went to Occidental College.

5. Harry K.'s essay began, "I can balance a shot glass on my head." But he had never had a drink. The shot glass balancing act was part of traditional Greek dancing, an art form he taught to little kids at his Greek church. I can only imagine what a welcome relief it must have been for admissions officers to read an essay about an activity they hadn't already read about from countless other applicants. Harry went on to Yale and then to Georgetown Law School.

KEEP IT FRESH

A lot of students write essays about something mentioned elsewhere in their application just to make sure the admissions office notices it. Unless that essay shares something new, it's like telling a stale story you've already told.

College essays should share new information the admissions office wouldn't know from just reading your application. Colleges know that editors of school newspapers have to work well with people. They know helping the less fortunate feels good, football is hard and England is different from the United States. Sharing stories the colleges already know just wastes an opportunity to help them get to know you better.

The best ways to make sure your essays don't repeat information:

- Pick a topic that has not been mentioned anywhere on your application, or

- Share new information about something you already listed.

One Collegewise student, Raquel, wrote an essay sharing that her festive family loved celebrating together so much, they were the only Mexican family she'd ever known who threw an annual St. Patrick's Day party, one to which her grandmother always arrived with her Chihuahua, "Chiquita," in tow.

Colleges didn't need Raquel to explain the concept that family is important. But the great lengths to which her extended family would go just to spend time together was brand new information colleges never would have known.

Another Collegewise student, Kenny, was a proud Boy Scout. He wrote an essay about the fact that his friends had nicknamed him "Dr. Kenny" because he carried a first-aid kit with him everywhere he went.

The colleges already knew Kenny was a Boy Scout because he'd listed it on the application. They didn't need him to explain what Boy Scouts do. But the story about Kenny carrying the first-aid kid everywhere he went (and the surprising number of times it had come in handy), was new information.

Repeating a story in an essay is like serving leftovers at a dinner party. Keep it fresh and give your reader something new to chew on.

AVOID CLICHÉS

One of our counselors referred to his last year working in admissions at Caltech as the year of the blood drive essay. That year, an unusually high number of applicants told the same tale of how one on-campus blood drive changed their lives and made them appreciate the importance of serving humanity.

Writing such grandiose statements into your essays won't help you stand out. The statements sound cliché. So here are the five most overused clichés I—and every admissions officer I've spoken with—see most often, and which you should avoid.

1. **The aforementioned "blood drive essay" or "How community service taught me the importance of helping others"**

Colleges appreciate students who are concerned about their communities. But one blood drive does not a humanitarian make. A claim to have learned how important it is to help people needs to be substantiated with evidence of a sincere, long-term commitment to helping people. Otherwise, your message loses some oomph.

If you had an experience during your community service that really meant a lot to you, say so. And be honest. Otherwise, consider doing a good deed for admissions officers and avoid the community service cliché.

2. **"Hard work always pays off," and other life lessons learned while playing sports**

The problem with many sports essays is they explain what life is like for every athlete. You go to practice. You work hard. You compete.

Then the student makes it worse by saying sports taught him the importance of hard work and commitment, which is almost certainly not something he would say to his friends.

Be original. Tell *your* sports story that nobody else can tell. If you can't find a story you own, just write about something else. The sport will still be listed on your application.

3. **"How my trip to another country broadened my horizons"**

This essay essentially says, "France is very difference from the United States—the food, the language, the customs. But I learned to appreciate the differences and to adapt to the ways of the French."

Visiting a country and noticing that it is different is not a story that you own. The admissions office doesn't want to read your travel journals. Instead, make yourself, not the country, the focus of the essay.

One of my students who had never previously ventured onto any sort of dance floor wrote that his trip to Spain was the first time he'd ever danced in front of other people. That wasn't an essay about how Spain was different—it was an essay about how *he* was different in Spain.

4.   "How I overcame a life challenge [that wasn't really all that challenging]"

Essays can help admissions officers understand more about a student who has overcome legitimate hardship. But far too many other students misguidedly manufacture hardship in a college essay to try to gain sympathy or make excuses (e.g., for low grades). That won't work.

If you've had a difficult hardship and you want to talk about it, you should. Otherwise, it's probably better to choose a different topic. Note: The pet eulogy falls into this category. Lovely if you want to write one. Just don't include it as part of your college essay.

5.   Anything that doesn't really sound like you

Your essays are supposed to give the readers a sense of your personality. So give your essays a sincerity test. Do they sound like you, or do they sound like you're trying to impress someone?

Don't use words you looked up in the thesaurus. There really is no place for "plethora" in a college essay. Don't quote Shakespeare or Plato or the Dali Lama unless that is really you. If your best friend reads it and says it sounds just like you, that's probably a good sign.

COMMITTEE NOTES

No McEssays

Ninety percent of the applications I read contain what I call McEssays— usually five-paragraph essays that consist primarily of abstractions and unsupported generalization. They are technically correct in that they are organized and have the correct sentence structure and spelling, but they are boring. Sort of like a Big Mac... If an essay starts out: "I have been a member of the band and it has taught me leadership, perseverance and hard work," I can almost recite the rest of the essay without reading it. Each of the three middle paragraphs gives a bit of support to an abstraction, and the final paragraph restates what has already been said. A McEssay is not wrong, but it is not going to be a positive factor in the admission decision. It will not allow a student to stand out.[11]

Parke Muth
Associate Dean of Admissions
University of Virginia

SOUND LIKE A TEENAGER

When writing college essays, some students mysteriously transform themselves into aging philosophers. They mention how they were enchanted by lush scenery during their travels, how they experienced a profound epiphany during a volunteer shift at the homeless shelter, or the moment on the soccer field when a teammate was injured and they realized that soccer was, after all, just a game.

None of those stories sound like the teenagers who wrote them.

College essays aren't formal, academic pieces of writing like those you write in your English classes. College essays should sound like you, so the reader can figuratively hear your voice and get a sense for your personality. The admissions officers are trying to get to know you, and they don't expect you to think or sound like anything but a teenager. As the Brandeis University dean of admissions told *The Boston Globe*, "We expect people to write like 17- and 18-year-olds."[12]

I'm not suggesting you should write your essays the same way you would text message a friend. I'm saying: relay the world the way you really see it. Colleges will find you much more charming if you're honest than they will if you try to be something you're not.

Here's a good way to strike the right tone without being too informal.

1. **For everything you write in your college essays, ask yourself, "Would I say this to someone else?"**

No athlete in the history of high school sports has ever said the words, "I personally feel very fortunate to have participated in varsity athletics because it has taught me the value of committing to my goals."

If you wouldn't say it to someone else, don't say it in your college essays. That will keep you from being too formal.

2. **Pretend you're telling your story to your favorite teacher.**

If you'd tell a story one way to your high school principal and another way to your best friend, your favorite teacher is probably the happy middle ground. Go to that middle ground when you're writing your college essays.

> Too formal:
>
> "I found chemistry to be a particularly challenging subject, as my natural academic strengths lie with writing."
>
> Too informal:
>
> "Chemistry blows. I'd pretty much rather do anything else than do even one problem set in chemistry."

Just right:

"Chemistry and I just don't get along. I don't know what it is about my brain, but it works a lot better when I'm reading Shakespeare than it does when I'm trying to memorize the periodic table."

ADMIT YOU'RE NOT PERFECT

Have you ever known someone who could admit when he wasn't good at something? Someone who laughed at herself easily? Or a person self-confident enough to own when he made a mistake? It's hard not to like those people. Since your college essay is all about helping the admissions officers like you, it doesn't hurt to occasionally poke a little fun at yourself.

Sometimes colleges ask essay questions about failures you've experienced or mistakes that you've made. Don't be afraid to answer those questions honestly. And never try to spin a positive as a negative, like, "Sometimes I can be too focused on my academics and can neglect time with my friends at the beach." That sounds like you're afraid to admit a real fault.

No successful person has been great at everything she's attempted. Admit you struggle in physics, you make the world's worst chocolate chip cookies, or no matter how hard you try, you can't paint a single image your classmates could identify. These things don't make you sound inferior—they make you sound human.

I'm not suggesting you should write an entire essay about your failures or shortcomings. I'm saying don't shy away from including those things when they're part of a topic you care about.

A kid who writes about working at a summer camp should absolutely share all the reasons he loved his job. But when he also mentions that the first night it was his turn to cook dinner, he undercooked all the hotdogs and none of the 40 campers would eat them, it makes him that much more likeable.

Admitting the occasional fault makes it easier to believe you when you claim to be really good at something. As long as you aren't admitting something that suggests you're a danger to yourself or others, doing so will probably help you get into college.

COMMITTEE NOTES

Admit a fault

I may be guilty of exaggerating, but the student I remember [most] quickly admitting a few years back was a young man who told us straight-out that after four years he was still the 'worst soccer player on the worst soccer team in the state.' Another who I remember saying to myself was someone who, when asked if there was anything else we should know, wrote, "As you will have noticed, my SAT scores are low. They are accurate." [13]

Fred Hargadon
Former Dean of Admissions
Princeton University

SEEK FEEDBACK OUTSIDE THE FAMILY CIRCLE

A student once asked me to review an essay in which he'd written that he struggled with "standardized testes." I swear I am not making that up. Spell check doesn't catch everything, so it's a good idea to have a fellow human review your essay, too.

The best reviews are people you trust, and who actually know what they're doing. They should meet both criteria, not just one. For most students, your counselor and English teacher usually can. Friends, parents and friends of your parents usually can't.

Some parents are offended when I suggest they shouldn't serve as their student's college essay advisors. They swear things are different in their families. Trust me, they're not. Your parents love you too much and are way too close to the subject matter to be impartial observers.

If your parents push you on this, show them the following excerpt from the American Medical Association's "Code of Medical Ethics," which advises against doctors treating their own children for similar reasons.

> Professional objectivity may be compromised when an immediate family member or the physician is the patient; the physician's personal feelings may unduly influence his or her professional medical judgment, thereby interfering with the care being delivered...If tensions develop in a physician's professional relationship with a family member, perhaps as a result of a negative medical outcome, such difficulties may be carried over into the family member's personal relationship with the physician.[14]

If a trained doctor should avoid diagnosing her daughter's flu-like symptoms, why should an untrained (or even trained) parent try to help her daughter with a college essay?

Take a proverbial page from the AMA and me here. Parents can and should be included in the college process with their kids. But the essays are one of those places where parents should step out and let someone else help.

Too much advice can hurt

Also, beware of seeking advice from too many people. When you shop around your essays for feedback, they end up sounding like they were written by a committee. When too many people give you too much advice, it just confuses you and leaves you unsure about what to write. "Don't let more than three people critique your essay. If you do, you'll get conflicting messages and your voice will be lost forever," advises Bryan Nance, former director of minority recruitment at MIT.[15]

Again, your English teacher and/or your counselor should be able to provide enough feedback. Everybody else—parents, uncles and siblings—can support you in other ways.

REWRITE BEFORE YOU REUSE

Great stories for college essays tend to be recyclable. If your topic is something that really was important to you, you can apply that significance to a lot of college essay prompts.

But there's a difference between repurposing a story and reusing the exact same essay. I once worked with a student who wrote an essay about how she had lost every high school election she'd ever run in. She wrote that each time she lost, she shrugged off the defeat and found another activity where she could be successful. It was a funny, self-deprecating peek into her personality, and it helped admissions officers get to know her better.

My student used the experience as the basis for great responses to several colleges' essay prompts:

> "Describe a time when you failed or made a mistake. What did you learn from the experience?"

> "What is a talent, skill, activity, accomplishment or personal quality that makes you proud?"

> "How do you hope to contribute to our campus community?"
> "Describe a time when you faced a challenge or adversity."

Each time she used the story, many of the details were the same, but she tailored the essay to answer the prompt. Those tailored versions addressed what each prompt asked for, and they were really well done—honest, engaging and focused.

When her real answer to a prompt had nothing to do with losing elections, she wrote different essays. But her "I am a good loser" theme worked for the essay prompts from more than half her colleges.

There's nothing wrong with recycling a story—especially if it does a great job answering the prompt. Just make sure you tailor it. Rewrite before you reuse.

BAD ESSAY ADVICE

Do a search on "college essay advice" and some of the results are just plain bad. Here's a sampling of some of the worst advice I've heard.

"Use a hook to grab their attention."

A "hook" is usually a writer's attempt to inject drama, shock or suspense into the opening of their essay. All too often, it just comes off as trying too hard. "As I crouched into my starter's block, eyes fixed on the icy pool below me, I could feel the tense eyes of the crowd bearing down upon me in my Speedo..."

What swimmer actually thinks like that before a race? Good stories that are well written don't need hooks. Just say it. You're not fishing here.

"Start your essay with a famous quote."

Terrible advice. Admissions officers want to hear from you, not Socrates, Mother Teresa or John F. Kennedy. The exception to the quote rule is if you're quoting a person from your own life who is central to the story (and probably not famous), like, "My baseball coach always says, 'We're going to play smart baseball, gentlemen, because dumb baseball is no fun to play and even worse to watch.'"

That's personal and it makes the story more interesting.

"Avoid controversial topics."

What's controversial to one person may not be controversial to another. If a student spent two semesters volunteering for an organization committed to protecting women's reproductive rights, I don't think that story should be discarded just because some people might not agree with her politics.

Don't write anything just for the sake of shocking your reader. Don't shy away from a topic that's important to you, either. If you're not sure whether a topic is appropriate, ask your high school counselor for a second opinion.

"Use your essay to highlight your interest in the school."

Showing interest in a school is good. But what if the prompt is, "Describe a time you failed or made a mistake"? How are you going to tie that to your interest in Gettysburg College?

If a college wants to know about your interest, they'll ask. If a topic you choose actually does have something to do with the reason you're applying, feel free to discuss it. But don't wedge it into your essay unnecessarily.

5. "Use your essay to explain a weakness."

Charming self-deprecation is good. But using your essay to make excuses for a low grade or another shortcoming usually just shines a light on the very thing you're trying deemphasize. It's like taking your shoes off at the beginning of a first date and saying, "Before this goes any further, I need to explain why my toenails are so grotesque." Some situations really do merit explanation, but most don't.

PART V: HOW TO GET STRONGER LETTERS OF RECOMMENDATION

SEND ONLY WHAT THEY ASK YOU TO SEND

Many private colleges will ask you to submit letters of recommendation from teachers, counselors or people who know you personally. In most cases, you don't send these yourself; the writers send them directly to the school either by mail or electronically.

Colleges' applications will state very clearly how many letters they want (if they want any at all), and from whom they want them. A lot of the students I've worked with want to ignore the instructions and send more letters than are requested. They include a letter from their dad's business partner who's an alumnus, even though the application clearly asks for letters from two teachers. Don't decide you're a special case who should ignore the instructions.

Martha C. Merrill, dean of admissions and financial aid at Connecticut College, offered another reason to submit exactly what's requested: "Admission officers will likely read only the required number of recommendations. If you submit too many, you leave it to chance which ones will be read."[16]

Personal beats famous

Some colleges also give you the opportunity to include a personal recommendation from a boss, coach, pastor or someone else who knows you well. In those cases, the content of the letter is far more important than whether or not the person is famous or powerful. Asking the published author your mother treats at her medical practice to write a letter for you will not help your chances of admission if that author barely knows you.

I attended a conference where an admissions officer from University of Pennsylvania shared that he had read an application from a student that included a letter of recommendation from President Clinton. The admissions officer put the letter on his bulletin board so he could have something with the official presidential seal, but the student still wasn't admitted.

Pay attention to each college's directions and send only what they ask you to send.

CHOOSE THE RIGHT TEACHERS

Colleges have your transcript and your application, so they don't need a teacher to tell them what grade you earned in the class. They want the story behind the grades. Did you participate in class? Did you ask intelligent questions? Did you do reading outside of your English class, build a functioning greenhouse in biology or do an oral report in US history dressed up like George Washington?

To make sure you pick the right teachers to ask for letters of recommendation, consider the following questions:

1. What teachers have seen your very best work?

Don't just think about the grade you earned. In fact, your best work might have come in a class where you didn't necessarily earn an A, especially if it was particularly challenging and you still brought your best effort. Think about the projects you did, the questions you asked and the way you involved yourself in the class.

2. In which classes did you participate the most?

Where did you ask questions, contribute to class discussions or talk with the teacher outside of class about the subject matter?

3. In what classes did you find the material the most interesting?

Did the teacher know how interested you were? How? Did you talk with her after class, do additional reading or take on extra projects?

4. Which solid classes from your junior year fit the above criteria?

Unless a college requests something different, teacher letters of recommendation should come from solid subjects (e.g., math, English, science, social science or foreign language) that you took during your junior year. Why the junior year? It's the most recent full academic year from which to draw—the freshman and sophomore years are closer to ancient academic history.

COMMITTEE NOTES

It's not all about the grade

Teachers who gave you an A do not necessarily write better recs than those who gave you a lower grade. Students mature academically at different rates, and many colleges (including ours) are looking for students who are passionate about learning a tough subject, not necessarily those who are merely naturally talented.[17]

Evan Cudworth
Senior Assistant Director of Admissions
University of Chicago

ASK THE RIGHT WAY

Some high schools have established systems for requesting letters of recommendation. They may establish deadlines or ask you to fill out a questionnaire to make the teacher or counselor's job easier. First, check with your counseling office and make sure you're following their instructions. Once you know the protocol, there's a right way—and a wrong way—to approach your teachers.

Many students make the mistake of stumbling up to a teacher at the end of class, dumping paperwork on his desk and asking if the teacher can write a letter of recommendation for an application that's due in two weeks. Not good.

Here's what I recommend:

- Ask early, preferably as early as possible in your senior year (once you have the necessary materials).

- Ask the teacher if you can make an appointment to talk about your college applications.

- When you ask, give the teacher some indication of why you are asking. For example,

  "Mr. Trumbull, I'm applying to several small private colleges, and they recommend I find teachers who can comment on my participation and performance in their classes. I was wondering if you thought it would be appropriate for you to write me a strong letter of recommendation."

This is not only polite, but it also gently tells the teacher what you want him to say. It also gives the teacher an easy out. If he doesn't think he can write strongly about the characteristics you've described, he can say so, and you can move on to another teacher. Yes, it will sting a little bit, but it's better that you know and get the chance to ask someone else.

WAIVE YOUR RIGHT

Each letter of recommendation form includes a portion you fill out before you give it to your teacher. It asks if you agree to waive your right to access the letter in the future.

If you waive your right, it means once the writer sends the letter to the school, you have no right to view it. You will never know what the writer said about you or whether it helped or hurt your chances of admission.

You should always waive your right.

Declining to waive your right essentially tells the writer that you don't trust him or her to do a good job, which is never a good strategy. Also, the college will wonder why you didn't feel comfortable enough to waive the right. It makes you look like you're hiding something.

If you feel uneasy about waiving your rights, consider asking someone else to write the letter, someone who's more unwaveringly positive about you.

If you're still uneasy, try to relax. Teachers and counselors are out to help, not hurt, students. Just about all of them will do their best to say something positive about a nice kid.

Once your teachers agree to write letters, make their jobs as easy as possible.

- Fill out the required student information at the top of each recommendation form.

- For each college, provide the teacher with an addressed, stamped envelope (use the admissions office's address as the return address).

- If the forms need to be submitted electronically, email the link to your teacher, or print it on a separate piece of paper.

- When you've got everything together, put the materials in one large envelope or folder for each school and give them your teacher.

PART VI: WHAT TO DO AFTER YOU SUBMIT

RESIST LETTING FEAR HIJACK YOUR APPLICATIONS

Your mind does terrible things to you before you make a big, irrevocable decision. Maybe that's why so many people are nervous on their wedding days? Before you hit "Submit," you'll second guess your essays. You'll wish your SAT scores were higher. You'll be embarrassed that you got a B in French or don't have more community service hours or only played varsity softball for one year. Don't worry. This is completely normal and almost always irrational.

The finality of submitting an application can be scary. You might have to deal with rejection. Or you might have to face the reality of leaving home and going someplace new. Taking any big step always comes with some nerves. That's normal. Once you expect it to happen, it's a lot less uncomfortable when it actually arrives.

On the other extreme, I've seen students let this fear hijack their college applications. They leave our offices with their applications reviewed and ready to submit, then return three or four weeks later and reveal that they haven't sent them. Waiting longer to take the last step doesn't seem to make these students any surer of themselves. They never edit and revise their way to a sense of comfort. The applications usually just get older, not better, during the delay.

The best way to diffuse this fear is to expect it. I'm not trying to get all Dr. Phil on you, but you'll see what I mean once you're about to submit your applications. When I tell a student it's going to happen, they're much less affected when it does.

Give applications the time and attention they deserve. Then acknowledge that you've done your best and hit "Submit." The nerves will go away within a few days (maybe even in a few hours).

BANG A GONG

Applying to college is a major milestone, and submitting your final application should be a celebration-worthy event. So take a page out of our Collegewise book (not this one—the figurative Collegewise book) and bang your own gong.

As Collegewise seniors submit their final college applications, they bang a two-foot gong right in the middle of our office. The gong sits on a custom-made metal stand with its accompanying mallet beneath a four-foot high "Rules of the Gong" poster, which specifies that it may only be banged by seniors who have submitted all of their applications.

In 2010 when we bought the gong, we were looking for a memorable way to let seniors celebrate their application completion. We suspected our students might think it was lame.

They actually love it.

We have yet to have one senior be too cool to bang the gong. As our former student, Silvie R., now at the University of Washington, said, "I was so proud of myself when I got to bang the gong in the Collegewise office when all of my applications were finished."

We love seeing the grins and looks of accomplishment on their faces. We all applaud and offer our congratulations. And their parents—who smartly step back and turn this process over to their students and Collegewise counselors—snap photos to capture their kids' gonging celebrations. A few moms have even joined their kids for their own photos in front of the gong. Kids have uploaded their gonging pictures to their Facebook pages.

Big, loud

For us, the gong is a big, loud acknowledgement of a job well done and a teenager taking one step closer to starting college. Most of them haven't yet received any admissions news, but that's no reason not to celebrate this important step. It reminds our students and parents that no matter which colleges say "Yes," they still have reason to be proud.

Don't delay your celebration for when decisions arrive. Bang your own gong. Celebrate the completion of your college applications in your own way. Do something else fun you've been too busy with applications to do. You don't need a college acceptance to do a little celebrating.

MAKE FOLLOW-UP CALLS

When you submit a college application online, you usually get an online confirmation that it's been received. That doesn't necessarily mean the admissions committee has everything they need to consider your application complete. That's why it's a good idea to follow up with a phone call to each college a few weeks after you've submitted everything just to make sure they have what they need (and it's yet another reason to start the process early).

You aren't the only one contributing pieces of your college application. Testing agencies send test scores. Counselors send transcripts. Teachers send letters of recommendation. Colleges are absolutely inundated with materials at this time of year. It's easy for something to get lost in the shuffle.

Just call the admissions office (don't let your parents do this for you), tell them your name and that you recently submitted an application for admission, and ask if you can confirm that your application is complete. It's not rude to do this, and if they tell you they're missing something, don't panic. Just tell them you'll take care of it right away, and don't forget to thank them for their time. Remember: colleges are insanely busy during application season.

One follow-up phone call to each college can put your mind at ease and let you get on with your senior year.

GIVE THANKS

Nobody gets into college alone. There are always supportive people in your corner who help you get there. So as you submit the last of your applications, take some time to thank the people who helped you.

Your high school counselor

Even if you never actually met to discuss your applications, counselors do a lot of work for you behind-the-scenes that you might not be aware of. They write school profiles that colleges request. They write letters of recommendation. They send transcripts and field phone calls and set up visits from college representatives.

Anyone who wrote your letters of recommendation

These people did you a favor and deserve to be thanked. It's also not unusual for a college to contact your counselor or one of your recommendation writers if they have a question about something that was unclear on your application. If that were to happen, what impression have you left? You wouldn't want your teacher to think, "He's the kid who asked me to write his letter 10 days before the deadline, gave me no supporting materials and never bothered to say thank you."

Write a note

One way to make your thanks especially meaningful is to write a note that shows you recognize they did a favor for you and that you sincerely appreciate the effort made on your behalf. Write it on stationery (not over email). Use proper grammar and punctuation. (Seriously, use proper grammar and punctuation.)

There's no formula for what to say. The key is to just be sincere and take the time to give a proper thanks. It makes a difference.

> Dear Mr. Gerard:
>
> Now that the college admissions process is officially over, I wanted to thank you again for taking the time to write my letters of recommendation. I can only imagine how many letters you must have written for students this fall. I know that most of my friends planned on asking you to write their letters, too. I really do appreciate the time and effort that you took for me.
>
> I also wanted to tell you that I got accepted early decision to Hamilton College and I'm planning to major in history. I'm not sure I ever would have considered studying history in college if I hadn't taken your class, but after I did that oral report on the Hamilton-Burr duel in front of the entire class without passing out, I'm sure I'm ready for whatever college history throws my way.
>
> You're a good teacher, Mr. Gerard, and I always looked forward to going to your class every day. My younger sister, Jenna, is a freshman this year, and I've told her to do whatever it takes to get into your class. She's a much better public speaker than I am, by the way, so she won't be prone to fainting when it's time to do oral reports.
>
> I'm so excited to go to college, and I'm sure I would not have had as many options as I did

were it not for your help. Thank you again for everything you've done for me, and have a wonderful summer.

All my best,
Rebecca C.
Hamilton College Class of 2016

That's a student who took the time to give some sincere thanks.

While you're at it, don't forget to thank your parents. From providing moral support to paying for the SAT tutor, they likely deserve a healthy dose of your gratitude, too.

Anyone who provided emotional support, offered monetary support or just generally took an interest in your college quest and your happiness deserves to be thanked. It's so easy to say thank you, and you'd be surprised how often it comes back to you.

RESIST THE WORRIES

You're done. You've submitted your applications, celebrated, followed up and thanked people. Now you have to wait to hear from colleges. So, exactly how much time should you spend worrying about it?

None, if you can swing it.

First of all, if you had your counselor approve your list, you're going to get in somewhere. If you did a thoughtful college search and found the right schools, that somewhere is bound to make you happy.

Worrying about whether or not your dream college is going to say "Yes" doesn't do you any good. It won't do a single thing to influence the result. I suggest you resist the urge.

In my experience, the happiest students accept that what happens from here is out of their hands. They'll spend their time dreaming about how great college is going to be, how much they're going to learn and how much fun they're going to have no matter where they go.

They also keep in perspective that nobody's life is made or broken by an admissions decision from a particular college. If a school you love denies you, you're still going to college. You're still going make new friends and have four years of fun and learning no matter where you go. You have so much to look forward to; it just doesn't make sense to worry.

COMMITTEE NOTES

Stay focused after submitting

You have work to get through in the next few months and it's going to prepare you for the next step, which isn't going to be any easier. Besides that, worrying about an application that is already submitted isn't going to affect the outcome and it's apt to take you away from those pressing academic tasks.[18]

University of Virginia
Office of Undergraduate Admissions blog

KEEP UP THE GOOD WORK

"Keep your grades up" often sounds like one of those empty platitudes adults say to seniors who've applied to college. In fact, doing so really can make a difference where you get in.

Most private colleges, as well as public schools like the University of Michigan, will ask you to send a seventh semester transcript (also called a "Mid-Year Report") once you complete the first semester of your senior year. Those grades will be reviewed before the school makes a decision.

Also, if you get wait-listed by a college, they might ask to see your second semester grades from senior year. Since students often aren't taken off wait-lists until after they graduate from high school, those colleges have the opportunity to look at your entire senior year's academic work before they make a decision.

Students who are taking Advanced Placement or International Baccalaureate courses, who keep up the good work and score well on their associated exams, can also end up with college credit. That can let you skip certain introductory classes your freshman year and maybe even graduate from college early.

Finally, every college will ask you to send a complete transcript once you're admitted. They'll look at both semesters of your senior year to make sure that you finished the classes you told them you were taking and that you kept doing as well as you'd done in the previous years. If you haven't kept up the good work, they can rescind your offer of admission.

Senior party

I've seen students who let the senior party start too early, even straight-A students who ended up getting a couple C's or a D in their senior year, who lost their admission to their chosen colleges. If it's not quite such a steep drop, you might still end up starting your freshman year of college on academic probation, which is not a fun place to be.

So really, keep your grades up. If you've followed the advice in this book about managing your course load, you shouldn't be unreasonably burned out and sleepless. Finish strong and you'll never have to wonder if a little more effort in your last two semesters of high school could have made an admissions difference.

Keep up the good work

Students who have a slight decline get a letter noting our disappointment that their grades are different from the grades on which they were admitted. For students who've had a larger decline, we ask them to write back with their comments and explanation. For the more serious, we tell them we're going to review the case and decide if we are still offering admission, and in the most serious, we sometimes revoke the offer.[19]

Scott Meiklejohn
Dean of Admissions
Bowdoin College

UPDATE SPARINGLY

1. You find a major mistake on your application.

Errors are never good, but no college admissions officer is going to reject you because of one misplaced comma or a misspelled word.

But if in your mad rush to meet the deadlines you missed several typos...or you mistakenly told Duke how much you'd love to attend NYU...or you have a string of sentences cobbled together from other essays that you mistakenly pasted in the wrong order and now make absolutely no sense...it's worth doing something about it.

If you're in that situation, mail a hard copy of your corrected application or essay to the admissions office(s) with a cover letter asking them to replace the current version with the enclosed copy. Sign the letter with your full name and Social Security number. Be brief (no long explanation necessary) and courteous. If they haven't read, evaluated and decided on your file yet, they'll usually replace the materials.

The course of action I'm describing above is appropriate to correct potentially embarrassing mistakes, not to submit what you think are new-and-improved versions of your application materials. Parents, especially: please take note.

2. You drop a class or make another change to the "Current Year Courses" you listed on your application.

3. You have a new, significant award, honor or accomplishment.

I define "significant" as something that was important enough that you shared it with other people. If you're a volleyball player and win team MVP as well as first-team all-league honors at the late fall banquet, that's something you'll tell your family about.

If you got an A on a vocab quiz in English, you won't.

If something has happened that you're proud of, something that was a big enough deal to share with other people, send the college a short letter asking them to update your file.

RESEND MISSING INFORMATION

You may receive a notice in the mail that your application to a particular college is incomplete due to a missing item like test scores or a letter of recommendation. If this happens, don't panic. You didn't necessarily do anything wrong. Remember, admissions offices receive thousands of pieces of mail during application season and each one needs to be individually sorted and filed. The occasional missing item is a normal part of the process even for kids who did everything right. That's why colleges build in time to alert those students to resend the missing information.

If you receive a notice of missing information:

1. Double check to make sure the material has been sent.

If they're missing a teacher recommendation or a transcript, check with your teacher or counselor to make sure that information has been mailed. If they're missing test scores, verify that College Board or ACT has sent them.

2. Respond to the college.

Once you've verified that the material has been, or is being sent, inform the college. Look to see if there is a contact name or email address on the notification. If not, just call the admissions office. Thank them for alerting you to the missing part of your file, and let them know what actions you've taken to correct it.

I worked with a student once who responded to such an inquiry with an email that simply said, "Thanks so much for letting me know you hadn't received my letter of recommendation. I visited my English teacher and she promised she would mail it this week. Please let me know if there's anything else you need, and I'm looking forward to hearing from you."

Nothing special. But after he was admitted, the admissions officer called this kid's mother and revealed that more than 700 letters had been sent out to applicants whose files were incomplete, and this student was the only one who replied in this fashion.

Every little bit helps.

COLLEGE INTERVIEWS: WHAT TO EXPECT WHEN YOU'RE FACE-TO-FACE

Long gone are the days when a college interview involved a meeting with an admissions officer who stared down at you from behind his desk as he smoked a pipe and asked why you feel you are worthy of attending said institution. These days, college interviews are generally very relaxed, laid-back experiences. [1]

Swarthmore College
Office of Admissions blog

RELAX AND BE YOURSELF

Many students I meet have a lot more anxiety about the college interview than it really deserves.

The National Association for College Admissions Counseling annual survey of colleges revealed the majority of colleges who offer interviews view them as, "...supplemental to the main academic factors, and as such, rated them with low to moderate importance."[2]

Dave Marcus, author of *Acceptance* and an alumni interviewer for Brown University, wrote in the *New York Times*, "My questions rarely matter. Applicants don't seem to realize that relatively brief alumni interviews hardly ever make or break a candidate's case."[3]

I've also met students who hoped a good showing at their interview might make up for shortcomings in their application like grades or test scores that were below those of typical admitted applicants. But even the most glowing review from an interviewer isn't likely to make an admissions committee overlook a lack of qualifications.

When an interview does sway an admissions committee, it's usually in the case of a student who is very close to being admitted, and a glowing report from an interviewer tips the scales.

John Birney, senior associate director of admissions at Johns Hopkins, told *Forbes*, "They (interviews) are not a significant factor in the vast majority of cases. But for a kid who is on the bubble, where the decision could go either way, a fantastic interview with an alumnus could make the difference."[4]

What's the point?

So, if the interviews aren't really that important in most cases, why do colleges offer them?

Interviews are colleges' way of making a largely impersonal process a tad more personal. They let the applicant have a real conversation with someone from the school, and in the case of alumni interviews, give graduates a chance to stay in involved with their alma maters. In terms of their influence on the actual admissions decision, college interviews alone will not make or break your case. You're not going to erase the previous three years of hard work with one bad answer in an interview.

I tell my Collegewise students that a few nerves before an interview are normal and maybe even a good sign that you're looking forward to the interaction. But unless you say something outrageously offensive or act like you'd rather be someplace else, you're not going to destroy your chances of getting into college.

I'm not suggesting you call your interviewer "Dude." There's a difference between relaxed and disrespectful. But if you can be yourself and have a good conversation, that will be enough to impress your interviewer. The rest of this chapter will show you how to do that.

KNOW WHAT'S PREFERRED

While they're intended to make the application process more personal, college interviews can sometimes just make it more confusing.

Not all colleges offer interviews. Those that do may or may not actually use them for admissions purposes.

Some require that you schedule the interview. Others will contact you after you apply.

Some will take it as a lack of interest if you choose not to interview. Others sincerely don't care whether or not you decide to sit down face-to-face.

I understand why so many students are confused about the role interviews play and how to prepare for them. The only way to know your colleges' interview offerings and preferences is to visit their websites and get the answers to the following four questions:

1. Does the college offer interviews?

Most colleges that offer interviews are small, more selective private schools. A large state school like the University of Michigan gets more than 35,000 applications for freshman admission, and it wouldn't be logistically possible to interview them.

2. Are interviews used for admissions purposes?

"Informative interviews," as colleges call them, aren't used at all to evaluate you. They're an opportunity for you to learn more about the school from an admissions officer or a current student. It's a marketing tool for the school. These interviews usually take place on campus and can be a great way to learn more about a school you're really interested in without the added pressure of admissions judgment. As Carleton College's website advises for students scheduling interviews: " Interviews are informational, not evaluative. We're not making black marks against you on a checklist. The goal is just to get better acquainted."[5]

If you'd be excited to learn more about the school from someone who can really answer your questions, great. But don't schedule an informative interview just because you think you should.

One of our Collegewise counselors, Arun, conducted informative interviews as an assistant director of admissions at the University of Chicago and painfully recalls the awkward silences when a student knew seemingly nothing about the school and had no questions. In one of his better experiences, the student looked past him and said, "Hey, what books are those on your shelf?" They spent the next 30 minutes talking about their favorite authors.

"Evaluative interviews," on the other hand, mean that what you say can and will be used to judge you in the court of admissions. Colleges may offer them on campus with admissions officers or current students, locally with volunteer alumni who live near the applicants, or both.

Most colleges' websites will tell you whether their interviews are informative or evaluative. For example, Yale's website clearly states: "All Yale interviews, both those with alumni and those with current Yale seniors, are evaluative. We read interview reports along with all your other application materials."[6]

Claremont McKenna College's site says: "Interviews at CMC are informational in nature, not evaluative. You should expect to get answers to any questions you may have about CMC or the admission process."[7]

3. Does the college recommend that you interview?

Colleges express varying levels of desire to have prospective students interview. Some take a decision not to interview as a sign you're not that interested in the school. Others have no preference. Once again, most will make their feelings clear on their websites. Five examples:

Pomona College

"Southern California applicants are expected to interview and must do so on campus."

Wake Forest University

"Interviews are strongly recommended for first-year applicants."

Oberlin College

"Interviews are not required for admission, except in the case of homeschooled students and students graduating from high school in less than four years. We do recommend interviews for all applicants visiting campus."

Reed College

"Interviews are not required for application to Reed, and you will not be at a disadvantage in the admission process if you do not schedule one."

University of Pennsylvania

"Not having an interview will not be held against you. Since interviews are not required nor are they offered to all applicants at this time, we encourage you to rely upon your application for admission as a forum for presenting the many unique aspects of your candidacy."

Again: visit the colleges' websites to get the interview scoop. A college guidebook might tell you an interview is "not required for admission," but you can see from this limited sampling it's not always that cut-and-dried.

4. How are interviews scheduled?

On-campus interviews usually need to be scheduled ahead of time. The schools' websites will tell you when interviews are offered and how to schedule one.

The opportunity to interview with local alumni usually depends on whether a volunteer interviewer lives in your area. Most alumni interviews take place at a mutually convenient location, like a coffee shop or at the interviewer's workplace. Some colleges require that students request these interviews. Many other schools simply tell students once they submit their application, they'll be contacted by an interviewer if one lives in their area.

Bottom line: Before you buy a plane ticket or get your nice clothes pressed, find out the answers to these questions. And rely only on the colleges' own websites to get them.

MAKE CONVERSATION

Students who get nervous before their college interviews are usually worried that, like a job interview, their most important objective is to give the right answers. Instead of relaxing and having an interesting conversation with their interviewer, they sit there passively waiting to be asked questions, then trying to give what they hope are the right answers—all the while appearing like they're on the verge of cardiac arrest.

This is not a job interview. Your college interviewers don't have prepared questions in hand, and they aren't looking for you to give the right answers. The interviewer's goal is to get to know you and see if you can have a good conversation with an adult.

John Detore, an alumni interviewer for MIT, offered this interview advice on the school's admissions blog: "I've talked to lots of candidates and the ones who are just themselves, who can laugh at their mistakes and struggles, who seem comfortable in their own skin—inevitably show a bit more maturity, and inevitably make the best impression. Just my two cents."[8]

There's something likeable about a teenager who's confident and mature enough to sit comfortably with an adult and chat about a variety of topics. They smile easily, tell good stories and ask good questions. And most importantly, they're not afraid to admit what they aren't good at or what they don't know. That's why it's so important to understand that this is much more a conversation than it is a test to see if you can give the right answers.

If you can be that mature and comfortable with your college interviewer, it's a sign that you'll be able to do the same thing when meeting with your professors and your academic advisor in college. Your answers aren't being scored by a panel of judges. The best thing an interviewer could say about you is that you're an interesting student that he or she enjoyed meeting and talking with.

Goes both ways

Remember: good conversation goes both ways. Have you ever been on a first date with someone who was a terrible conversationalist and made you do all the talking? It's just about the most agonizing thing in the world. You sit there trying desperately to think of things to say so you can avoid the excruciating silence that you know is going to come unless you keep talking. After about 20 minutes of trying, you want to pull an imaginary ejection handle and catapult yourself out of there.

If you sit in your college interview waiting to be asked questions and then give short answers without any details, it's like putting the interviewer through a terrible first date. That leads to exchanges like this:
Interviewer: "Can you tell me about playing violin in the orchestra?"

"Yes. I am a first chair violinist in my school orchestra and I take lessons five hours every week."

A brief answer like that puts all the effort of conversation on your interviewer. What if this student had thought ahead of time what he might like to say about orchestra and given a more thoughtful response, like:

"Sure. My mom played the violin growing up and she really encouraged me to join my school's orchestra program when I was in sixth grade. I've been playing ever since. Sometimes it's been a little rough being the only guy at my high school who plays the violin, but I'm glad I stuck with it. Last year, my school's orchestra actually traveled to Amsterdam to play. It was the first time I'd ever been out of the country, so that was pretty great."

Rather than sounding like a line from a resume, the second response tells a quick story and made some interesting conversation. It gives the interviewer the chance to follow up with another question, like what it's like to be the only guy at school who plays the violin, or what you thought of Amsterdam, or whether or not you and your mom have bonded over the violin.

If you want to be impressive, make the interviewer's job easier. Give some detail to your answers and tell a story. Be a good conversationalist. Don't just sit there.

RESPOND PROMPTLY WHEN CONTACTED

If your target college requests an alumni interview, your interviewer will likely reach out to you by phone or email after you apply. When they do, it's important to respond promptly.

I've heard several college interviewers tell stories about leaving voicemails or sending emails to kids who don't respond for four to five days. That makes it much harder for them to schedule with you and doesn't send a very good message about your interest.

You don't have to be on high alert and respond within 15 minutes of being contacted. But during the college admissions process, it's a good idea to check to your voicemail and email at least once a day. And if you get a message from an interviewer, respond within 24 hours. If it's an email, observe the laws of grammar and punctuation. And always thank the interviewer for contacting you.

BE READY FOR COMMON TOPICS

While most interviewers don't have prepared questions, they'll tend to ask about the same topics. If you're ready to discuss these five things, you'll be ready for your college interview.

1. Why are you applying to this school?

2. What's your favorite subject (and what are you thinking about studying in college)?

3. What do you enjoy doing when you're not in class?

4. What are three interesting things about yourself that I wouldn't know from your application?

5. What's an example of a mistake you made, a failure you endured, something you aren't good at, or anything else that you probably wouldn't bring up unless somebody asked you about it? (Note: be honest, but don't admit anything scary, like, "I have a history of violent crimes when dealing with rejection.")

Could interviewers ask you about things not on this list? Absolutely. But there's only so much conversational ground an interviewer can hope to cover in your limited time together. Be ready to have a nice conversation about the aforementioned subject areas and you'll be ready for your interviews.

FIND YOUR STORIES

In a college interview, a good answer is one that reveals something about you and has a personal anecdote to back it up. So before your interview, find the stories you'd like to share and think about how you'd like to tell them.

For example, let's say you write for the school newspaper. If that were to come up during your interview, what would you like to say about it that might be interesting? You can't just say you've been writing for the paper for the last two years. That's a good start, but there's got to be more to it than that.

Maybe you write your own sports column and made it your mission to give attention to less popular sports. Maybe you wrote an editorial you're particularly proud of that lots of teachers complimented you on. Maybe you helped double advertising revenue, or did a one-on-one interview with the principal that was a first for the paper, or wrote the pieces that won awards at an annual ceremony.

Those would all be interesting stories about something that's important to you. The interview is the perfect time to share them.

Finding your stories ahead of time serves two purposes: (1) it can help you make sure you talk about what is important to you, and (2) it helps you avoid the unnerving feeling of leaving the interview only to think of something worthwhile that could have been mentioned. Try to spin the conversation to these stories at appropriate times.

The best part about finding your stories ahead of time is that it makes you feel more confident during the interview. You can be more relaxed and just enjoy yourself.

DRAWING A BLANK IS A GREAT OPPORTUNITY

It happens. In spite of all your preparation, the interviewer asks you a question you're totally unprepared for, and you're stumped.

In a college interview, being stumped is actually a big opportunity. If you don't get flustered and manage to handle yourself well, you'll look much better than the average applicant who panics and blurts out the first thing that comes to mind.

So relish drawing blank.

Pause for a moment to show the interviewer that you are considering the question carefully.

Tell the interviewer, "That's a great question, I've never really thought about it before." That will buy you a little time to think, and if there's silence while you're thinking, it's OK.

Taking 10 to 15 seconds to think hard about your answer shows your interviewer you are carefully considering the question—that you're not flustered. It shows you're the kind of student who likes being asked difficult questions and thinking about the answers—that's never a bad thing for someone who's about to go to college.

If you really can't come up with anything, just say something to the effect of, "I'd really like to think about that a little more. Would it be OK if we came back to it a little later?"

Guess what? They always oblige, and they never come back to it.

I have never once had a student tell me that their interviewer went back to a former question. As long as you don't take a pass on a basic question about your interest in the school or what you want to study in college, the interviewer will be happy to talk about other things.

Passing on a question won't work on your AP government final, but it works in your college interview.

CONSIDER QUESTIONS YOU'D LIKE TO ASK

Students often ask my Collegewise team, "What questions should I ask at my college interview?"

We always respond with our own question: "What would you like to know?"

A college interview is a rare opportunity for you to sit with someone who either works at a college you're applying to, or has already done what you want to do and has attended the school. If you're really interested in attending, it's hard to imagine there aren't some things you'd like to know.

If your interviewer attended the college, don't hesitate to ask about her experiences. How did she pick the school? What did she study? What surprised her most about her time there? Was there anything she didn't like?

All of those are reasonable questions if you'd really like to know the answers.

I'd avoid asking questions that show you haven't done basic research on the school, like, "Does the school offer a business major?" It's also fine to ask about the social life and what kids do, but I wouldn't ask if kids drink beer in the dorms.

Also, avoid asking questions just to ask them. Your interviewer will be able to tell if you're not really interested in the answers, and part of being a good conversationalist is being interested in the conversation. So think about what you'd really like to know about the school. What's something that you haven't been able to learn about from the website or the tour or the guidebooks? If you genuinely want to know and you're interested in the answer, you'll be asking a good question.

LEAVE YOUR PARENTS AT HOME

Never bring your parents with you to your college interview. Leave them at home. Or send them on vacation. Send them anywhere as long as it's far away from your college interview.

Bringing your parents with you sends a terrible message to your interviewer. You're saying you can't talk to an adult by yourself without your assigned parental counsel. That's not the kind of student who will do well in college.

Are your parents pressuring you to let them join you? Read them this sentence:

Parents, if you go with your kids to their college interviews, you will hurt their chances of getting into college.

If you don't have a car, it's fine to have your parents drop you off. Wave and watch them drive away to make sure they're gone. Then go have your college interview.

One exception: I have seen cases where a college interviewer asks a student to bring a parent. If your interviewer asks, disregard everything I just said about never ever under any circumstances bringing a parent to your college interview.

DRESS FOR THANKSGIVING

How should you dress for the interview?

Imagine your parents were making you dress up for Thanksgiving dinner at your grandparents' house where all of your extended family would be joining. What would your parents want you to wear?

Most parents I've met would say a T-shirt and jeans is too casual, but a full suit or formal dress is too much. Anything in between those two will probably be fine as long as you use good judgment.

That's a good rule of thumb for your college interview attire.

You need to show your interviewer you appreciate the importance of the meeting. Making an effort to look nice conveys that message, but if you dress up so formally that you feel awkward and uncomfortable, you're going to ooze tension during the interview.

If you really want to dress up more than you would for a visit to Grandma's, knock yourself out. The key is feeling confident about how you look. I worked with a student who told me that he wanted to wear a suit to his interviews because, "I always feel like a badass when I wear suits."

I told him to go ahead and get his suit pressed, but not to be surprised if he was dressed better than the interviewer. Keep this in mind if you're meeting at a coffee shop or other non-work location.

Also remember: you're not dressing for a date. It's fine to be fashionable, but you don't want your outfit (or overwhelming wafts of perfume), to speak for you. Wear something that would make your grandma say, "You look nice, dear."

WORK THE WAITING ROOM

If you're interviewing on campus, there's a good chance you'll be in a waiting room with other students who are also there to interview. You'll probably be able to feel the nervous tension in the room. That's why I always tell students to start a conversation with other students who are waiting. Introduce yourself. Ask people where they're from. Listen to their answers and maybe ask a follow-up question.

This accomplishes three things.

1. It will put you at ease. Sitting there in awkward silence will just make you and everyone else more nervous. But if you're the one kid who's confident enough to actually strike up a conversation, you'll feel empowered.

2. Talking to a few people you don't know is a conversational warm-up before the interview, like the way a miler does a few slow laps before the big race.

3. It helps make a good first impression on the interviewer. It's easy to notice the one student who seems to be interacting easily with the others who are waiting.

I've had a lot of students who did this tell me it helped them be more relaxed and more confident.

MAKE A GOOD FIRST IMPRESSION

The first impression you make on your interviewer sets the tone. In fact, if you can get the first five seconds right, your odds of getting the rest of the interview right increase dramatically.

Frank Bernieri, a psychologist at the University of Toledo, conducted an experiment where 98 volunteers were interviewed for 15 to 20 minutes. At the end of each interview, the interviewers filled out a six-page evaluation of the person they'd just interviewed.

Bernieri then got a series of strangers to watch a video of only the first 15 seconds of each interview. Those viewers didn't see any part of the actual interviews—just the subject entering the room, saying hello, shaking hands and sitting down to be welcomed. The strangers then filled out the same six-page evaluation based only on the 15 seconds of video they'd seen. Based only on their first impressions, the strangers reached virtually the same conclusions that the interviewers reached after 15-20 minutes.[9] "People do judge books by their covers," Bernieri concluded. "First impressions are going to predict final impressions."[10]

How to make a great first impression

Here are three things to do to make a great first impression on your interviewer.

1. Smile and look the person in the eye.

This is something of a lost art for a lot of teenagers. When you smile and look your interviewer in the eye, you project a certain confidence.

2. Provide a firm handshake.

Shake hands, introduce yourself and say, "It's nice to meet you." Make the handshake firm. Not crushing, just firm.

3. Fill the initial walk with some conversation.

No matter where the interview is taking place, there's a good chance that after meeting your interviewer, you'll have to walk to an office or a table at the coffee shop before the interview actually starts. This can be a potentially awkward walk of silence for a student that's not prepared. When you start the walk, initiate the conversation with something like, "Thanks so much for seeing me today," or "So, how many interviews do you have scheduled today?"

In just the first five seconds, you'll have shown your interviewer that you're confident, mature and a good conversationalist.

MAKE A GOOD LAST IMPRESSION

Parents often nag kids to write thank-you notes to their college interviewers. This is one of those times when your parents are right.

Your college interviewer has already been to college and doesn't need anything from you. They're giving up time for you and they deserve to be thanked. Our Collegewise counselor, Arun, recommends students send an email, not an old-fashioned card. "Cards get thrown away. An email gets printed and added to their folder," he says.

If your interviewer hasn't previously communicated with you over email, ask for his or her card at the end of the interview. And remember the laws of capitalization and punctuation are not suspended just because it's email. If you can't get an email address, go the old-fashioned route and write a thank-you card. Whichever route you choose, make the note a good one.

Not all thank-you notes are created equal. Some are only two or three sentences and sound like they were written by a corporation. They're the thank-you version of "We apologize for any inconvenience."

As covered in "Give thanks," good thank-you notes are sincere. This person gave up time for you and deserves to be thanked. Sound like a real human. And specifically reference something about the interview that was helpful or interesting to you, even if it wasn't relevant.

A student who writes, "I'm also glad to learn I'm not the only one who thinks Arrested Development was the greatest show in television history" wouldn't just personalize the note, it also would remind the interviewer of the conversation and the student—you.

Finally, send your email or write your card the day after the interview. You don't know how many students your interviewer is seeing after you, and if you wait a couple weeks to send your thank you, your name and face might be figuratively fuzzy.

AFFORDING COLLEGE: HOW TO GET FINANCIAL AID AND SCHOLARSHIPS

Since we used one of the FAFSA estimation calculators, we knew with two high tech incomes that we wouldn't qualify for any need-based financial aid. Because our son has excellent grades and test scores, we made sure that some of the colleges on his list were reputed to give good merit scholarships. Chapman University offered him a $25,000 per year presidential scholarship, bringing the total close to in-state costs at a University of California campus. It was also a great boost to my son's confidence that his hard work was paying off—it's not every day someone offers you $100,000 to go to college. Even University of California, Berkeley where he enrolled offered us unsubsidized loans for the full cost of attendance.

Lynn C.
Mother of Noah K., former Collegewise student, Class of 2012
University of California – Berkeley

SAVING IS YOUR BEST STRATEGY

According to the College Board's publication "Trends in College Pricing 2011," current one-year average costs are roughly $17,000 for an in-state public four-year college and $38,000 for a private one. That's $70,000 over four years for a public school, $154,000 for a private. Bottom line up front: saving is your best college financing strategy.

The more a family manages to scrimp, sacrifice and save, the less you'll need to rely on financial aid and the more control you'll have over your college destiny.

Since money you save earns interest, while money you borrow to pay for college incurs interest, it's cheaper to save than it is to borrow. The sooner you start setting aside money and letting compound interest work for you, the better. According to finaid.org, saving $50 a month from the day your child is born would yield about $20,000 by the time the child turns 17, assuming a 7% return on investment. Saving $200 a month would yield almost $80,000.[1]

How much to save

You don't necessarily have to save the full amount to pay for college. College financing expert Mark Kantrowitz recommends families aim to save one-third of their expected college costs. When the student starts college, the family would pay one-third of the remaining cost from using their current income, and one-third from a combination of parent and student loans.[2]

Of course, it would be better if you didn't have to borrow at all, but Kantrowitz believes this is the realistic reflection of many families' finances.

More from Kantrowitz on how to save: http://www.finaid.org/savings/

Don't lose hope

Even if parents didn't start setting aside money as soon as they left the hospital delivery room, it's never too late to start. Put aside what you can, even if it's just $50 a month. Colleges are much more likely to look financially favorably at a family who has made an honest effort to save for college than they are at a family who's lived beyond their means and now expects financial aid to make up for it. Start early.

The best way to save

529 college savings plans (which include Section 529 College Savings Plans and Section 529 Prepaid Tuition Plans) are one of the best ways to save for college. Here are a few reasons why:

- **No federal income tax**
  As long as the withdrawals are used to pay for college expenses, money earned in a 529 plan isn't subject to federal income tax.

- **Fewer restrictions**
  Anyone—a parent, a relative, or even a generous family friend—can contribute to a student's 529 plan. There are also no age limits for contributors, no income restrictions, and much higher maximum allowed contributions than those for many other types of accounts.

- **Parents retain control**
  While the child is named as the beneficiary, the parent controls the 529 account and will never lose control of the money. Parents can also change the named beneficiary to one of their other kids, or name themselves if they decide to go back to school.

- **Less impact on eligibility for financial aid**
  Because the parent owns the 529 account, the financial aid formulas treat that money as a parent asset. In financial aid formulas, parent assets are assessed at a rate of 5.6 percent as opposed to 20 percent if the money is saved in an account owned by the student.

529 plans are sponsored by individual states and you can invest in any state's plan. For more information and advice on choosing a 529 plan, including a list of which states provide deductions for 529 plan contributions, visit the "State Section 529 Plans" section of finaid.org: http://www.finaid.org/savings/529plans.phtml

DON'T MAKE AID ASSUMPTIONS

I often hear families make assumptions like, "We can't afford private schools," or "We'll never qualify for aid." Be careful—aid assumptions like those tend to work against you when it comes to paying for college.

Assuming your family can't pay for some (or any) colleges just takes options off the table. You may not be as motivated to work hard to get in. You may also eliminate certain colleges that are right for you, which are often the schools most likely to give you aid.

The College Board reports in the 2010-11 school year, undergraduate students received an average of $12,455 in financial aid —roughly $6,000 in grant aid (free money that doesn't have to be paid back), $5,000 in federal loans, and $1,000 in a combination of tax credits and deductions and Federal Work-Study. Why not apply for your fair share of what's being distributed?

With the price of some colleges exceeding $150,000 over four years, many families who are otherwise financially comfortable, even affluent, can qualify for aid. There's no shame—or admissions risk—in applying for it. The worst a college can do is say no.

One difficult part of planning for college is you don't know your financial aid package until you actually apply and are accepted. So you have to choose colleges without really knowing exactly how much they'll cost. There are ways to estimate your aid, which I cover in this chapter. But as you factor the cost for college into your search, make no assumptions. Plan well, choose the right colleges and apply for any aid that's available to you.

PARENT TO PARENT

No assumptions

I had heard that applying for financial aid wasn't worth all the trouble, and the forms were time-consuming, complicated and confusing. They sure were time-consuming, but pretty straightforward. And both the FAFSA and PROFILE forms have a help desk you can call with questions, which I contacted several times. Although some schools weren't able to offer any aid (only loans), there were a few that offered a grant and loan package that makes it more manageable. So applying was definitely worth my time and effort. I would advise every parent to apply for financial aid.

Amy A.
Mother of Mike, former Collegewise student, Class of 2012
Syracuse University

KNOW THE COST OF ATTENDANCE

The price of attending college can be far more than the price of just the tuition and fees. Families will also need to pay for room and board, personal expenses and travel. That total annual cost of attendance (COA) can often be two to three times the listed tuition. So the COA, not just the tuition, is what families need to factor into college budgeting and research.

This can actually be good financial news. The COA is what will be used to determine whether or not your family receives any need-based financial aid. When colleges evaluate your ability to pay, they'll consider all of the costs you would incur, not just the listed tuition.

Most colleges calculate the COA for you. Just visit the financial aid section of colleges' websites to find it.

COLLEGE COSTS AND AID RECEIVED

Source: National Center for Educational Statistics

School	2011-12 Tuition	2011-2012 Cost of attendance	2009-2010 % of students receiving aid*
Sarah Lawrence College	$45,212	$60,116	62
Yale University	$40,500	$58,250	66
George Washington University	$44,148	$57,148	67
Colgate University	$42,920	$55,570	41
Hamilton College	$42,640	$55,270	56
**University of California – Berkeley	$12,834	$32,632	68
**University of Colorado – Boulder	$9,152	$27,236	76
**University of Michigan	$12,634	$25,204	65
**University of Texas – Austin	$9,794	$24,714	68

*Includes students receiving Federal Work Study aid and aid from other outside sources.
**Costs listed are those for in-state residents.

Behind the numbers

The "College Navigator" tool (http://nces.ed.gov/collegenavigator/) will let you look up detailed financial aid information for particular colleges, such as:

- **The full cost of attendance.**
  Not just the tuition— the full "COA"

- **Average financial aid award for all students, not just freshmen.**
  This is important, because if the aid for all students is significantly lower than that for freshmen, it could mean the college gives more generous aid to encourage students to attend only to decrease that aid once they've spent a year or two at the school and are less likely to want to leave.

- **The average price paid by families, sorted by income.**
  This indicates how much financial aid is given out to families at each income level, and can be helpful when you try to approximate your aid eligibility.

MEET THE NET PRICE CALCULATOR

Imagine you had to buy a car without knowing the sale price, how much money you could borrow or what your monthly payment would be. You'd have no idea how much car—or which one—you could afford.

For a long time, college financial aid worked much the same way. Families knew the cost of attendance (COA), but without a financial aid offer in hand, they didn't know what portion of the COA they would need to pay. The only way to know what a college would cost was to apply and wait to see if any aid was offered upon admission. That made college financial planning a lot harder than it needed to be. It got a little easier in October 2011.

The federal government mandated that by October 2011, colleges had to post a new tool called the "net price calculator" to their websites. You input information common for financial aid forms (like income and savings). Then the net price calculator estimates your financial aid eligibility, subtracts that from the college's COA and tells you how much they estimate you will need to pay next year to attend each school. You reapply for financial aid each year that you're in college, so the calculator is only estimating the upcoming year's costs. The calculator does the estimate for you.

Not a promise

The net price calculator estimate is not a promise (or a denial) of future financial aid. Colleges will eventually ask you for a lot more detailed information when you fill out your official financial aid forms, and the result then might be different than what the calculator tells you now. Your qualifications as an applicant can do a lot to influence the aid you receive beyond what you qualify for (see: "Apply to plenty of targets and safeties"). But a well-calculated estimate is better than no information at all. You'll be able to make better-informed decisions about which colleges you likely can afford to attend.

As of the writing of this book, not every college has posted the net price calculator on their websites. If you don't see it on a particular college's site, use the one at www.collegeboard.com.

It's going to take a couple cycles to see just how effective the net price calculator is. But college financial aid had long needed to be reengineered so families didn't have to apply and just cross their fingers with no idea whether or not they'd qualify for aid. The net price calculator is a good first step.

Be as accurate as you can when inputting the numbers. If you and your parents decide to change your college list based on the results, ask your high school counselor if she can recommend some schools that would be appropriate.

LOOK BEYOND STICKER PRICE

We naturally make decisions whether we can afford things based on how much they cost. That makes it easy to tell what's in—and out—of our price range. But paying for college works differently.

The Free Application for Federal Student Aid (FAFSA)—which you file in January of the year you plan to start college—is the starting point for applying for aid for any four-year college.

When you file the FAFSA, the figure the government returns to you is your Expected Family Contribution (EFC). That's the amount your family will be expected to pay for the upcoming year at any college. It will be up to the government and the colleges to come up with a financial aid package (that may include loans that will need to be paid back) to make up the difference between your EFC and the full cost of attendance at each school.

For example, if your EFC is $20,000, and you apply to a school that costs $30,000 a year to attend, you've demonstrated $10,000 in financial need.

So in theory, whether a school costs $10,000 a year or $50,000 a year, you will pay the same EFC amount at the time of enrollment at each school—$20,000 using the example above. That's what you've demonstrated you can afford.

There's more

I say "in theory" because about 270 private schools believe that the FAFSA doesn't tell them enough about your ability to pay. They may require you to fill out additional forms that enable them to calculate their own EFC, and that number can be higher or lower than the number the FAFSA gives you. Still, using the aforementioned net price calculator removes a lot of that guesswork.

Of course, the amount of aid you can receive isn't dependent only on how much money you have (or don't have). Your academic strength, match with the school, and the college's desire to have you on campus can also influence a financial aid award.

I would never recommend applying to a list of schools that are all out of your price range. But since you're dealing with estimates, I also don't recommend crossing schools off your list just because they exceed a certain sticker price.

PARENT TO PARENT

Kami was awarded grants, academic scholarships and performance scholarships from all of the colleges she applied to—everything Collegewise told us about not letting the price tag of some colleges scare you off. You never know what they will award you!

Kim K.
Mother of Kami, former Collegewise student, Class of 2012
Point Loma Nazerene University

APPLY THE ADMISSIONS ADVICE

Applying for financial aid is a totally different process than applying for admission. There are different forms with different deadlines, all of which are handled by an entirely different office on college campuses. But my advice about applying for admission is exactly the same when applying for financial aid: Start early, find out what's required and follow the directions.

The only guaranteed, mistake-free way to make sure you file the correct forms by the deadlines is to visit the financial aid section of each college's website and verify what they require. That's your first step. In the fall of your senior year, visit the financial aid sections of your colleges' websites and find the answers to three crucial questions:

1. **What forms do you need to fill out to apply for need-based financial aid (e.g., Free Application for Federal Student Aid, school-specific forms, etc.)?**

2. **Do the financial aid offices require any supporting documentation?**

For example, some colleges require information from stepparents, or parents' income tax returns or business statements.

3. **What are the deadlines to submit all of those required forms?**

Narrow window

You'll notice many of the deadlines fall between January and March of the senior year, and many of the forms you need to fill out can't actually be started until after January 1. It takes time to gather all this information and January to March is a narrow window to complete everything that's required. Even if you can't officially start filling out forms now, you can at least set yourself up to finish everything as early as possible once the filing window opens.

Just like when you fill out college applications, always follow directions. Send colleges what they ask for, when they ask for it. You aren't the one to decide that your situation necessitates a better way. If you have questions, contact the college's office of financial aid directly.

TALK TO YOUR PARENTS ABOUT COSTS

A lot of parents believe they should shield their kids from the economic realities of attending college—that it's your job to get accepted and their job to pay for it. I think it's honorable. Still, I think it's good for students to have honest, open discussions with their parents about college costs.

It's not unreasonable for a student to know what her parents can afford to pay for college, the sacrifices they've made to save or the continued sacrifices they'll make during the four years they have to write tuition checks. Having that conversation now, however unpleasant it might be, is much better than having it later, when you have an offer of admission in hand, but your family can't afford the school.

Says Kate P., a Class of 2012 Collegewise student who went on to the University of Arizona: "I'm glad my parents shared our financial abilities with me because it helped me realize that some of my schools were very unrealistic. Knowing what my family was able to sacrifice to send me to college helped me choose schools that I knew were affordable."

Financial aid impact

Even a student who isn't aware of his family's finances might be impacted when applying for financial aid. Not all financial aid is free money. Sometimes it includes loans, and those loans will be taken out in your name, even if your parents pay your tuition. That means you'll be legally obligated to start paying back that money (once you graduate from college).

Another type of financial aid is "work study," where you're offered a part-time job on campus to help defray college costs. You—not your parents—will be the one washing dishes, manning the front desk of the library or filing papers in the dean of student's office. That's why college financing is often a family decision, whether your parents want it that way or not.

If you're mature enough to go to college, you're mature enough to know what it'll take to pay for it. So even if your parents haven't brought it up, talk to them about college costs. Ask them if they'd be willing to share that information with you. Even if they insist on keeping it secret, you'll at least have given them one more example that you're taking this seriously and that you appreciate everything they're doing to send you to college.

APPLY TO COLLEGES THAT MAY PAY

Financial aid isn't all cold, hard numbers measuring costs and what your family can afford to pay. Financial aid offices have a lot of power to offer more generous packages to students they think are right for the school and are more likely to attend. That's why one of the best ways to get more financial aid is to apply to plenty of "target" and "safety" schools (see "How to Finalize Your List").

At a minimum, most colleges will offer you the financial aid you qualify for. But the specific aid package you're offered, and whether or not that package is even more generous than what you're eligible for, can have a lot to do with how badly the admissions office wants you at that school.

If you're a strong student who fits well with that college, the financial aid office may give you an award package that has more free money, with fewer loans or work-study components.

If they're not as interested in you, the opposite might be true.

If a school really wants you, they also can give you a scholarship that has absolutely nothing to do with financial need.

Financial aid offices earmark a certain percentage of money every year just to lure academically appealing students. This practice is called preferential packaging, and it's not a dirty secret. Note the following from the financial aid office at Muhlenberg College in Allentown, Penn.:

> Preferential packaging means, simply, that the students a college would most like to enroll will receive the most advantageous financial aid packages. A preferential financial aid package includes a far greater percentage of grant aid than self-help (loans and work). Because they have discretion over how much grant aid they choose to award a student, a college can award a bigger grant to a student they would really like to enroll. In some cases, the total of grant from the college and the loans the student is entitled to may exceed the student's financial need.[3]

Rule of thumb

The simple rule of thumb: if you want more financial aid, apply to the schools most likely to accept you.

Every year, we have B and even C students at Collegewise who get generous and unsolicited offers of aid from colleges. They do it by applying to plenty of target and safety schools that fit them well, and where they have a good chance of being admitted. The better the fit between you and a college, the more likely that school will entice you to attend.

Regardless of your GPA, you can find target and safety schools and avail yourself of potential scholarships. One former Collegewise student with a 2.8 GPA and an 18 on the ACT got a $6,000-per-year merit-based scholarship from Westminster College in Salt Lake City, Utah.

Find a financial safety school, too

I also recommend that you pick a financial safety school, one you're sure you can get into and pay for even if you get no financial aid.

If you apply to the right colleges, use the net price calculator and file all the appropriate forms, you probably won't need a financial safety school. Still, it's always good to have a fallback position when things don't go as planned. If there's one thing families have learned since the US economy collapsed in 2008, it's how fast our family financial situations can change for the worse.

If you're not sure there are any schools you could afford without financial aid, take a look at the public universities in your state, ask your counselor which ones you have the best chance of being admitted to and make one your financial safety school.

Remember, nobody is saying you necessarily have to go to your financial safety school. But it's much better to at least have the option if things don't work out as you expected them to.

UPDATE SCHOOLS IF CIRCUMSTANCES CHANGE

When you file your financial aid forms, you give the colleges a financial snapshot of your family. If the snapshot changes before you get your financial aid award, it's important to update schools so they have the most recent information.

Financial aid offices want to know if there's a significant change to the information you shared on your forms. If your parent loses a job, or your family has unforeseen medical expenses, or your parents get divorced, all of those things impact how much your family can afford to pay for college. All of them are worth sharing with the financial aid office.

If you're not sure whether a change is substantial enough to share, update the school anyway. The worst thing that can happen is that the school doesn't use the information.

COMPARE AWARDS

A lot of families get swept up by the total figure in the financial aid award letter.

When a college says you've been awarded $16,000 in financial aid, the figure sounds great. But it doesn't necessarily mean you're getting a $16,000 discount off the college's sticker price.

Financial aid awards can be a combination of free money (scholarships), loans and work study. To figure out who's giving you the best offer, you need to consider the total cost of attendance for the college, the amount of free money, the amount of the loans and accompanying interest rates. It's a challenging project even for someone who loves math and spreadsheets—and there's an easier way.

Visit www.finaid.org and use their Award Comparison Tools. http://www.finaid.org/ You plug in the numbers for each school—the cost of attendance, the amounts of the scholarships, loans and work study. They'll give you the bottom-line figure of how much each school will cost.

You may or may not decide to pick your college based just on the price. But no matter how much you plan to factor cost into your final choice, compare your award letters so you know the real cost of each school.

TELL COLLEGES ABOUT BETTER OFFERS

If you receive two very different offers of aid from two different schools, consider calling the college that gave you less aid and asking if there is any way they will reevaluate your package.

Families have often heard that you can leverage one financial aid offer into a more attractive offer from another school; that if you call a school and point out that another college is giving you a lot more money, you can almost negotiate your way to a higher package.

That scenario doesn't always pan out. You're not buying a used car here. Financial aid officers aren't likely to do anything that feels like haggling.

But I've seen it work. There are times when making that call can lead to a good outcome, especially if the two schools compete for the same applicants, and if the offers are very different.

Here are two things to keep in mind when making such a call.

1. Financial aid officers have an unstated sense of a collegiate pecking order.

If you call a prestigious school that rejects most its applicants and tell them you've been awarded a more generous aid package from a school they've never heard of, they won't likely be inclined to give you more money. I'm not saying you shouldn't ask, but know your argument will have less oomph.

2. Approach this like a civil business discussion.

Leave your emotions out of it. Be polite and respectful. If there are substantial differences between the two awards, the college will probably ask to see a copy of the other award. Offer to provide any additional documentation that might be helpful. And always thank the person no matter what the outcome.

Enlist your parents

This is an appropriate call for a parent—not the student—to make. Students should always make contact with colleges themselves, but when it's time to discuss how to pay the bill, colleges expect the majority of those calls will come from parents.

Paying for college is a big deal and you want to know you've done everything you can do to get the aid you qualify for. So don't get your hopes up that you'll somehow negotiate your way to a higher aid package. Don't hesitate to call and ask, either.

ANSWER THE $2,800 QUESTION

I meet a lot of families who have the impression there is oodles of money available from outside or private scholarships. These are little-known awards from private companies, foundations, community organizations, churches and other benefactors. There is money to be had from those sources, and they may be worth applying for, but you won't likely get a free ride from outside scholarships alone.

According to *Paying for College Without Going Broke*, the money from outside scholarships accounts for only about *5 percent* of the aid that is available. The author points out that the biggest chunk of scholarship money comes from funds provided by the federal and state governments, and from the colleges themselves, all of which you access by following each college's directions to apply for financial aid.

That said, and even if the amount of money available from outside scholarships is comparatively small, free money for college is always a good thing. So here's how I recommend families go about deciding whether or not to apply: consider the time investment.

Survey says

In 2008, the National Postsecondary Student Aid Study surveyed 140,000 undergraduate students about how they paid for college. Among students enrolled full time at four-year colleges, 10.6 percent received scholarships. So the odds of winning a scholarship for students pursuing a bachelor's degree are about 1 in 10.[4] The average award was roughly $2,800.

Applying for outside scholarships is a time-consuming process. Kids have to research and find the scholarships, fill out the applications, and often write essays, get additional letters of recommendation and maybe even interview. If you devoted 10 to 15 hours of work to win $2,800, would you think it was worth it?

If your answer is, "Of course!" apply for outside scholarships.

If you'd feel like a $2,800 return on your investment of time and energy just wouldn't be worth it, you might reconsider.

My experience

Of course, that figure is an approximation. You could win more or less than $2,800, depending on your qualifications. My experience with our Collegewise students has supported the logic in the aforementioned book; the biggest awards don't come from the outside scholarships. I can't recall ever hearing one of our students won a $15,000 scholarship from a private foundation or company. I see it happen all the time from the other sources, particularly from the colleges themselves.

If you decide to search for outside scholarships, all the information is available free to you. Two of the best places to search: www.scholarships.com and www.fastweb.com.

DECIDING: HOW TO HANDLE ADMISSIONS DECISIONS AND PICK YOUR COLLEGE

We did acknowledge each acceptance with high fives and congratulations on the specifics. "Wow! You got invited to apply for honors." "Just think about the great snowboarding." "That $5,000 scholarship will really help." "Getting the Presidential Scholarship must mean they really want you." When the last notice came in, we went out to dinner to celebrate all of them. And when his decision was made, we immediately placed a web order for a college logo sweatshirt so he could wear it at admitted students' day.

Lynn C.
Mother of Noah K., former Collegewise student, Class of 2012
University of California – Berkeley

CELEBRATE EVERY OFFER OF ADMISSION

As acceptances start to roll in, some seniors hold off their excitement until the dream school's decision arrives.

I say, celebrate every offer of admission. I don't care if it's your safety school. You're going to college.

As soon as you get more than one acceptance, you'll get to pick which college you want to attend. Whether you get three or five or 12 acceptances, life is good. Be proud that you worked hard enough to earn this, and enjoy the process of deciding where you're going to spend the next four years.

HOW THEY CELEBRATED

Our Collegewise families celebrate every offer of admission. Here's how a few of them did it.

Collegewise Student	College attended	How they celebrated each acceptance
Noah K.	UC Berkeley	Noah's family gave each other group high fives as each decision arrived, and enjoyed a family dinner out to celebrate his choices at the culmination of the process.
Mike A.	Syracuse University	Mike's parents sent an email to their extended family around the country as each acceptance arrived (even for the safety schools).
Aaron F.	Southern Methodist University	When each acceptance arrived, Aaron's mother bought two Mylar balloons in the school colors to display in their house. When the next acceptance arrived, new balloons were added to the others. Soon there was a giant bouquet of balloons in the kitchen.
Lizzie H.	University of Arizona	For each acceptance, Lizzie's mother baked a cake frosted in the school's colors.
Amy D.	Loyola Marymount University	Amy's parents bought T-shirts from every college that accepted her, saving the sweatshirt purchase for her final college of choice.

MAKE REJECTION PAIN TEMPORARY

It's never a great day when bad news arrives from a college. If this news comes from one of your dream schools, it's a pretty bad day. I would never minimize that disappointment. I can only offer that like bad hair cuts and embarrassing moments, the pain associated with the rejection will eventually pass.

You are allowed to be disappointed by a rejection. But (warning, a little tough love coming here), you are not allowed to treat the rejection like a tragedy.

This isn't a tragedy; it's a disappointment, and all successful people have their share of them. It's important to remember how lucky you are to be living in a country with the best system of higher education in the world. Wherever you go, you will carve out a college experience that you'll one day tell your kids about. It's still going to happen, and that's something worth appreciating.

College rejections often feel bitterly personal. But a rejection does not necessarily mean the admissions office didn't love your essay or appreciate your activities or think you wouldn't be a great addition to the campus.

"The truth is that there is always a reason that colleges accept a student, but very often there is not a reason that they don't," writes A. Lucido, vice provost for enrollment policy and management at the University of Southern California. "It's truly nothing you did—or even didn't do... There are many more applicants than spaces in the class at selective universities, and we cannot take all the students that we would love to have on our campuses."[1]

Look ahead

One of the best ways to get over a college rejection is to look ahead six months from now.

You'll move into a dorm. You'll meet your new roommate while your parents exact your promise to call home on a regular basis. You'll buy a sweatshirt bearing the name of your new college. You'll go to your first college class, start making your new friends and officially begin your life as a college freshman.

Do you have any idea just how exciting that's going to be for you?

When we reach out to our former students who are in college, the overwhelming majority are blissfully happy where they are, regardless of whether they're attending what was once their first-choice school. Can you blame them? Have you ever been to a college party? Have faith that you'll be happy, too.

Six months from now, the college rejection that stings today will be a distant memory. So you're allowed a brief period of mourning if necessary. But as quickly as you can, move on. The sooner you begin falling in love with a college (if you're not already) that said, "Yes," the sooner you'll be excited about the next four years.

"I didn't get into my number one choice and now I can't believe I wanted to go somewhere else besides SMU," says former Collegewise student Taylor O. "College is literally the best thing that's happened to me and I can't see myself anywhere besides the place I ended up. I can't believe I am almost done with my first year here. I wish I could go back and start all over again."

RESIST THE URGE TO APPEAL

An appeal is a formal request you send in writing, asking a college to reconsider your application for admission. I meet a lot of students whose knee-jerk reaction to a rejection is to appeal as a way of not taking "No" for an answer. In most cases, that's like asking for a second opinion from the same doctor who's already diagnosed you, which is why I rarely see appeals work.

Those few cases where I've seen an appeal lead to an admission is when a student provides new and compelling information that wasn't originally in the application. For example, if your seventh semester grades were a dramatic improvement over your previous grades, or a club you started raised a large amount of money for a charity event you planned, or the new internship you just secured happens to be in the field you plan on majoring in, these are things that can be taken into account when reconsidering your application. None of these scenarios mean a college will necessarily overturn their decision, but at least you're presenting new information.

Some students want to appeal a decision because they simply believe they are stronger applicants than other students from their school who were admitted. Colleges won't consider this a valid reason to overturn their original decision. Don't point out the reasons you think you deserve the admission more than other students did. That just makes you look bitter.

Read and research

If you decide you want to appeal, carefully read the decision letter the college sent you, and research the admissions section of the college's website to see if any information about appealing decisions is provided. Then write a letter as soon as possible explaining why you want the admissions committee to reconsider your application for admission. Be polite and respectful, and make sure to present new information. If the college indicates extra letters of recommendation will be accepted in appeals cases, consider asking a teacher to write a letter of recommendation (a different teacher than you asked before).

I know it's disappointing not to be accepted to a school you really wanted to attend, but you'll be able to move past the disappointment faster if you let yourself start getting excited about your other colleges.

Unless you have new information the college didn't have when you submitted your application, resist the urge to appeal and start moving on.

CONSIDER DECLINING THE WAIT-LIST SPOT

Instead of receiving an acceptance or a rejection from a college, some students are offered a wait-list spot and told they might be admitted later if more space becomes available.

It's the college admissions version of purgatory.

Colleges don't know how many accepted students will ultimately decide to enroll. A wait-list is a school's way of hedging its bets and making sure their freshman class is ultimately full.

Wait-lists help schools but create a lot of stress for the students placed on them. That's why I tell every student offered a spot on a wait-list to seriously consider saying, "No thanks."

A spot on a wait-list makes your college future uncertain. You don't know if you'll be taken off the list, and the statistics aren't encouraging. The National Association for College Admissions Counseling reported that nearly half of all colleges used wait-lists in 2010, but only 28 percent of wait-listed students were ultimately admitted (the most selective colleges admitted only 11 percent).[2]

It's also quite common for schools to have little or no financial aid left for students admitted off the wait-list. The University of San Diego's website says, "Typically, there is no financial aid available to students admitted from the wait-list."

Meanwhile, by May 1, you still have to commit to another college that accepted you. I've seen students make their commitment to a school but refrain from buying a sweatshirt or otherwise celebrating because they were still holding out hope to be admitted from another school's wait-list.

Again: college admissions purgatory.

No thanks

Your alternative is to say, "No thanks."

A student who declines a spot on a wait-list takes control of his college destiny. Instead of hoping for a change in his wait-list status, he can focus on real options that are available to him and plan visits to schools he knows he could attend. He can compare offers from schools that gave him financial aid, commit to a college that's ready to commit to him and know where he's going to school in the fall.

It wasn't your choice to get a wait-list decision, but it's your choice whether or not you want to keep your spot on it.

I wouldn't decline a wait-list offer rashly, and I certainly wouldn't recommend doing so without talking it over with your parents and counselor. Just remember you're in charge. You aren't obligated to accept a spot on a wait-list. There's no shame in deciding to attend a college that accepted you outright.

Accept an offer

I can't overemphasize the importance of accepting an offer of admission by May 1 from one of the colleges that accepted you. The fact you're on a wait-list someplace else doesn't mean the colleges who said "Yes" will hold a spot. So even if you're holding out hope for a wait-list school, commit by May 1 to another college.

When you officially do commit, allow yourself to be excited. At least one school you've picked said, "Yes."

They didn't need to wait to see who else enrolled before they admitted you. They deserve some excitement, and so do you. Make an emotional commitment to your new school and keep the wait-list school as your back-up plan.

Improve your odds

If the school that wait-listed you really is your top choice and you want to pursue the option, the best way to improve your odds is to make contact with an admissions officer and express your desire to attend.

1. Call the admissions office.

Since admissions officers will rarely tell you something specific kept you from being admitted, the purpose of this phone call is primarily to show the admissions officer your level of maturity and your sincere interest in attending the school.

Explain you intend to accept the offer to be placed on the wait-list, and you are calling to find out if there might be anything specific you could address that would improve your chances of admission. Before you hang up, write down the person's name (you're going to write a letter to him or her next).

2. Meet with your counselor.

It's also a good idea to meet with your high school counselor and tell her about your wait-list situation.

If you've followed the advice in this book (you've already established a relationship with your counselor and you asked her to approve your college list), you can ask her if she would call the admissions office on your behalf to see what you can do. Admissions officers can sometimes be more candid with a counselor than they can be with a student.

3. Write a letter.

Many admissions officers tell me they are instructed to only pull kids off the wait-list who have made the effort to express their interest in the school. They don't want to pull kids off the list who aren't really interested.

Your letter can be just two or three paragraphs. Thank them for taking the time to speak with you, update them on any recent achievements or awards you've earned since applying and reiterate your interest in the school.

If the school is your first choice (and it really should be if you're accepting a spot on the wait-list), make that clear in the letter.

SAMPLE WAIT- LIST FOLLOW-UP LETTER

Below is a sample letter from a wait-listed student to an admissions officer at a college they are hoping to attend. This letter is something you want the admissions office to have in their office by the third week of April. Do not copy what you see below. Use it as a guideline. In order make the effective impression on the admissions officer, you need to be honest and specific with your reasons. Don't just copy from their viewbook or website, either. Being genuine and enthusiastic goes a long way with admissions officers.

Name of admissions officer you've spoken with
Title
Name of college
College's address
City, State, Zip code

Dear Mr. Burns,

Thank you for taking the time to speak with me last week about my status on the wait-list. While I was disappointed, I'm still excited about the possibility of attending this fall. When I first visited the University of Pennsylvania last summer, I made the smart decision and sat in Professor Hibberts' introductory vertebrate biology class and really enjoyed the discussion that took place. I also appreciated the balance Penn students I met in the student union showed with their academics and activities. I love the fact that I can work hard as a biology student and still enjoy supporting a competitive basketball team and study abroad at the Barcelona campus.

> The opening paragraph should thank them for taking the time to speak with you (be specific and mention the date you spoke on the phone) and explain that you are sending this letter to update the office on your progress. Feel free to express your disappointment at not being accepted, but keep the tone upbeat and optimistic as you share why you want to attend this college.

Since I submitted my application in December, there have been some updates to my academic and extracurricular record.

In the most rigorous program of study available at Springfield High School, I received four A's in AP courses (including AP physics) and one B in honors calculus in the 3rd quarter. I continue to do just as well in my final semester and will graduate in the top 3% of my class with high honors.

> List your academic and extracurricular updates in bullet form. Resist the urge to repeat too much information that was in your application. Instead, focus on recent developments.

In addition to continued involvement with Teen Line and volunteering at the local animal shelter, my water polo team won our league and finished second in CIF. I started every game and was named 2nd team All-District and Most Improved Player.

I was awarded a "Superior" rating in the Alta Monte Unified School District Science Fair for my project on "Hydroponics: The Future of Agriculture." I will be competing in mid-May at the state level.

I would like to make valuable contributions to the Penn community as a member of the Botany Club as well as continue my volunteer work at a local Philadelphia animal shelter. I also look forward to the opportunity of working closely with professors and conducting original research through the URF program. If there is any additional information I can provide you with, please don't hesitate to contact me at *your email address* or *your phone number*. Thank you for your careful consideration. Penn is absolutely my top choice for college. If admitted off the wait-list, there is no doubt I would attend as there's no other place I'd rather be.

In your third and final paragraph, state that the school is your first choice (if it actually is) and that you will accept a place in the class if you are given a space off the wait-list (if that's true). Thank them for taking the time to consider your application.

Sincerely,

Your name
Your high school
Your city, state, and zip code
Your social security number

Trust your instincts

A lot of high school students expect they should be certain of their choice when they decide where to go to college.

I'll make this easier for you: don't expect to be certain. In fact, expect to be uncertain. Selecting a college is a big decision. Big life decisions almost always come with some uncertainty. You likely won't be sure you've made the right college choice until you get there, eat some dorm food and get lost trying to find a class.

If you're feeling unsure about your choice, don't worry. It just means you're giving this big life decision the care and attention it deserves.

There is no college that will be perfect in every way for you. It's going to be up to you to make your college experience perfect for you. So whatever you do, accept admission to a college where you feel excited to spend four years, a place where you can't wait to go to class, meet new friends and find what college life has in store for you.

If you own that it will be your responsibility to make the most of your college experience, your instincts likely will lead you to find a school you'll look back on after graduation, knowing you made the perfect choice.

Pros and cons

Some students try to weigh the positive and not-so-positive traits of their college choices, but in most cases, you can't pros-and-cons your way to a college decision.

No matter what the pros and cons are, and no matter what anyone tells you, you are the one who will spend four years at the college you choose. At some point, your gut instinct has to kick in. So listen to it. You'd be surprised how right it usually is. "Clemson was never a school that I envisioned myself attending, but when I visited, it just felt right for me," says former Collegewise student, Mackenzie K. "So I decided to go with my gut. Joining the Clemson University community has been one of the best decisions I have ever made. Going with my gut feeling definitely paid off."

ADULTS ONLY: HOW PARENTS CAN HELP WITHOUT HURTING

Our son applied to schools that he chose, filled out all essays completely on his own (good thing as I probably would have rewritten it differently), and got into every college he applied to, ending up with his first choice. So, whether I helped or not by "letting go," I still enjoyed watching him go through the process with me on the sidelines cheering him on.

Melanie L.
Mother of Brandon, former Collegewise student, Class of 2012
Cal Poly – San Luis Obispo

FOCUS ON WHAT'S REALLY IMPORTANT

Parents, the college admissions process can be a stressful one for you, too. You deserve to enjoy this time with your kids. So to start this section, I'm going to share a dirty but effective trick with you.

When I tell groups of parents that one of the most important things they can do to manage college admissions stress is take a deep breath and remember what's really important, I ask them to picture these scenarios.

Imagine making the trip to college with your new college freshman and helping her move into her new dorm room.

Imagine welcoming her home at Thanksgiving, hearing her talk over turkey about how much she loves college, and then rolling out the family red carpet again a few weeks later when she's finally home for the holidays.

Imagine visiting her at Family Weekend, where you meet her new friends and buy yourself a sweatshirt that proudly identifies you as the parent of a college student.

Imagine receiving her phone calls and emails when she tells you how much she's learning, how much fun she's having and how happy she is in college.

Imagine following her progress during college and seeing for yourself how much your former high school senior is maturing.

Imagine hearing her tell you about the professor who sees great potential in her work, the summer internship she's so excited about and how she's finding her passions and thinking about what she'll do after graduation.

Imagine graduation day. You'll think back to changing diapers, to the terrible twos and the elementary school years. You'll remember her braces in junior high and watching her start high school. You'll remember teaching her how to drive, taking pictures before school dances, watching her apply to college and leaving the nest to start life as a college freshman.

Imagine her walking across the stage and accepting her diploma. She's done it. You have raised a beaming, grown-up, happy college graduate.

Now, when you were imagining those things, did it matter whether or not the college was a prestigious one?

I have never once done this exercise and had a parent answer, "Yes."

When you feel the stress of admissions starting to take its toll, just remember that your son or daughter is going to go to college, and someday, you'll be in the audience at graduation. Is anything more important than those two things?

You'll enjoy the college admissions process a lot more if you keep this truism in mind.

THINK LONG TERM

How would you react if a colleague told you, "I just haven't had much success in my career, but that's because I got a mediocre SAT score."

You'd laugh the guy out of the office. The SAT he took 20 years ago is obviously not the problem. You'd probably feel the same way if he blamed his lack of career advancement on his rejection from Georgetown when he applied at age 17.

During the college planning years, it's easy to assign lifelong importance to things that won't matter even a few years from now. The C+ in French, the SAT score that won't budge or the rejection from a dream school—those things matter today. But the long-term, life-changing opportunity for our kids to go any college—to be better educated, discover their talents, learn, grow, make lifelong memories and have fun while there—that's what matters in the long run.

Going to college is important. But your student's SAT score, grade in math or admissions decision from one dream college won't impact whether she's successful in her career, who she marries or how many grandkids you'll get to spoil one day.

When you focus on the long term, it's easier to see that your kid's work ethic to study like crazy in a physics class he struggles in is more important than whether or not he eventually gets an A.

The fact that he gets up at 5 a.m. every morning to practice with the water polo team—and does so with an inexplicable but endearing smile on his face—is more important than whether or not he ever starts a game.

Your kids' character traits—like their work ethic, interest in learning and how they treat other people—are much more important in the long run than whether Georgetown says "Yes."

Anytime you find yourself panicking about the college process, think about the bigger picture. Remember what will matter in the long run.

SET GOOD EXAMPLES

When a tearful parent tells me her daughter is "just devastated" by a rejection from Stanford, I think two things:

1. Is devastation really an appropriate reaction to a rejection from college?
2. Are you sure it's not you who's devastated?

I understand parents are connected to their children and you're going to take on whatever your kids are feeling. You have an important role to play in this process—you're the parent of a college applicant. Kids need you to guide and encourage them, to calm them down and most importantly to set good examples as the mature voice of reason. Your kids need you to not spiral out of control on their behalf.

If you fall apart in the face of a college rejection, your student is just going to feel even worse. One of my students was accepted by eight colleges and rejected by his dream school. His mother was so upset by the one rejection that he said to me, "I got into eight out of nine colleges, but it seems like my parents aren't happy at all."

Instead of showing him how a mature adult handles disappointment, his mother just couldn't make peace with the outcome and left her son feeling like he'd let her down.

Clear message

If you spend the college planning years trying to strategize how your student can get into Dartmouth, you're sending a clear message to your student that anything less than an admission to Dartmouth is failing.

You don't have to rain on your student's love for Dartmouth. But you can also set a good example and be excited about other less-selective schools.

If you place deposits down at more than one college so your student can have more time to decide after the deadline where to enroll—even though colleges make it explicitly clear this isn't allowed—you're telling your student it's OK to break the rules in life as long as it benefits you.

Don't be surprised if your student mimics that behavior while in college.

Parents who live vicariously through their college applicants never seem to enjoy the process. Worst of all, they end up neglecting the important job of showing their kids how adults deal with stressful situations.

Your kids are going to take their cues from you about how to approach the college admissions process. Remember you're on stage all the time. You don't have to be perfect, but when you sense yourself losing your perspective, revert back to setting good examples.

Enjoy the ride

We have had two daughters go through the college application process. Our goal as parents was to minimize the anxiety for everyone involved. We would present them with considerations, yet not be involved in the details. As a family, we were able to keep the discussion we did have about colleges at a higher, and more importantly, less stressful level. We enjoyed the ride and have absolutely no regrets. One more daughter to go!

Carol S.
Mother of former Collegewise students:
Becca, Class of 2010, St. John's College (MD)
Katie, Class of 2012, Boston University

SUPPORT WITHOUT HOVERING

You're not going to college—your kid is. If you want admissions officers to see your kids as capable young adults who are ready for college life, the best thing you can do is let them take charge of their college application process—not to hover and do it for them.

When parents pick all the activities, research the colleges and even fill out the applications, they can actually hurt their kids' chances of getting into college.

Bruce Jones, assistant director of admissions at Whitman College, told *US News & World Report*, "A too obviously involved parent, almost always a mom, hurts a kid in the admission office."

He shared an example of one applicant he downgraded because the majority of early contact with the school came in the form of emails from the applicant's mother.[1]

Jeanine Lalonde, assistant dean of admissions at the University of Virginia, blogged: "There are days when almost every call that comes into the office is from a parent filling out the Common Application for a student. To be frank, I'm disappointed...If you are headed for UVA, you should be more than capable of completing the Common Application."[2]

Kids blame

Parents may justify their hovering in the name of securing a better future for their kids. Clinical psychologist Mark Crawford points out that when kids with helicopter parents later neglect their responsibilities or make bad choices as adults, they tend to blame other people. "I see a lot of parents who hold their kids' hand across the high school graduation stage and think when they send them off to college all will be well," Crawford said. "They are not doing them a favor. They are actually doing them a disservice."[3]

Long-term effects

A study by sociologists Terri LeMoyne and Tom Buchanan of the University of Tennessee at Chattanooga found that college students with helicopter parents had higher rates of persistent anxiety and depression and were more likely to indulge in recreational drug use.[4]

The researchers even noticed these effects among the students in their classes. Buchanan says when today's students have trouble with a class or grades, instead of handling the situation themselves, "they sic their parents on their professors."

His students need far more detailed direction than they used to, repeatedly ask for study guides and even answers to essays, and are "very anxious when they face uncertainties."[5]

Gradual transition

As your kids progress through high school, it's time for you to step back and refrain from doing things for your kids that they should be able to do for themselves.

This transition can be a gradual one. Start by letting kids choose and pursue their own activities, rather than finding volunteer work or summer programs for them.

Students impress admissions officers by showing the initiative, skills and drive to locate and secure those activities on their own, not by participating because parents told them to.

If your student has trouble in a class, don't contact the teacher for him to find out what can be done. You won't be able to call his professor in college or email his boss later in life. Encourage him to visit the teacher on his own to ask for help.

If your student needs to raise funds for the lacrosse team, don't take over the project, send the emails and make all the fundraising calls for him. Let him do his own earning and learning. He's not too busy. The people he's asking for money are busy, too. Trust me, they'll have a harder time saying no to a high school kid than they will to his mother.

Is a 17-year-old ready?

Some parents want to step back from the college application, but get too involved out of concern for their 17-year-old who isn't taking it seriously enough.

I understand. It's especially tempting if you feel your kid is making a mistake he's going to regret later.

If your teen isn't exactly driving his college application process, resist the urge to jump in and do it for him.

Instead, be honest about your concerns. Tell him how excited you are about his college future. Let him know the efforts you've made to save for his college tuition and the sacrifices you're willing to make to send him. I think a mature teen will appreciate how much emotional and financial investment you're willing to make in him. He might then be a little more open to hearing your concerns about the looming deadlines and the lack of application action.

College-bound kids need to develop their own initiative and independence if they want to get in and be successful at college. In spite of some teenagers' behavior that might give parents pause, if they're mature enough to go to college, they're mature enough to take responsibility for the process of getting there.

I know it's not easy, but stepping back and letting them make the choice sets the right tone.

Manage stress

Letting go is also a good way to manage the stress of the process, especially when tied to the potential outcomes.

You can't make Yale say, "Yes," no matter how badly you or your student may want it. That outcome is not in your control.

College admissions disappointment can be minimized by making good decisions. But it can't be avoided through parental influence anymore than you'll get to control job advancement, friendships or romance in your kids' adult lives.

It is not your job to protect your kids from the disappointment of college rejection. In fact, rejection can be a good learning experience for kids. Occasional disappointment is part of life. Successful people learn from it and move on. This is the time for kids to start learning that skill.

When he was 30, Steve Jobs got fired by Apple. He went on to start two new companies, met and married his wife, and later returned to resurrect Apple. "I'm pretty sure none of this would have happened if I hadn't been fired from Apple," he said at a 2005 Stanford commencement address. "It was awful-tasting medicine, but I guess the patient needed it. Sometimes life hits you in the head with a brick. Don't lose faith."[6]

Part of a parent's successful adjustment to life after a child leaves for college is letting go of that need to influence every area of their lives. The more you try to control the college admissions outcomes, the more likely you are to experience stress, frustration and even alienation from your kids who may feel you don't trust them to do it themselves.

Instead, cheer them on. Offer a supportive ear and occasional parental guidance when they need it. Accept that like most of life's transitions, you can't control the outcome for your kids.

Let kids take ownership

We decided it was time for our son to take some control of his life and start figuring things out for himself. We felt that successfully attending college had to be something he wanted to do and not something that we wanted him to do. Our instincts were right. He took a real interest in researching colleges and the application process. He knew the deadlines well and finished his essays so early that he became a resource to many of his friends. When he had questions, we gave factual answers and were careful not to give strong opinions that would influence him. He was accepted to many colleges and felt so proud of himself. After visiting several schools, he decided to attend Arizona State University where he was awarded a $10,500 yearly academic scholarship and was selected to participate in the business school Leadership Academy. He feels "grown up" and so excited for the future. Our advice to parents is to give kids the freedom to plan and decide their college future. You will always be looking over their shoulders checking on them, but let them feel like it's their plan, not yours. Let them take ownership—you may be pleasantly surprised.

Dave C.
Father of Kevin, former Collegewise student, Class of 2012
Arizona State University

HELP WITH BALANCE

It's possible to be too focused on getting into college.

A student once told me, "I never do anything without thinking about how it's going to look on my resume."

Used to making straight A's in high school, when she earned her first B+, she and her parents waged a year-long campaign to get the grade changed. (They weren't successful.)

She was a competitive equestrian rider who wanted constant reassurance the activity would help her get into a selective college.

She spent nearly 100 hours (and her parents spent thousands of dollars) preparing for the SAT in hope of matching the scores of kids admitted to Ivy League schools. She also worried that her high school's lack of a numerical ranking system for students would hurt her chances of admission to a prestigious college. So she transferred.

It didn't work. She was rejected from all of her reach schools (12 total), and half-heartedly went to Vassar after she was taken off the wait-list.

My student wasn't made so obsessive by overbearing parents. She had a severe case of namebranditis that proved contagious within her family.

It's a cautionary tale.

I always encourage kids to care about their college futures. But if that focus leads them to make every decision in high school based on how it will look to colleges, they're trying to game the system rather than follow their own interests. That never works in college admissions.

Beyond admissions impact

A student can love playing the trumpet even if he's not good enough at it to play in a college marching band.

A student can take a cooking class over the summer with no regard for whether or not colleges will appreciate it.

A student can be happy with her part-time job at the mall even if it's not as impressive sounding as an internship at a law firm.

Students can also get adequate sleep, read books about baseball, hang out with friends and enjoy general teenage goofing off. Not everything a student does in high school needs to be measured by its potential impact in college admissions.

It's no accident so many college applications ask students to talk about their favorite subjects or teachers, the activity that's meant the most to them, what they do for fun and what part of college they're most excited about.

Kids who've approached high school with a single-minded devotion to pleasing colleges never have answers to those questions like the kids who've led balanced lives do.

Learned skill

Fulfilled adults have learned how to balance a devotion to their work with their enjoyment of family, friends, hobbies and things that will never earn them a raise.

Kids need to do that, too.

Don't tie everything kids do to college admission. Help them separate and find a balance between college planning and the other parts of their lives. They'll be happier, more successful college applicants if you do.

RUN WITH THE RIGHT CROWD

Some parents approach college admissions like it's some sort of battle to be won.

They're intent on turning the entire process into a status competition with other parents.

They talk about how many hours of community service their kid has done, how expensive the SAT tutor is that they're housing in the guest room this summer or how they plan to use their connections to wangle an advantage at Yale.

They ruin the ride to college for their peers and, sadly, don't ever seem to find any joy in watching their kids make this transition.

These are not the parents you want at your next dinner party.

As you no doubt tell your kids, the fact that other people are doing something is never a good reason to do it yourself. Still, I've seen too many parents buckle to peer pressure.

When other parents want to turn their kids' college process into some sort of bizarre academic arms race, don't join in. Walk away. Talk about something else. Associate with other parents who care more that their kids end up happy in college than they do about whether or not those schools are Ivy League schools. Parents who share that belief are more fun to be around at dinner parties anyway.

While you're at it, let your kids know you're not keeping score, and they shouldn't either. You're not comparing them to other kids or to their siblings. This is about them, not about anybody else.

PARENT TO PARENT

Learn which parents to avoid

You learn early on which parents to avoid. Back in 8th and 9th grade, some parents were already talking about GPAs, extracurricular activities and "key" colleges. It's easy to see which parents are working on building their kids' resumes for the college application. These were often the overscheduled kids in elementary school. By early high school, the focus shifts to "leadership" opportunities, even more sports, band, music or theatre, an Eagle Scout award perhaps, oodles of service hours and the list goes on. I never understood why all these different kids would want to go to the same 10 to15 schools; so if I heard from parents about the "key" schools and what they were looking for, I tended to discount what the parent was saying because I didn't think their opinion was one that I would learn from.

Tanya B.
Parent of Ryan J., former Collegewise student, Class of 2012
Northeastern University

IGNORE BAD ADVICE

When I get an "I heard..." question at seminars, it's usually followed by something ranging from partially inaccurate to absolutely ridiculous. The source of the story is never a high school counselor or a college admissions officer. The person always heard it from a neighbor, a fellow parent or somebody else who isn't a college admissions expert of any kind.

This is why college admissions seem so complicated for so many kids and parents. You hear so much conflicting information that it seems impossible you could ever make all the right decisions.

The subject of college admissions is one for which people with wildly varying experiences liberally give—and accept—unsolicited advice. It's up to you to ignore people who don't know what they're talking about.

I'm not saying college admissions is as complicated as building satellites. But your student's education is important enough to not just listen to anybody who offers advice. There's a reason you don't ask your doctor to do your taxes or your accountant to diagnose your knee pain. Go to the right sources.

Your child's high school counselor, colleges' websites, college guidebooks, admissions officers, representatives at college fairs and students who attend the schools are good sources. Shameless self-promotion: so are well-recommended private counselors—but not before you exhaust the other resources.

FIND THE FUN

The worst part of the frenzy surrounding college admissions is it can ruin what should be an exciting, positive experience for parents. At Collegewise, we encourage families to make it fun.

You can get caught up in the race and make the entire process about GPAs, test scores and whether or not one dream college will say, "Yes."

You can spend hours trying to fix your kid's perceived college admissions weaknesses. You can join other parents in a status competition and base the success or failure on the prestige of the college your student attends (or doesn't attend).

Or you can decide to enjoy this time together as a family.

Go watch every volleyball game.

Never miss an orchestra performance or dance recital. Cheer loudly from the literal and figurative sidelines of their activities.

Take way too many pictures before school dances.

Buy ice cream at the shop where your daughter works so you can see her scoop in person.

Celebrate just how many great colleges there are from which to choose. Ask embarrassing questions on college tours like, "Where is the parent dorm?"

Threaten to move in next door to your kid when she leaves for college.

Celebrate every offer of admission.

Buy the loudest, proudest sweatshirt you can find when she finally picks her school.

There are hundreds of colleges that accept almost everyone who applies, so nobody is forcing your hand to make the process more stressful than it needs to be. Like most milestones in your kids' lives, this time will pass quickly. You get to decide how to approach it.

Decide to enjoy it, and you probably will. It's up to you.

TREAT REJECTIONS LIKE HIGH SCHOOL BREAKUPS

If your daughter came home in tears and told you her boyfriend broke up with her, would you think she was now going to be alone forever? Would you strategize about what she could change to win him back?

I doubt it. You'd tell her how wonderful she is, and the boy who rejected her is a dope who obviously doesn't understand what he's missing. You'd remind her that another boy—the right boy—will see the same great qualities that you do.

That's exactly what to do if a college says, "No."

Some parents react to college rejections by second-guessing the approach their kids took, wondering what would have happened if the test scores had been higher or if the essay topic had been different.

They want to appeal the rejection and claim that other students who were admitted were less qualified.

I understand disappointment. But I believe wallowing in the rejection is akin to refusing to move on after a breakup. It will only make kids feel worse and delay their opportunity to find a better match.

They blew it

If a college rejection arrives, the best thing you can do as a parent is to tell your student you think the offending college blew it, and there are plenty of other collegiate fish in the sea. Then encourage your student to move on to one of the colleges who had the foresight to offer her a spot.

It's your job as a parent to model the right behavior in the face of disappointment. It may feel devastating, but anyone who's suffered legitimate hardship would tell you that Princeton saying "No" is not a tragedy. Lots of kids are denied admission to their first-choice schools. None of the ones I know still hurt when they make friends in a dorm someplace else.

Some names you may recognize of people rejected by their first-choice colleges:

- Warren Buffett
- Meredith Vieira
- Ted Turner
- Steven Spielberg
- Tom Brokaw

They turned out OK. Your student will, too.

Temporary disappointment is normal, but like a breakup, the faster you can move on, the better.

BUY THE SWEATSHIRT

I'm a proponent of the magical powers of a college sweatshirt worn by mom or dad.

If the sweatshirt actually has the word "mom" or "dad" on it (like, "NYU Mom"), that's even better. When your student decides where she's going to college, your first order of business should be to get yourself a sweatshirt.

A parent who's proudly decked out in her kid's new school colors vividly tells the world just how proud she is of her soon-to-be-college freshman. Your kids might feign embarrassment when you wear it in public. That's fine. Deep down, they'll be beaming, too.

Managing the cost

One family who put four kids through Collegewise came up with a great system for managing the cost of the sweatshirts. After the acceptances were all in, they would decide with their student which four or five schools to visit before making the final decision. At each of those schools, they'd buy her a T-shirt bearing the school's name. Once she made her final decision, they'd buy the more expensive sweatshirts for the entire family.

Magnified power

The sweatshirt's power is magnified when a student might still be smarting over the rejection from another college. I always tell kids that the healing power of signing your name to a college that said "Yes" is the best way to get over a rejection from a dream school. When you add a sweatshirt to the mix, your student won't be thinking about that rejection anymore.

Buying and wearing college paraphernalia shows your kids you're happy for them and that your pride was never tied to an offer from one specific college.

The more excited you are about their college, the happier they'll be in their new setting, too.

ENDEARING: TEN SECRETS OF "GREAT KIDS"

Charisma isn't everything. It actually makes a difference to have substance. And those quiet people can be incredibly easy to miss in college admissions, but they can be brilliant and wear incredibly well over the long haul.[1]

William Fitzsimmons
Dean of Admissions
Harvard University

CULTIVATE GREATNESS

"He's a great kid."

That's just about the best thing you can have a parent, teacher, counselor, coach, boss or admissions officer say about you.

When people call you a great kid, they're almost never referring to your SAT scores. Being a great kid has more to do with your character—how you treat other people, the impression you make and your maturity, etc. Being a great kid can make all the difference when you're trying to get into college.

The more personal a college makes its admissions process, the more important it is for applicants to be likeable, especially if it's a competitive school. If the straight-A student with high test scores comes off as arrogant, if his letters of recommendation don't mention anything about how much his teachers actually enjoyed having him in class, if he writes an essay that makes weak excuses for the B he got his sophomore year, he just doesn't sound likeable.

Likeable students tend to stay likeable once they get to college.

I see the importance of likeability play out every year at Collegewise. When a student repeatedly shows up late to our meetings and never apologizes, or seems to think he's smarter than all of his classmates and isn't afraid to declare so, or makes fun of awkward kids, we know our office isn't the only place he's doing those things. Those students are never as successful in the admissions process as the great kids are.

In this chapter, I'll share 10 traits great kids seem to exhibit. I would never suggest you change who you are to try to get into college. But these are life skills that will serve you long after you leave high school.

Many people, myself included, took a lot longer than 12 grades of school to learn some of these. Consider my sharing them with you now your opportunity to get a head start.

MEET PEOPLE WELL

People make judgments about you within the first few seconds of meeting you. We all do it. It's just human nature. So why not give yourself an advantage and start strong?

Meeting people well and making a good first impression is one of the more important skills you can have. It sets a tone. For example, when a family visits Collegewise for the first time, we can't help but make judgments about their kid based on how well he meets us. If he steps forward, looks us in the eye and smiles, shakes our hand and says, "Hi, I'm <insert name>—nice to meet you," we get the impression the kid has his act together.

On the other hand, if he shuffles forward meekly, looks at the ground and offers us a handshake that resembles a lifeless salmon, he might as well have told us, "I have the personality of a lifeless salmon."

Smile

When you meet someone, smile. Look the person in the eye when you introduce yourself. Offer a firm (not crushing) handshake. It's easy to do, and you'll be pleasantly surprised how positive the impression you make for yourself can be in just three seconds before you've even started a conversation.

Whether you're meeting a fellow student, the new tennis coach, the boss at the store where you want a part-time job or the Duke representative who's visiting your school, if you meet them well, you get to build on a great first impression rather than having to rebuild from a bad one.

WRITE GOOD EMAILS

Today's college applicant is likely to communicate over email as often, if not more so, than face-to-face. Just as people size you up when you talk face-to-face, the person on the receiving end of your email is going to make judgments about you based on what you write and how you write it. Here's a checklist to review before you email anything to an admissions officer, teacher, counselor or anyone else with whom you want to make a good impression.

1. **Make the subject line something descriptive.**
   "Question" isn't descriptive. "Question about how to get involved at your center" is.

2. **Address the person by name at the beginning. Looks like: "Hi, Ms. Harrington:"**
   Imagine if someone walked up to you and just started asking you a question without even first saying, "Hi." Wouldn't it be rude (and a little weird)?

3. **If the person doesn't know you or may not remember you, identify yourself in the first paragraph.**
   "I met you last weekend at your son's baseball game (my brother David is on the same team). You mentioned that you might need some summer help at your office and asked me to email you."

4. **Keep your email to one screen.**
   Don't write something so long they have to scroll through it.

5. **Observe the laws of punctuation, capitalization and good grammar.**
   Nobody ever looked stupid for sending a properly capitalized and punctuated email, but they have looked that way for ignoring the rules. This is not a text message.

6. **Don't ever type in all caps.**
   When you write "PLEASE RESPOND TO ME ASAP," it reads like you're yelling at the person (or hopped up on espresso).

7. **Be careful with exclamation points for the same reason.**
   "I really hope you can write my letter!" sounds like you're yelling.

8. **It's OK to write like you talk as long as you're respectful.**
   "The purpose of my email is to request your assistance with my college applications" is too formal.

   "I'm writing to ask you if you might be able to help me with my college applications" gets the job done.

9. **Use a normal font.**
   Think black type and normal size. No bright colors, cursive, blinking lights or animated creatures of any kind.

10. **If you're asking for something, say "please."**

11. **At the end, always say, "thank you."**

12. **Proofread carefully.**

13. **Type your full name at the end of the message.**
    If you need a reply back, leave a phone number, too, so the person has the option of calling.

14. **Use cc sparingly.**
    Especially if the person you email doesn't know the people you cc. Imagine if you walked into this person's office and didn't introduce the two people you brought in tow.

15. **Are you angry?**
    Be careful sending an email to someone who's made you angry. "You can always tell a guy to go to hell tomorrow," said Warren Buffet, CEO of Berkshire Hathaway and one of the richest people in the world. "You don't give up that opportunity."

    Once you put your anger out there, it's there. You can't take it back. So write it, but don't send it. Come back tomorrow and read it again. If you're still comfortable with what the email says, then send it.

REMEMBER PEOPLES' NAMES THE FIRST TIME

Here's a quick way to make anybody you meet like and respect you more: remember their names after you meet them the first time.

When you meet someone new and you remember his or her name, they notice.

When you use their name during your first conversation ("How long have you played in the marching band, Kevin?") and you remember it the next time you see them, it's like giving them a compliment. It shows you pay attention and care enough to remember their name. You're demonstrating your willingness to make the effort.

When you interview for a part-time job and you say to the boss at the end of the interview, "Thanks so much for your time, Mr. Dillinger," you show your potential boss you pay attention to details.

When you meet the new kid at school and introduce him to your friends, "Hey guys, this is Jason," you'll see the wave of relief wash over the new kid's face now that people actually know who he is.

When you're introduced to a group of two or three people at a time, see if you can remember—and use—all of their names. It's not a coincidence that the few people who actually make the effort to do this are always the ones with the most friends.

Popular excuse

A lot of people say, "I'm really bad with names." But that's just an excuse for not actually trying to remember. Dale Carnegie, late author of the best-selling "How to Win Friends and Influence People," compares remembering names to any other skill (e.g., learning to ski). Your progress depends on how important it is to you to do it.

Three of Carnegie's tips for remembering names:

1. **Focus on the name when you're introduced, and ask the person to repeat it if you don't hear it clearly.**

2. **When you are introduced to a person, repeat the name immediately.**
    Don't just say, "I'm Kevin," in return. Say, "Hi Tony, I'm Kevin."

3. **Use the person's name during your conversation together.**[2]
    So make the effort. Practice it. And if you forget a name, it's OK. Just own up to it and say, "I'm really sorry, but I don't remember your name. Can you remind me?"

That's a lot better than trying to fake it every time you run into the person again.

LEARN FROM FAILURE AND MOVE ON

Most successful students—and adults—have experienced failure. If you put yourself out there enough times to go after things that aren't easy to achieve, you're going to fail every now and then. There's no shame in it, especially if it's a good failure.

If you try out for the varsity volleyball team and get cut, it's not fun. But that doesn't mean it's a bad failure. Maybe you use that free time to do something else you're excited about? Maybe you use getting cut as motivation to come back even stronger next year? Maybe you find a way to be a part of the team anyway by being the team manager, taking photos of the games or running the fundraiser? Any of those scenarios turns that failure into something good.

One of our most successful applicants at Collegewise wrote her essay about how she had lost every election she had ever run in…badly. But she used each of those opportunities to find activities that were even better suited to her. She ended up at Notre Dame.

Sure, not all failures are good. If you blow off studying for your biology midterm and get an F, that's a bad failure. But if you try your best, things don't work out and you take something productive from it, that's a good failure. Don't be ashamed about it.

Here are a few steps to help you turn a failure into a something positive in the long run.

1. **Accept your failure gracefully.**
Don't blame anyone else or get too down on yourself.

2. **Think about what you've learned from the experience.**
Is there something you could have done better or differently, or did this failure point out that your talents might be better put to use elsewhere?

If you're not sure, ask for advice from someone who observed your attempt.

3. **Decide a next step.**
Is there another way to stay involved or contribute? Are you going to improve and come back strong for another try? Are you going to try something else you might be better suited for? Wallowing won't turn this experience into something valuable. Learn as much as you can, and then decide on your next step.

It takes a mature, confident person to admit defeat and to move on positively.
Nobody, including colleges, expects you to be perfect. In fact, most people will be impressed by good failures.

Learn from failure

I've spent enough time in high schools to know teenagers will never be perfect. They do silly things, mess up, fall down and lack confidence. The ability to bounce back is a fundamental life skill students have to learn on their own. The lessons of failure can't be taught in a classroom; they are experienced and reflected upon.[3]

Angel B. Perez
Dean of Admissions
Pitzer College

ACCEPT RESPONSIBILITY

Some people have an excuse for everything. Nothing is ever their fault.

In high school, it's the kid who says he got a C in history because the teacher didn't like him, not because he just didn't study as much as he should have. It's the football player who says he isn't a starter because "it's all political," not because the kid who got the starting nod works harder.

Sure, there are times when something happens to you that really is not your fault. Other times, you're just making excuses. If you're not sure which one it is, use the $1 million scenario.

When we have a student who repeatedly misses or arrives late to meetings but always seems to have an excuse (e.g., "traffic," "too busy" or "I forgot"), we ask, "What would you do if you knew you'd win $1 million if you arrived at your next meeting on time?"

The student inevitably says something like, "I'd leave earlier to beat traffic," or "I'd write it down so I wouldn't forget."

The $1 million scenario exposes when you're making excuses for things that you really could do if you wanted to.

That shouldn't push you to do things that will make you unhappy. If there were $1 million riding on you getting a 4.0 this semester, but in order to do it, you'd have quit the jazz band you love and sleep three hours a night, that's not improving your life. But when you eliminate excuses, you take responsibility for what you do and don't do. You get out of your own way.

Recommend yourself

Westmont College in California once asked applicants to write a letter of recommendation for themselves. It was a big reach school for my student who started his letter, "There is no doubt about it, Joey is an underachiever. He didn't have a learning disability. He didn't have a problem at home. He didn't have bad teachers who didn't care about him. He just didn't work as hard as he should have in high school. But there is more to Joey than his 2.65 GPA..."

He was admitted.

Excuses rarely make someone like and trust you more. Excuses don't work on colleges, either. Make fewer excuses. Take more responsibility.

LEARN TO APOLOGIZE WELL

Sometimes we do things that hurt or inconvenience other people, even if we don't mean to do it. When that happens, forgiveness comes a lot faster if you apologize like you mean it.

A half-hearted "Sorry about that" is not a good apology. That's like an airline telling delayed passengers, "We regret any inconvenience this may have caused."

Does anyone ever feel a lot better after a company says that?

A real apology is sincere. There's emotion to it, which conveys you actually feel bad.

If you break curfew and your parents waited up until 2 a.m. wondering where you were, give them a good apology. "Mom, I'm really sorry I made you worry last night. If I had to wait up until 2 a.m. worrying if you were OK, I'd be really upset. I should have called you."

If you goof off in class and your teacher has to discipline you, stop by after class and offer up a good apology. "Mr. Cunningham, I'm really sorry I was talking so much in class today. I know it's not easy to teach trig to a room full of 40 kids. I won't do it again."

Even if something wasn't your fault, you can still give a good apology. If you're supposed to meet a friend to study and your softball practice runs too late, just apologize well. "I'm so sorry I never showed up for our meeting. My practice ran late and my coach wouldn't let me get to my phone to call you. I can't believe I left you waiting for 45 minutes."

I learned the hard way

When I was in college, I applied for a job to run the summer orientation program. When I didn't get the job, I wrote the boss a letter outlining all the reasons I thought she'd made a big mistake. She hadn't made a mistake. She hired good people and I was just taking my disappointment out on her. It was a stupid thing to do and I regretted it immediately after I sent it.

So I made an appointment to meet with her, and I told her how embarrassed and sorry I was. When I reapplied the following year, she hired me.

Fourteen years later, she invited me to come back to campus and give the welcome address to new freshmen. The year after that, she enrolled her son with me at Collegewise, and she and I are good friends today.
None of those things would have happened if I hadn't apologized to her.

None of us can go through life without occasionally doing things we have to apologize for. When it happens, apologizing well can actually improve your relationship with the person you let down. It shows that you care about how you treat people. Anybody can do it.

LAUGH AT YOURSELF REGULARLY

Successful people always have some missteps along the way. The most likeable of them aren't afraid to talk about those times. They share those stories openly and even laugh at themselves when something embarrassing happens. They know that's a much healthier approach than wallowing in embarrassment and hiding from those opportunities in the future.

Let's say you decide to run for student body president and your speech doesn't go well. You lost your place a few times. The joke you thought was supposed to be funny didn't go over well at all. And you ended up suffering what you're sure was the most lopsided loss in school history.

You have two options.

1. You could be morbidly embarrassed, resolving never to put yourself in that situation again, and replaying the loss over and over again in your mind and getting mad at your friends if they ever mention it.

2. Or you could laugh at yourself.

You could joke that it's hard to lose your place twice when the speech is only three paragraphs long.

You could sarcastically tell your friends that you won't be able to hang out with them as much because prominent politicians are asking you to run their campaigns. You could tell your hockey teammates you have great news—due to your absolutely terrible showing in the election, you'll have even more time to work on your slap shot next year.

Picking Option 2 lets you get over the loss faster. It lets you recognize you tried your best and be proud that you at least took the risk to run for something only two other people at your school had the guts to run for. And it will almost certainly make people like you even more.

Psychology study

Ursula Beermann of UC Berkeley and Willibald Ruch of the University of Zurich studied 70 psychology students to test their ability to laugh at themselves. The findings showed that the ability to laugh at yourself linked with having an upbeat personality and good mood, and may be the foundation for a good sense of humor.[4]

One of my Collegewise students worked over the summer as an ocean lifeguard in Laguna Beach, Calif. He wrote his college essay about his first day on the job, a hot Saturday when the beach was packed to capacity.

A group of swimmers had gotten caught in a riptide and were yelling for help. As he climbed down from his lifeguard tower, he tripped and fell eight feet, face first into the sand. He was still spitting sand out and regaining his bearings when he finally got to the water.

My student still laughed about it when he told me the story six months later. He even wrote one of his college essays about the face plant and titled it, "Save yourselves!" He got into almost every college he applied to.

When you can laugh about a failure, a weakness or something that was outright embarrassing, it's endearing. It shows confidence and how comfortable you are just being yourself. People love hanging out with others who are like that. Colleges love those people in their classes and dorms.

GIVE OFF POSITIVITY

"Be positive" can be hard advice to follow. Some people are just naturally a lot cheerier than others. You can't be expected to radically change your personality if it's not your style to skip down the hallways at school every day.

But anybody can make a choice to *give out* positivity—to be complimentary, thankful and congratulatory.

If you really enjoyed a class, tell your teacher. If your teacher stayed after school to help you, tell her how much you appreciated it and how much good it did you. If your teacher helped you with your college essay, read over a rough draft and gave you good feedback or offered you any good advice that really helped you, thank her.

If you got a low grade on a test and your parents were understanding and supportive, tell them how much it helped you to know they were in your corner. If your parents helped you through a situation where you needed guidance, thank them and let them know how much you benefitted from their advice. If they cheered you on when you had a big success, tell them how much their praise meant to you.

Congratulate the members of the cross country team when they win the league championship, the cast of the school play when they close out their final performance or the writer on the school newspaper who wrote a particularly good article you appreciated.

If one of your friends was there for you in a time of need the way we all need a good friend to be every now and then, let your friend know the support didn't go unappreciated.

Be sincere

I'm not saying you should lavish thanks and praise on everyone for no good reason. It doesn't mean anything if you aren't sincere.

Heartfelt positivity is free to you and so ridiculously easy to give if you're conscious about it. It will make you feel good about your relationships with people in your life. And it will go a long way toward making people want to be there for you again in the future.

RISE ABOVE THE DRAMA

Some parts of high school are wonderful. Other parts, not so much—like the popularity contests, social backstabbing and insecurities. It's rough out there. But you actually get to choose whether or not to engage in it.

My advice: the more you avoid it, the more it will avoid you.

Try not to worry too much about all the drama that goes on in high school. Just be yourself. Be confident. Don't worry about what other people think. Reject the idea of popular versus unpopular. Be proud of who you are and what you stand for. Do what you want to do rather than what other students say you should.

It's never a good idea to invest too much emotional energy into something that just doesn't matter. You know all the drama about who's popular and who's not, who gets invited to the right party and who gets left home, who looks right or wrong, and all the other bad drama that's so rampant in high school? Nobody will care about any of it once you get to college. In fact, pretty much everyone looks back on it and realizes just how silly all of it was.

Have you ever heard your parents make fun of someone based on what that person did or wore back in high school? Probably not. People grow out of it.

When you go to your 10-year high school reunion, the roles you used to play will be ancient history. The former popular kids and the former social outcasts will all be part of the same club— adults trying to make it in the world.

Until then, just try to stay out of the drama as much as you can.

NICE IS UNDERRATED

The word "nice" has such an undeservedly bland connotation in high school. Referring to someone as "nice" is like saying, "Well, he's not *awful.*"

It's too bad, because nice is just about one of the best things you can be.

Everybody likes the kid who's genuinely nice. Nice kids are good to their friends and family. They don't make fun of other people or hesitate to say "Hi" to the socially less fortunate. They're easy to trust and hard to criticize. There will probably never be a time in your life after high school when just being nice will make such a difference for people around you. And it's something you can do every day.

Tell people at the junior prom that they look great.

Say "Hi" to your English teacher in the hallway.

Congratulate the kid who beat you in the election.

And for that one poor soul who's the easy target, the one who always gets laughed at and maybe even bullied, pull him aside or send him an email saying, "Those kids are as*holes. I'm so sorry about what they're doing. Keep your chin up."

Extra help

Nice kids get extra help from teachers and counselors when they ask for it.

They get more glowing letters of recommendation from teachers and counselors and make better impressions on college interviewers. Nice kids are more likely to have people in their corners, ready to work and lobby and fight on their behalf. They've earned those benefits by just being good to other people.

When he could tell that the new exchange student from France was having a hard time fitting in at school, my Collegewise student, David, went out of his way to introduce the new student to people and make him feel welcome, going as far as to set him up with a date for the spring formal. David's English teacher mentioned his efforts in her letter of recommendation as an example of the kind of great kid that David was.

He went on to attend one of his reach schools, Santa Clara University.

Being nice is free and easy. And it gives you a chance to impact a lot of people without really having to do much. And even though there's no place to list "I'm a nice kid" on a college application, I have noticed that all the nice kids I've worked with always seem to end up with plenty of college options.

PARTING WORDS

College has been the most amazing experience of my life so far. I joined a sorority, started writing for the school newspaper and even spent this last year studying abroad in London and Athens. I really feel like I have grown up in college, but the responsibility isn't something that weighs me down; it's what I love about it. I couldn't wait to get out of high school, but I never want college to end!

Katie S.
Former Collegewise student, class of 2006
Pepperdine University

FIND COLLEGE MEMORIES

Congratulations—you're done with this book. I hope you're excited to find the right colleges and have a little fun while you're at it.

Your college process deserves to be taken seriously, but the families who enjoy this time the most care less about the name of the college and more about the experiences their kids will have once they get there.

There are plenty of great colleges out there. The challenge is finding and eventually deciding on the schools that fit. You now have all the knowledge you need to find, apply, get in and pay for those schools that fit you. I now invite you to put those lessons to work, so you can start enjoying a defining four years in college.

In college, you'll take classes you actually want to take. You'll learn from professors who have dedicated their professional lives to one particular subject and are willing to share their knowledge with you. Every single day of your college career, you'll learn something—maybe from a professor, maybe from a friend or maybe from a meaningful experience. That means every morning you wake up, you'll be a little bit smarter than you were the day before.

You'll go to good parties.

You'll date—a lot.

You'll meet more new people and make more friends than you've ever made before. Some of those friends will be in your life forever. Some will stand at your wedding one day. Some will one day tell your kids how you both pulled an all-nighter together in your dorm studying for your chemistry final.

College memories have a long shelf life.

Your college memories

There likely will be an experience in college—one you may not recognize when it happens—that you'll look back on when you're 40 and realize how important it was. It might be the class that makes you realize just how much you love literature.

It might be the professor who takes the time to tell you she sees great potential in your work.

It might be an internship, time you spend abroad or the day you meet the person you'll eventually marry.

Whatever it is, your defining memory is out there waiting for you at your future college.

Now, you have to go make it.

Defining memories aren't limited to the schools atop the *US News & World Report* rankings. They can be found at more than 2,000 four-year colleges out there. You're most likely to find your memories at the right college, the place where all your college soul searching, the college visits, your counselor and just plain gut instinct told you to go.

The right college is the one that fits you.

That concept, summarized in nine words, led me into this business. It's why I wrote this book, and why I spend so much time trying to convince students (and their parents) to stop worrying about getting into what they think are the best colleges and start working on finding the right ones.

The right school is out there waiting for you. Go find it.

Best of luck with your college admissions journey.

Relax. It will be OK. You're going to enjoy it.

How's it going?

Thank you for reading my book. I hope it inspires you to take control of your college planning, find the colleges that are right for you and have some fun while you're at it. If so, drop me a line at iftheufits@collegewise.com and let me know how it's going. I hope to hear from you.

WANT MORE?

If you'd like more help finding, applying and getting accepted to the right colleges for you, here's where to find more information about Collegewise.

Collegewise
www.collegewise.com

College counseling
www.collegewise.com/services
Collegewise counselors work with students in person and online.

Online store
www.collegewise.com/store
The online store has guides, videos and other college planning resources.

If the U Fits site
www.iftheufits.com
The official book site

Wise Like Us
www.wiselikeus.com
Company blog written by Kevin McMullin.

Subscribe to the Collegewise newsletter
www.collegewise.com/subscribe

Email
iftheufts@collegewise.com

ACKNOWLEDGEMENTS

Adam Kleiner, my college buddy, fellow English major and the intrepid editor of this book, you helped transform my first draft of ramblings into something we think people will want to read, all while balancing your day job and a new baby in the house. We used to talk back in college about how we both wanted to be writers someday. You got there first, then helped me follow suit. Thank you.

Mom and Pop, who exemplified the "Parent" section of this book back when I was applying to college, thank you for all your support and for believing in me even when I announced I was quitting my steady job to start Collegewise.

Rosie Bancroft, thank you for encouraging me and for waiting so patiently to get a peek at the book. Everyone should be so lucky to live life with such a supportive partner.

Thank you to the current and former Collegewise counselors for helping so many students find their perfect college fits, and to Allison Cummings for watching over our office while I huddled in front of my keyboard writing this book.

Arun Ponnusamy, Paul and Abby Kanarek, thank you for all your support and cheerleading. I write best alone, but I work best with good friends and partners.

Katie Konrad Moore, Collegewise counselor and proud college nerd, thank you for finding so many willing students and parents to share their stories here.

And to the Collegewise students and parents who trusted us, let us ride shotgun on their rides to colleges and allowed their stories to be shared here, thank you. Keep wearing those sweatshirts proudly.

ABOUT THE AUTHOR

Kevin McMullin is the President of Collegewise, a college admissions counseling company that he founded in 1999 using his last paycheck from his previous job. Today, with offices in Southern California, New York, New Jersey and Washington State, Collegewise has helped over 5,000 students find, apply to and attend the right colleges. Kevin is also a popular public speaker and has given over 500 presentations at high schools and conferences to discuss smarter, saner college admissions planning. As long as the speeches don't require him to do any math problems, he always does a bang-up job. Kevin is a graduate of UC Irvine with majors in English and history and earned his college admissions counseling certification from UCLA. He also writes a daily college admissions blog at www.wiselikeus.com.

APPENDIX I: ENDNOTES

Basic Retraining: How to Approach the College Admissions Process

[1] Parsishbeachpatrol, "Reality Check: I love you just the way you are," *Swarthmore College Admissions: The Blog*, September 28, 2007, *Swarthmore College*, parrishbeachpatrol.wordpress.com/2007/09/28/reality-check-i-love-you-just-the-way-you-are/

[2] Blake Ellis, "Harvard, Princeton post record low acceptance rates," *CNNMoney*, March 30, 2012, http://money.cnn.com/2012/03/30/pf/college/acceptance_rates_ivy_league/index.htm

[3] Melissa E. Clinedinst, Sarah F. Hurley, David A. Hawkins, "2011 State of College Admission," *National Association for College Admissions Counseling*, October 19, 2011.

[4] Caroline M. Hoxby, 2009. "The Changing Selectivity of American Colleges," *Journal of Economic Perspectives*, American Economic Association, vol. 23(4), pages 95-118, Fall.

[5] Hoxby, "The Changing Selectivity of American Colleges."

[6] "Myth: It's impossible for regular students to get in anymore," University of Wisconsin, Madison, accessed April 19, 2012, http://www.news.wisc.edu/admissions/myth6.html

[7] Jay Mathews, "10 Ways to Survive 11th Grade," *Washington Post*, April 11, 2006, http://www.washingtonpost.com/wp-dyn/content/article/2006/04/11/AR2006041100484.html

[8] Bureau of Labor Statistics, "College Enrollment and Work Activity of 2010 High School Graduates," *United States Department of Labor*, April 8, 2011, http://www.bls.gov/news.release/hsgec.nr0.htm

[9] Malcolm Gladwell, *Outliers: The Story of Success* (Little, Brown and Company, 2008), 48.

[10] "Seth Rogen," Internet Movie Database, accessed June 4, 2012, http://www.imdb.com/name/nm0736622/

[11] Mark Cuban, "Success and Motivation P4." *Blog Maverick: the Mark Cuban weblog*, May 25, 2004, http://blogmaverick.com/2004/05/25/success-and-motivation-p4/

[12] Andrew Flagel, "Will hyper-involvement help you get admitted (and would that be worth your time)?" *Not Your Average Admissions Blog: A Beneath the Surface Look At Everything College Admissions (with a few shameless plugs)* (blog), June 25, 2010, http://notjustadmissions.wordpress.com/2010/06/25/will-hyper-involvement-help-you-get-admitted-and-would-that-be-worth-your-time/

[13] "2012 College Hopes and Worries Survey," The Princeton Review, Accessed June 27, 2012, http://www.princetonreview.com/college-hopes-worries.aspx

[14] Tara Parker-Pope, "College's High Cost, Before You Even Apply," *The New York Times*, April 11, 2006, http://www.nytimes.com/2008/04/29/health/29well.html?_r=1&ref=health&oref=slogin

[15] Vivian Giang and Eric Goldschein, "Killing Elephants, Space Travel, Running Marathons: What 12 CEOs Do In Their Spare Time," *Business Insider*, February 23, 2012, http://www.businessinsider.com/here-are-12-crazy-activities-ceos-do-in-their-spare-time-mark-zuckerberg-bob-parsons-2012-2?op=1#ixzz1nKwVM0zG

[16] "Hidden Talents of Politicians," Zimbio, accessed June 26, 2012, http://www.zimbio.com/Hidden+Talents+of+Politicians

[17] Kaja Perina, "The Genius of Play," *Psychology Today*, January 0,1 2003, http://www.psychologytoday.com/articles/200301/the-genius-play

[18] Ben Jones, "There is no formula," *MIT Admissions* (blog), *MIT*, December 16, 2004, http://mitadmissions.org/blogs/entry/there_is_no_formula

[19] Parsishbeachpatrol, "Reading season: a brief explanation," *Swarthmore College Admissions: The Blog, Swarthmore College*, March 4, 2010, http://parrishbeachpatrol.wordpress.com/2010/03/04/reading-season-a-brief-explanation/

[20] "Fast Facts: Income of Young Adults," National Center for Education Statistics, Accessed June 26, 2012, http://nces.ed.gov/fastfacts/display.asp?id=77

Finding Fits: How to Find the Right Colleges for You

[1] Robert Samuelson, "Prestige Panic," *Newsweek,* August 2006, http://www.thedailybeast.com/newsweek/2006/08/21/prestige-panic.hml

[2] Peter Ewell, "No Correlation: Musings on Some Myths About Quality," *Change Magazine*, November 2008, http://www.changemag.org/Archives/Back%20Issues/November-December%202008/full-no-correlation.html

[3] Seth Godin, "*Do elite trappings create success? (Causation vs. correlation),*" *Seth Godin* (blog), December 20, 2010, http://sethgodin.typepad.com/seths_blog/2010/12/do-elite-trappings-create-causation.html

[4] "Undergraduate Colleges," Harvard Law School, accessed June 26, 2012, http://www.law.harvard.edu/prospective/jd/apply/undergrads.html

[5] "Fortune 500: Our annual ranking of America's largest corporations," CNNMoney, accessed June 26, 2012, http://money.cnn.com/magazines/fortune/fortune500/2012/full_list/

[6] Clinedinst, Hurley, and Hawkins, "2011 State of College Admission."

[7] "The 7 Most Common Schools For Google And Apple Employees," *Huffington Post,* March 29, 2012, http://www.huffingtonpost.com/2012/03/29/where-did-google-apple-college_n_1387567.html#s822713&title=Stanford_University

[8] Gayle B. Ronan, "College Freshmen Face Major Dilemma," *MSNBC*, November 29, 2005, http://www.msnbc.msn.com/id/10154383/ns/business-personal_finance/t/college-freshmen-face-major-dilemma/#T4I_8dmiYoM

[9] "Undecided Major," Marquette University, accessed June 26, 2012, http://www.marquette.edu/explore/major-undecided.shtml

[10] "National University Rankings Methodology," US News, accessed June 26, 2012, http://colleges.usnews.rankingsandreviews.com/best-colleges/rankings/national-universities

[11] Malcolm Gladwell, "What College Rankings Really Tell Us," *The New Yorker*, February 14, 2011, http://www.newyorker.com/reporting/2011/02/14/110214fa_fact_gladwell

[12] Justin Pike, "Love your list," *Inside Admissions: Behind the scenes with Tufts admissions officers* (blog), *Tufts University*, October 21, 2011, http://admissions.tufts.edu/blogs/inside-admissions/post/love-your-list/

Preparing: How Any Student Can Become a More Competitive College Applicant

[1] "Our selection process, Academic Preparation," Stanford University, accessed June 26, 2012, http://www.stanford.edu/dept/uga/basics/selection/prepare.html

[2] Clinedinst, Hurley, and Hawkins, "2011 State of College Admission."

[3] "Important Factors in Admission to JMU," James Madison University, accessed June 26, 2012, http://www.jmu.edu/admissions/process/freshman.shtml

[4] "Preparing for College," Vanderbilt University, accessed June 26, 2012, http://admissions.vanderbilt.edu/facts/preparing-for-college.php

[5] "Applying to Ole Miss/Freshmen," University of Mississippi, accessed May 5, 2012 http://www.olemiss.edu/admissions/fap.html

[6] Parrishbeachpatrol, "Making the Best of High School," *Swarthmore College Admissions: The* Blog, Swarthmore *College*, January 19, 2010, http://parrishbeachpatrol.wordpress.com/2010/01/19/making-the-best-of-high-school/

[7] Andrew Flagel, "A in Regular or B in Advanced Placement," *Not Your Average Admissions Blog: A Beneath the Surface Look At Everything College Admissions (with a few shameless plugs)* (blog), October 27, 2007, http://notjustadmissions.wordpress.com/2007/10/27/a-in-a-regular-or-b-in-advanced-placement/

[8] Kaiser Foundation, "Generation M2: Media in the Lives of 8- to 18-Year-Olds," 20 January 2010, http://www.kff.org/entmedia/entmedia012010nr.cfm

[9] Marcel Adam Just, Timothy A. Keller, Jacquelyn Cynkar, "A decrease in brain activation associated with driving when listening to someone speak," Center for Cognitive Brain Imaging, Department of Psychology, *Carnegie Mellon University*, February 19, 2008, http://www.distraction.gov/research/PDF-Files/carnegie-mellon.pdf

[10] Department of Transportation, *Driver Distraction in Commercial Vehicle Operations*, Federal Motor Safety Administration, September 2009, http://www.distraction.gov/research/PDF-Files/Driver-Distraction-Commercial-Vehicle-Operations.pdf

[11] Cal Newport, *"Anatomy of an A+: A Look Inside the Process of One of the World's Most Efficient Studiers," Study Hacks: decoding patterns of success*, May 18, 2011, http://calnewport.com/blog/2011/05/18/anatomy-of-an-a-a-look-inside-the-process-of-one-of-the-worlds-most-efficient-studiers/

[12] Jean Johnson, Jon Rochkind, Amber N. Ott and Samantha DuPont, "Can I Get a Little Advice Here? How an Overstretched High School Guidance System Is Undermining Students' College Aspirations," A Public Agenda Report for the Bill and Melinda Gates Foundation, *Public Agenda*, March 3, 2010, http://www.publicagenda.org/files/pdf/can-i-get-a-little-advice-here.pdf

[13] Clinedinst, Hurley, and Hawkins, "2011 State of College Admission," page 31.

[14] Ibid., page 31.

[15] "The Pleasure of Finding Things Out," BBC Television, last modified October 2008, http://www.bbc.co.uk/sn/tvradio/programmes/horizon/broadband/archive/feynman/index_textonly.shtml

[16] Tom Rath, *StrengthsFinder 2.0*, (New York: Gallup Press, February 2007).

[17] Shane Lopez, *The Encyclopedia of Positive Psychology*, (Wiley-Blackwell, August 2011).

[18] Rath, StrengthsFinder, page iii.

[19] Wendy Livingston, "Overheard in Committee: What Happens in Committee Doesn't Stay in Committee," *Admit It! True Confessions from W&M's Admission Officers* (blog), College of William and Mary, February 29, 2012, http://blogs.wm.edu/2012/02/29/overheard-in-committee-what-happens-in-committee-doesnt-stay-in-committee/

[20] Jose Antonio Vargas, "The Face of Facebook: Mark Zuckerberg opens up," *The New Yorker*, September 20, 2010, accessed June 26, 2012, http://www.newyorker.com/reporting/2010/09/20/100920fa_fact_vargas

[21] "Tips for Writing a Great Essay," University of Michigan, accessed May 3, 2012, http://www.admissions.umich.edu/essays/tips

[22] Valerie Strauss, "Question 3: Do colleges want well-rounded students or those with a passion?" *Washington Post*, November 3, 2009 http://voices.washingtonpost.com/answer-sheet/college-admissions/question-3-do-colleges-want-we.html

[23] Greg Roberts, "The Rumor Mill," *The UVA Admissions Blog: Notes from Peabody*, February 17, 2012, http://uvaapplication.blogspot.com/2012/02/rumor-mill.html

[24] Strauss, "Question 3."

[25] Strauss, "Question 3."

[26] Strauss, "Question 3."

[27] Strauss, "Question 3."

[28] "The Happy Wackiness of Zappos.com," ABC News, October 26, 2011, http://abcnews.go.com/blogs/business/2011/10/the-happy-wackiness-of-zappos-com/

[29] Strauss, "Question 3."

[30] Jessica Godofsky, M.P.P.; Cliff Zukin, Ph.D.; Carl Van Horn, Ph.D; "Unfulfilled Expectations: Recent College Graduates Struggle in a Troubled Economy," *Worktrends: American's Attitude about Work, Employers, and Government*, John J. Heldrich Center for Workforce Development, Rutgers University, May 2011, http://www.heldrich.rutgers.edu/sites/default/files/content/Work_Trends_May_2011.pdf

[31] Charles Fishman, "Face Time With Jeff Bezos," *Fast Company*, January 31, 2001, http://www.fastcompany.com/magazine/43/bezos.html

[32] "Q. and A.: College Admissions," *Questions/Answers, The New York Times* (blog), December 17, 2008, http://questions.blogs.nytimes.com/2008/12/17/qa-college-admissions/

Testing: Planning and Preparing for Standardized Tests

[1] Matt McGann, "What's the big deal about 40^2?" *MIT Admissions* (blog), *MIT*, November 20, 2004, http://mitadmissions.org/blogs/entry/whats_the_big_deal_about_402

[2] Drawn from multiple sources including:

Dan Fletcher, Brief History: Standardized Testing, *Time U.S.*, December 11, 2009, http://www.time.com/time/nation/article/0,8599,1947019,00.html

"Where Did the Test Come From? A Brief History of the SAT," Frontline: Secrets of the SAT, PBS, accessed April 27, 2012, http://www.pbs.org/wgbh/pages/frontline/shows/sats/where/history.html

Ida Lawrence, Gretchen W. Rigol, Thomas Van Essen, and Carol A. Jackson, "A Historical Perspective on the SAT 1926-2001," *The College Board*, 2002, http://professionals.collegeboard.com/profdownload/pdf/rr20027_11439.pdf

"Examined Life," Malcolm Gladwell, *gladwell.com*, December 17, 2001 http://www.gladwell.com/2001/2001_12_17_a_kaplan.htm

"History of the ACT," American College Testing, accessed April 16, 2012, http://www.act.org/aboutact/history.html

"History of the Tests," The College Board, accessed June 4, 2012, http://sat.collegeboard.org/about-tests/history-of-the-tests

John Cloud, "Should SATs Matter?" *Time U.S.*, March 4, 2001, http://www.time.com/time/nation/article/0,8599,101321,00.html

[3] "National Merit Scholarship Program," National Merit Scholarship Corporation, accessed June 24, 2012, http://www.nationalmerit.org/nmsp.php

[4] "Prepare for College Level Studies," The College Board, accessed June 26, 2012, http://professionals.collegeboard.com/k-12/prepare

[5] "Fee and Liability Policies," The College Board, accessed April 5, 2012, http://www.collegeboard.com/sss/help/feesandliability/basicuserfee/index.html

[6] Clinedinst, State of College Admission.

[7] Robert S. Clagett, "Middlebury Dean Says SAT or ACT Score Is 'Seldom a Deal Breaker,'" *The Choice, Demystifying College Admissions and Aid* (blog), *The New York Times*, October 15, 2010, http://thechoice.blogs.nytimes.com/2010/10/15/middlebury/

[8] "Test Optional," Lawrence University, accessed June 21, 2012, http://www.lawrence.edu/admissions/about/testoptional.shtml

[9] "Test Optional Frequently Asked Questions," Sewannee University, accessed May 28, 2012, http://admission.sewanee.edu/apply/test-optional-frequently-asked-questions/

[10] "10 Myths about the SAT," Fairtest: The National Center for Fair and Open Testing, August 20, 2007, http://fairtest.org/10-myths-about-sat

[11] "Issues in College Success: The Relative Predictive Validity of ACT Scores and High School Grades in Making College Admission Decisions," *ACT*, 2008, http://www.act.org/research/policymakers/pdf/PredictiveValidity.pdf

[12] "The ACT: Biased, Inaccurate, and Misused," Fairtest: The National Center for Fair and Open Testing, August 20, 2007, http://www.fairtest.org/facts/act.html

[13] "Interview: John Katzman," Frontline: Secrets of the SAT, PBS, accessed April 25, 2012, http://www.pbs.org/wgbh/pages/frontline/shows/sats/interviews/katzman.html

[14] Cloud, Should SATs Matter?

Applying: The Art of College Applications

[1] Angel B. Pérez, "Want to Get Into College? Learn to Fail," *Education Week*, February 1, 2012.

[2] Carolyn Pippen, "Behind the Scenes of the OUA," *Undergraduate Admissions Blog, Vanderbilt University*, February 17, 2012, http://admissions.vanderbilt.edu/vandybloggers/2012/02/behind-the-scenes-of-the-oua/

[3] Ben Jones, "It's More Than A Job," *MIT Admissions* (blog), *MIT*, March 17, 2006, http://mitadmissions.org/blogs/entry/its_more_than_a_job

[4] "Hot Chicken and Data Days," *Undergraduate Admissions Blog* (blog), *Vanderbilt University*, February 24, 2009, http://admissions.vanderbilt.edu/vandybloggers/2009/02/hot-chicken-and-data-days/

[5] Clinedinst, 2011 State of College Admission.

[6] Clinedinst, 2011 State of College Admission.

[7] "Applying to Duke: How to Apply: Regular and Early Decision," Duke University, accessed June 27, 2012, http://admissions.duke.edu/jump/applying/apply_RD-ED.html

[8] "Q. and A.: College Admissions," *Questions/Answers, The New York Times* (blog), December 17, 2008, http://questions.blogs.nytimes.com/2008/12/17/qa-college-admissions/

[9] Peter Schworm, "College applications can be too good: Admissions officers wary of slick essays," *Boston Globe*, February 12, 2008, http://www.boston.com/news/education/higher/articles/2008/02/12/college_applications_can_be_too_good/?page=full

[10] William Honan, "Personal Essay Questions: Turning Torture Into Fun," *The New York Times*, December 27, 1995, http://www.nytimes.com/1995/12/27/us/personal-essay-questions-turning-torture-into-fun.html?pagewanted=all&src=pm

[11] Parke Muth, "Writing the Essay: Sound Advice from an Expert," Office of Undergraduate Admission, University of Virginia, accessed June 27, 2012, http://www.virginia.edu/undergradadmission/writingtheessay.html

[12] Schworm, "College applications can be too good."

[13] Valerie Strauss, "Admissions Officials Tell What They Like (and Don't Like)," *The Daily Gazette*, May 5, 2002, http://news.google.com/newspapers?nid=1957&dat=20020505&id=Q-EqAAAAIBAJ&sjid=E4oFAAAAIBAJ&pg=4091,1288889

[14] Code of Medical Ethics of the American Medical Association, "Opinion 8.19 - Self-Treatment or Treatment of Immediate Family Members," June, 1993, http://www.ama-assn.org/ama/pub/physician-resources/medical-ethics/code-medical-ethics/opinion819.page

[15] Bryan G. Nance, "I've Got 99 Problems… Admissions Is Not One," *MIT Admissions* (blog), *MIT*, October 25, 2005, http://mitadmissions.org/blogs/entry/ive_got_99_problems_admissions

[16] Martha C. Merrill, "Note to Applicants: Admissions Officers Do Read What Your Teachers Say," *The Choice: Demystifying College Admissions and Aid* (blog), *The New York Times*, October 8, 2010, http://thechoice.blogs.nytimes.com/2010/10/08/teacher-rec/

[17] Evan Cudworth, "Phoenix Tip #2: Letters of Recommendation," The Uncommon Blog (blog), *University of Chicago,* September 6, 2011, https://blogs.uchicago.edu/collegeadmissions/2011/09/phoenix_tip_2_letters_of_recom.html

[18] Greg Roberts, "It's Time to Focus," *The UVA Admissions Blog: Notes from Peabody* (blog), *University of Virginia*, February 2, 2012, http://uvaapplication.blogspot.com/2012/02/its-time-to-focus.html

[19] Tamar Levin, "A Warning: Colleges Can Change Their Minds," *The Choice: Demystifying College Admissions and Aid* (blog), *The New York Times*, March 18, 2009, http://thechoice.blogs.nytimes.com/2009/05/18/a-warning-colleges-can-change-their-minds/

College Interviews: What to Expect When You're Face-to-Face

[1] Parishbeachpatrol, "The College Interview," *Swarthmore College Admissions: The Blog*, Swarthmore College, September 4, 2009, http://parrishbeachpatrol.wordpress.com/2009/09/04/the-college-interview/

[2] Clinedinst, 2011 State of College Admission.

[3] Dave Marcus, "Advice for the College Interview: Girls, Dress Discreetly; Boys, Mind Those Hands," *The Choice: Demystifying College Admissions and Aid* (blog), *The New York Times*, October 25, 2010, http://thechoice.blogs.nytimes.com/2010/10/25/october-interview/

[4] Steve Cohen, "Do College Interviews Really Count?" *Forbes*, October 10, 2011, http://www.forbes.com/sites/stevecohen/2011/10/10/do-college-interviews-really-count/

[5] "Arrange an Interview," Carleton College, accessed June 27, 2012, http://apps.carleton.edu/admissions/interview/

[6] "Interviews for Freshmen Applicants," Yale University, accessed June 27, 2012, http://admissions.yale.edu/interviews

[7] "Prospective Students Visiting Campus," Claremont McKenna College, accessed June 27, 2012, http://www.claremontmckenna.edu/admission/visit/

[8] John DeTore, "Thoughts On The MIT Interview," *MIT Admissions* (blog), *MIT*, October 19, 2006, http://mitadmissions.org/blogs/entry/thoughts_on_the_mit_interview

[9] Malcolm Gladwell, *What the Dog Saw*, (New York: Little, Brown and Company, 2009), 381-382.

[10] Jenni Laidman, "Making an Impression," *Toledo Blade,* June 25, 2001, http://cjonline.com/stories/062501/pro_impressions.shtml

Affording College: How to Get Financial Aid and Scholarships

[1] "Saving for College," FinAid, accessed June 27, 2012, http://www.finaid.org/savings/

[2] Mark Kantrowitz, "College Q&A: How Early Is Too Early to Start Saving?" *Main St.,* November 10, 2010, http://www.mainstreet.com/article/moneyinvesting/education-planning/college-qa-529-or-trust-account-0

[3] "The Real Deal on Financial Aid," Muhlenberg College, accessed June 28, 2012, http://www.muhlenberg.edu/main/admissions/realdeal.html

[4] "Number of Scholarships," FinAid, accessed June 28, 2012, http://www.finaid.org/scholarships/awardcount.phtml

Deciding: How to Handle Admissions Decisions and Pick Your College

[1] Valerie Strauss, "Why Students Get Rejected from College," *Washington Post*, March 26, 2010, http://voices.washingtonpost.com/answer-sheet/college-admissions/college-rejection-its-not-abou.html

[2] Clinedinst, 2011 State of College Admissions.

Adults Only: How Parents Can Help without Hurting

[1] Lucia Graves, "The Perils and Perks of Helicopter Parents," *US News*, December 18, 2007, http://www.usnews.com/education/articles/2007/12/18/the-perils-and-perks-of-helicopter-parents

[2] Jeanine Lalondem, "Family roles during the application process," *The UVA Admission Blog: Notes from Peabody* (blog), *University of Virginia*, December 28, 2011, http://uvaapplication.blogspot.com/2011/12/family-roles-during-application-process.html

[3] Judy Fortin, "Hovering Parents Need to Step Back at College Time," *CNN*, February 4, 2008, http://articles.cnn.com/2008-02-04/health/hm.helicopter.parents_1_helicopter-parents-college-students-students-with-higher-levels?_s=PM:HEALTH

[4] Dr. Terri LeMoyne and Dr. Tom Buchanan, "Does 'Hovering' Matter? Helicopter Parenting and Its Effect on Well-Being," *Sociological Spectrum*, July/August 2011, http://blog.utc.edu/news/2012/01/professors-study-effects-of-helicopter-parenting/

[5] LeMoyne and Buchanan, "Does 'Hovering' Matter?"

[6] "'You've got to find what you love,' Jobs Says," *Stanford Report*, *Stanford University*, June 14, 2005, http://news.stanford.edu/news/2005/june15/jobs-061505.html

Endearing: Ten Secrets of "Great Kids"

[1] Rebecca R. Ruiz, "The Ideal High School Graduate," October 27, 2011, *The Choice: Demystifying College Admissions and Aid* (blog), *The New York Times*, http://thechoice.blogs.nytimes.com/2011/10/27/ideal-grad/

[2] "Quick and Easy Ways to Remember Names," Dale Carnegie Training, accessed June 27, 2012, http://www.dcarnegietraining.com/resources/remembering-names

[3] Perez, Learn to Fail.

[4] American Psychological Association, Ursula Beerman and Ruch Willibald, "Can people really laugh at themselves?"—Experimental and correlational evidence, http://psycnet.apa.org/index.cfm?fa=buy.optionToBuy&id=2011-11794-003, (June 2011).

NOTES

CPSIA information can be obtained at www.ICGtesting.com
Printed in the USA
LVOW111452180613

339157LV00008B/392/P